THROUGH FIFTEEN REIGNS
A Complete History
of
The Household Cavalry

THROUGH
FIFTEEN REIGNS

A Complete History
of
The Household Cavalry

by

J N P WATSON

SPELLMOUNT

Staplehurst

All photographs not attributed © J N P Watson 1997
Maps © Derek Stone 1997

British Library Cataloguing in Publication Data:
A catalogue record for this book is available from the British Library

Copyright © J N P Watson 1997

ISBN 1-873376-70-7

First published in the UK in 1997 by
Spellmount Limited
The Old Rectory
Staplehurst
Kent TN12 0AZ

1 3 5 7 9 8 6 4 2

Designed by Banbury Pre-Press Centre
Printed in Great Britain by
Hillman Printers (Frome) Ltd
Frome Somerset BA11 4RW

CONTENTS

Dedicated
by Gracious Permission
to
Her Majesty The Queen
Colonel-in-Chief

FOREWORD

by Major General Lord Michael Fitzalan Howard
GCVO CB CBE MC DL Colonel, The Life Guards and
General Sir Desmond Fitzpatrick GCB GCVO DSO
MBE MC Colonel, The Blues and Royals

THIS addition to the existing histories of the Regiments of Household Cavalry is the first book to trace together the stories of both the 1st and 2nd Life Guards, the Royal Horse Guards and the Royal Dragoons, providing the only complete history of the Household Cavalry under one cover.

The story is told by reigns which makes for easy reference. It is interesting to note the number of occasions over fifteen reigns when some or all of the regiments served beside each other. It also emphasises the close bond which has existed between successive monarchs and their Household Cavalry since the raising, by King Charles II, of the original troops of Life Guards as his most immediate and trusted bodyguard.

Over nearly three and a half centuries the Army has altered in shape and size on many occasions to mirror developments in weapons, tactics and doctrine. As is shown in this book, these changes have been felt as much by the Household Cavalry as anywhere else. What has been remarkable is the resilience of our Regiments to cope with revolutionary and often abrupt changes, not least of which were those seen recently as a result of the overall reduction in the size of the Regular Army.

The book demonstrates the difficulties brought about by the requirement to provide ceremonial troops in London, while at the same time training for or taking part in operations and general war, first on horses and now in armoured vehicles. The dichotomy exists to this day when our two Regiments are manned from one pool of manpower. It is to the great credit of our officers and soldiers that they minimise the difficulties and master both roles with distinction. Indeed it is a constant source of pride to see the number of medals for active service worn by those on ceremonial duty.

The text is well-researched and accurate. In addition the author is to be congratulated on bringing together the richest collection of photographs ever assembled on the subject. The book tells a stirring story and is strongly commended to anyone with an interest in our Royal and military heritage.

Colonel The Life Guards

Colonel The Blues and Royals

Preface

JUST as I was embarking on this book I was fortunate to be offered assistance from my Household Cavalry contemporary Major General Sir Desmond Langley, formerly of The Life Guards. He has held every conceivable appointment in the Corps, both at command and on the Regimental staffs. With his knowledge of its history and his eye for detail he scrutinised every chapter, checking the details with the proverbial 'fine tooth comb'. My profound thanks are due to him, too, for providing the interesting Introduction which follows.

In addition I am most grateful to Colonel James Hamilton-Russell, late of the Royal Dragoons, who went on to command The Blues and Royals and, subsequently, the Household Cavalry. Similarly, he read through the entire manuscript and made many useful suggestions. Another former Life Guardsman with a keen interest in Regimental history, who cross-checked my typescripts, was Captain Alastair Ingham Clark. His help, too, has been much appreciated.

When I started this project I was warned to 'refer to Sir George Arthur's three volumes...' – *The Story of the Household Cavalry*, which took the history of the Corps up to 1919 – '...with considerable caution and circumspection. They are riddled with errors...' Yet I sympathise with Sir George. Notwithstanding the pains I took to have the chapters of my *Story of The Blues and Royals* read over and cross-checked by numerous experts, several mistakes were overlooked and emerged in print. Considering the even closer attention which the following account has received, however, I trust it will not be much criticised for inaccuracy.

A history of the Household Cavalry of this depth has required considerable research beyond what has been recorded by previous writers on The Life Guards, the Royal Horse Guards and the Royal Dragoons. My thanks go to Colonel W H Gerard Leigh, formerly commanding the Household Cavalry, and Colonel D de C Smiley, formerly commanding the Royal Horse Guards. And to Colonel Peter Rogers, commanding the Household Cavalry, Colonel William Rollo, commanding the Regiment at Windsor and to Lieutenant-Colonel Toby Browne, commanding the Mounted Regiment – all of whom held those appointments throughout the time of my work.

To Major Valentine Woyka, Blues and Royals, from whom I received much advice on the mysteries of the tanks and armoured cars of today, and who organised the photograph of his squadron at 'crews front', which concludes the book. To Major Paddy Kersting, the curator of the Regimental museum, for permitting me to pester him on numerous occasions. To Major M D Vickers, commanding 20 Transport Company RLC, for his help regarding the history of Regent's Park Barracks.

And to the staffs of the Imperial War Museum, the National Army Museum, the London Library and *Soldier* Magazine each for their substantial assistance. Gwyneth Campling of the Photographic Services at Royal Collection Enterprises, Windsor Castle, was also most cooperative.

Above all, my wife, Lavinia, is owed a huge debt of gratitude, not only for typing the book and printing out several copies of it, but also for helping me to deal with all the copious correspondence, visits and visitors connected with it.

Regarding the Capital 'T' for the definite article of The Life Guards and The Blues and Royals, the usage began with The Life Guards in 1928 to emphasise the fact that they had been two Regiments. They were, from 1922 to 1928, the Life Guards (1st and 2nd). The Blues, not to be outdone, endowed themselves with a capital, too – the Royal Horse Guards (The Blues). Notwithstanding that the usage is relatively recent, I have, for the sake of simplicity, given the capital throughout the book.

JNPW
Pannett's, Shipley
1997

ix

MAPS

INTRODUCTION

by Major General Sir Desmond Langley
KCVO, MBE

THERE can be few organisations with a longer continuous existence than the older regiments of the British Army. The Church, Parliament and the Judiciary have certainly better claim, but a regiment of some six hundred men who have lived for well over three hundred years in a closed community passing on from generation to generation their expertise, standards, prejudices (and probably their weaknesses) is a remarkable phenomenon. But although the members of these unique organisations are in many ways fashioned by their inherited characteristics, they are surprisingly unaware and unconscious of the activities of their forebears.

In this book Johnnie Watson has most successfully removed any excuse for ignorance about the Household Cavalry, which can claim as long a history as any, starting from the formation of the Standing Army. Their dual role in forming the Sovereign's cavalry of the Guard and taking their place in the Line in time of war gives them a unique character and provides a fascinating story in this case skilfully told.

I worked on four separate occasions in the Horse Guards building in Whitehall which was the original home of the Household Cavalry at the time of the Restoration and still houses their headquarters and the Queen's Life Guard, which they daily provide. Every time I entered or left the building I passed their sentries wearing the uniform of my own or its sister Regiment. Each time I was reminded that they had been marching up and down virtually the same beat or sitting on their horses watching the approaches for over three centuries. The building has a most interesting history and in my last appointment there I worked in the lovely room above the centre arch at the desk of the first Duke of Wellington, once Colonel of the Royal Horse Guards, whose office it was

when Commander-in-Chief of the Army. When I took my seat behind it on my first day I looked through the window at the statue of the Duke of York, an earlier Commander-in-Chief, the one who 'marched his men to the top of the hill and down again', but also reorganised the troops of Life Guards and Horse Grenadier Guards into the 1st and 2nd Regiments in 1788. I gave thanks for being in his seat and asked him to keep an eye on me.

Thirty years earlier I was a trooper in a squad of Household Cavalry potential officers, mostly National Servicemen, sent to the Guards Depot at Caterham to do our basic training. The impact of history came early when two of our number in The Blues were placed on charges for saluting an officer when not wearing their headdress. In what was then a totally Foot Guards environment the influence of the Marquis of Granby, Colonel of The Blues and patron of innkeepers, who lost his hat and wig in battle yet saluted bald-headed, was unrecognised. Happily the case against our comrades was eventually dismissed. Our own knowledge of Lord Granby was very limited, and regimental history was only administered in small doses by a Household Cavalry officer sent over from Windsor. He might indeed have been the author of this book, for Johnnie Watson's reputation as an historian dates from early in his career. We also learnt the importance of the capital letter in the definite article preceding the title of my Regiment: Johnnie has for the sake of consistency called us The Life Guards from the very start although it was not until 1928 that the amalgamation of 1st and 2nd Life Guards brought about this usage.

Several other regimental customs and traditions are connected with the Horse Guards building. The Queen's Life Guard turns out dismounted at four o'clock every afternoon, a punishment, it is still believed, inflicted by Queen Victoria when she drove through the Arch one afternoon early in her reign and the Guard failed to turn out to pay her compliments. The sentence was one hundred years of Four O'Clocks and the centenary occurred during the Second World War when the Guard had been discontinued. In the late forties and early fifties we lived in hope of being signed off but the Four O'Clock Inspection had become a major tourist attraction and we are now well on our way to a second century.

The arcane ceremony of Hanging the Brick carried out by members of The Life Guards non-commissioned officers' mess at Christmas time, after which work is limited to the barest necessities, was alleged to have originated in a mysterious event at Horse Guards in the distant past. So many were the interpretations that another historian wrote a definitive history of the custom, eliminating most of its mystique and perhaps rather spoiling the story.

Living when in England, as the Regiments do, in barracks at Windsor and in London occupied exclusively by their predecessors for some two hundred years, the past is ever present although the buildings have been replaced more than once. Those with longer memories will continue to bore the young with details of earlier soldiers' accommodation and horses' stables. Overseas it is of course different, but four decades of periodic service in Germany produced its own traditions. Frequent handovers between the two Regiments were sometimes marred by exaggerated memories of earlier discord. Happily when Johnnie's squadron once took over from mine nothing could have gone more smoothly. There was also in Germany a more distant past for those who looked for it. The Life Guards' competitiveness towards their sister Regiment was crystallised when both Regiments' Standards were paraded simultaneously. Those of the Royal Horse Guards bore the battle honour Warburg (1760) while the Standards of The Life Guards did not. A short detour to Warburg in Westphalia while fishing in the Diemel gave me a much better appreciation of a battle which earned great distinction for The Blues and indeed for the Royal Dragoons. A visit to the monument at Zandvoorde, near Ypres, was a more solemn reminder of the severe losses suffered by the Household Cavalry in 1914-15.

Service in the Suez Canal Zone in the early 1950s enabled us to visit the battlefields of Kassassin and Tel-el-Kebir where the Household Cavalry fought in 1882. To the regret of some, operations in the Gulf War were not pursued for long enough to reach Habbaniyah in Iraq where the 1st Household Cavalry Regiment had moved to protect the RAF airfield during the Second World War.

The chapters in this book match the reigns of successive monarchs emphasising the continuing connection between them and their Mounted Bodyguard. When I commanded the Household Cavalry the Silver Stick I carried when in-Waiting on The Queen had been used by my predecessor in the reign of King William IV whose cypher it bore, a reminder of the unchanging nature of my duties. The Queen's interest in, and knowledge of, her Household Cavalry has been greatly appreciated by its members throughout her reign. This book is the history of all the Regiments that now constitute the Household Cavalry and includes that of the Royal Dragoons whose amalgamation in 1969 with the Royal Horse Guards (The Blues) as The Blues and Royals made their proud history part of that of the Household Cavalry, as did that of The Blues when they finally and officially joined the two Regiments of Life Guards as Household Cavalry from the beginning of the reign of George IV. The many strengths brought by the Royals can now be shared by all in the Household Cavalry Regiment which currently comprises the operational elements of both Life Guards and Blues and Royals.

Readers of this book will realise that the conflict between the operational and public duty, or ceremonial, roles was detrimental to the efficiency of the Household Cavalry for much of its life. The Life Guards were in England for sixty years between the War of Austrian Succession and the Peninsular Campaign and initially found the going very hard in Spain. Retained at home during the Crimean War the Composite Regiment which went to Egypt in 1882 had not seen service overseas since Waterloo. Both in the South African War and the First World War the demands of London duties limited the contribution that could be made in the initial stages. In the Second World War the tardy mechanisation of the cavalry left the Household Cavalry till last and it took them some time to catch up.

But all this is history now as, since 1945, the Household Cavalry has served in an operational role in every theatre where armour could be employed and has maintained the very highest standard of tactical and technical expertise with whatever weapons and vehicles it has been equipped. The ever increasing demands have necessitated a degree of professionalism that may have caused a moderation in the style of some by comparison with days past, but neither the spirit nor the pride nor the constant demand for nothing but the best has diminished in any way. These characteristics have been demonstrated equally in the Mounted Regiment which has performed the State duties of the Household Cavalry in an exemplary fashion often before the eyes of all the world. Whether it be the crew of an armoured fighting vehicle or the mounted trooper on guard in full dress, the standard is as good as it ever was and often very much better.

Author's note: General Langley joined The Life Guards in 1948, commanded the Regiment in 1969–71 and held most of the pivotal posts in the Household Cavalry before commanding the Household Division (Household Cavalry and Foot Guards) from 1979–83.

1 EVOLUTION AND PRECEDENCE

The edifice of the British Army, the fount of all its spirit and pride, resides in the regimental system. From the beginning until the present day the cornerstone of that edifice is the Household Division, not only because its Regiments of Horse and Foot were the first to be raised, but also because of their uninterrupted record of esprit de corps and excellence and their special relationship to the Monarch, to whom all Britain's armed forces swear allegiance.

The first to be recognised at the Restoration were The Life Guards, who, as we shall see, began their story during Charles II's exile in the 1650s. They remain the Army's senior regiment. For the next six decades the term Household Cavalry would be exclusive to The Life Guards. In 1661 came the Royal Regiment of Horse – later the Royal Horse Guards (The Blues) – which was destined to be raised to the status of Household Cavalry in 1820. Also in 1660 the nucleus of the Foot Guards was formed, the Royal Regiment of Guards (Grenadiers)[1] and the Lord-General's Regiment (Monck's Coldstream).

In the same year, too, a regular troop of horse was raised to give England's new colony, port and trading post of Tangier, on the Moroccan coast, some cavalry support. That troop would, on its return to England, be expanded to become the Royal Regiment of Dragoons, the regiment which, in 1969, was absorbed into the Household Cavalry by amalgamation with the Royal Horse Guards - thus the Blues and Royals, the second regiment of the Corps of Household Cavalry.

No corps in the British Army has enjoyed, or suffered as the case may be, so many changes of organisation and role. They were exclusively a mounted force, but have always been employed either mounted or on foot as their functions as guardians of the Monarch, or on duty for the Monarch abroad, has demanded. Besides their first role as guards, sentries and escorts to the Sovereign and other members of the Royal Family, they have acted as policemen and customs and excise officers, horse grenadiers, infantry, cameleers and heavy machine gunners. They have also gone to war in armoured cars, tanks and helicopters, by parachute and on bicycles, while their ceremonial

The Duke of York's Troop of Life Guards at the Coronation of Charles II

James, Duke of Monmouth,
the eldest illegitimate son of
Charles II. He was the second
Captain-Commandant of
The Life Guards (1669)
and the first Gold Stick
(1678)

Combermere Barracks, Windsor, between the wars.

A composite mounted regiment was put together for active service in 1939. This, the 1st Household Cavalry Regiment, campaigned briefly in the Middle East with their horses. But, with the irrevocable eclipse of the warhorse, the regiment converted, in 1941, first to lorried infantry, then to armoured cars. For the duration of the Second World War they formed themselves into two composite armoured car regiments.

When peace came again those two were reorganised, one as Life Guards, one as Blues, each deploying a mounted squadron at Hyde Park Barracks to furnish, as of old, the King's Life Guard and other ceremonial duties. The two armoured car regiments alternated between Windsor and a foreign station. Then, in 1969, at about the same time that Household Cavalrymen learned that they were to be trained for tanks, as well as armoured cars, the amalgamation took place of the Royal Horse Guards (Blues) and the Royal Dragoons (1st Dragoons), to form a new second regiment of Household Cavalry, The Blues and Royals.

Twenty-three years later, meeting further defence cuts in reply to the dismantling of the Warsaw Pact, came the reduction of the corps to a single service regiment, with two squadrons of Life Guards and two of Blues and Royals, and a mixed headquarters squadron. The Mounted Regiment, however, remained untouched.

That, in the briefest outline, describes the evolution of the Household Cavalry down to its present state. But, although it shows the Corps to stand at the head of the British Army, it does not tell of its singular significance in relation to the Monarch. That status may be summed up in the words Gold and Silver Sticks, those military appointments closest to the Sovereign, which senior officers of the Household Cavalry have been privileged to hold continuously since 1678.

GOLD AND SILVER STICK

Their innovation came about in that year from the supposed threat to the lives of Charles II, his Queen Catherine and his brother, the Duke of York. The danger amounted to little more than a freak scare felt by anti-Catholic England at large. This was fomented by the radical

activity and displays have won, as they continue to win, the delight and admiration of the world.

The Household Cavalry dwindled from three troops (each about the size of a modern squadron) in the 17th century to two troops (supported by Horse Grenadiers) in the 18th; then expanded to two regiments (1st and 2nd Life Guards) in 1788; and to three regiments, with the inclusion of the Royal Horse Guards in 1820. The Household Cavalry was again cut to two regiments with the amalgamation of the 1st and 2nd Life Guards in 1922, and narrowly avoided contraction to one, since the Geddes Axe, as the instrument for the defence reduction of that year was known, had, at one moment, been poised to bring The Blues into the same fusion. Saved, however, as two horsed regiments the Corps alternated between Hyde Park Barracks, London, and

and mischievous Whig leader, the Earl of Shaftesbury and the vindictive, lying, rabble-rousing Titus Oates, and was primarily designed to prevent Catholic York from succeeding to the throne.

Be that as it may Charles's eldest natural son, the Duke of Monmouth, then Colonel of The Life Guards, and Captain of the King's Troop of the Regiment, persuaded his father to appoint him, Monmouth, or one of the captains of the other two troops to act as the King's personal bodyguard, day and night. Although, with the eclipse of the so-called Popish Plot, the need for such close protection was perceived to have passed, those appointments, and the prerogative which went with them, continued to be jealously kept; and, albeit now largely ritualistic, the Household Cavalry still holds them proudly. Constitutionally, the Monarch's instructions for the Household Cavalry are passed to the Gold Stick currently in-Waiting, and he transmits them to the Silver Stick for implementation.

During the Napoleonic Wars The Life Guards' sister-regiment, The Blues, came to share the duties of Gold and Silver Stick, which was the first step to their being raised to Household Cavalry status. In 1807 The Blues' commanding officer was instructed to draw his Standards from the Lord Chamberlain's office as The Life Guards did. Then on March 1, 1820, the Duke of York, Commander-in-Chief, wrote to the Duke of Wellington, then Colonel of The Blues, informing him that, from that day forward, The Blues were to be granted 'the same privileges in every respect as are possessed by the two regiments of The Life Guards.'

Thus, in 1820, The Blues became a fully fledged regiment of Household Cavalry on an equal level with The Life Guards, as The Blues and Royals have stood since 1969. The duties of Gold Stick alternates between the Colonel of The Life Guards and the Colonel of The Blues and Royals, and the post of Silver Stick, while conventionally held by the officer commanding the whole Corps, may be temporarily delegated to any Household Cavalry officer of field rank.

Towards the end of the 19th century the appointment of Field Officer-in-Brigade-Waiting having been devised to give senior officers of the Brigade of Guards a liaison at Court, the Household Cavalry perceived it as a challenge to the precedent of Silver Stick, and were at pains to see that it should not be so. Soon after, the Prince of Wales (later Edward VII) was appointed Colonel of both regiments of Household Cavalry. Queen Victoria instructed the Master of the Rolls, Lord Esher, to adjudicate. Lord Esher found as follows:

> From the time of the inception of Gold Stick, Silver Stick has been placed close to the Sovereign's person, and thus his office is one of personal service to the Monarch, whereas the Field Officer-in-Brigade-Waiting is only at court for the purpose of taking commands for his Guards. Therefore Lord Esher advises the Queen to give precedence claimed to Silver Stick.

Nor, during the present century, has that position altered. The Household Cavalry remain closest, in military terms, to the Monarch (which is why the chapters of this book are arranged by successive reigns). The precedent of the Household Cavalry to do duty within the Royal palaces is emphasised, incidentally, by their mounting of the 'Staircase Party' at the House of Lords (the Palace of Westminster) for the annual State Opening of Parliament, and by the provision of their State Trumpeters within the palaces.

Great prerogative and privilege carry with them great responsibility. Household Cavalrymen have duly striven to be the best. They have been ever famous for their dash and elan both at home, in overseas garrisons and on active service. They have carried out their daily guard and other ceremonial duties with promptitude and a glittering style essentially their own. Following the high reputation with which they emerged from the Second World War they have been engaged in most of the small campaigns and peacekeeping roles which have occupied the British Army during the second half of the 20th century down to the present. They have served with the United Nations forces in Bosnia. The Life Guards took part in the Gulf War where one squadron was in the forefront of the short land battle. The two troops of The Blues and Royals, which alone represented British armour in the Falklands campaign, received this accolade from their brigade commander: 'I was most impressed...They did all that was asked of them in great style. I found them all well-mannered, well turned-out in all circumstances, calm and collected, which is, if I may say so, what I would have expected of Household Cavalrymen'[2]. And so it has been for three-and-a-half centuries.

1. Their claim to seniority, like that of The Life Guards, goes back to the 1650s, but, officially, it can only be from the year of the Restoration

2. Letter from Brigadier Julian Thompson commanding 3 Commando Brigade during Operation Corporate to Lt Colonel James Hamilton-Russell commanding The Blues and Royals.

2 CHARLES II (1660-85)

ORIGIN OF THE LIFE GUARDS

Many of those gentlemen who had formed themselves into a Life Guard of Horse and of Foot for the protection of Charles I during the Civil Wars, accompanied the Prince of Wales into his Continental exile. Prince Charles, then a youth in his teens, dreamed of a new monarchy and court shining with splendour, military splendour. And, as the impoverished guest of his cousin, Louis XIV, he cast an envious eye on the Sun King's brave and swaggering army, particularly the Household troops, the French Monarch's Maison du Roi.

A contingent of Prince Charles's bodyguard joined him in his expedition to Scotland, attempting to claim his crown, in 1651, and from there into England, to the debacle that closed with the Royalist defeat at Worcester.

During the 1650s first in France, then – following the treaty of alliance between Louis XIV and Cromwell in 1656 – when Charles was obliged to move on to Germany, then to the Netherlands, the numbers of his Royal Guards burgeoned, those of the Life Guard of Horse numbering 80 on Lord Gerard of Brandon[1] assuming command of them at Brussels in the following year.

Those Life Guards took as their emblem a sprig of oak with acorns, in commemoration of the tree in the forest of Boscobel, in Shropshire, among the branches of which their Prince lay hidden from Cromwell's men after Worcester. But the financial affairs of Prince Charles and his attendant exiles being always in a parlous state, it is likely that neither those cavaliers, nor their comrades in the Royal Lifeguard of Foot, cut much of a dash however frightening their aspect.

However, there was a good deal more to Charles's army in the late 1650s than his Life Guard of Horse and Foot. After Cromwell signed his pact with Louis, Charles formed an

alliance with Spain, promising to support the Spanish Netherlands against the French invader. For that purpose he contrived to raise three regiments of foot besides the Guards. Cromwell's expeditionary force was placed under command of the great Marshal Turenne who, in May, 1658, took Dunkirk and the fortress of Mardyke for the Commonwealth regime after trouncing the ragged English Royalists and their Spanish allies at the Battle of the Dunes. But in the wake of defeat hope for the Prince of Wales was soon to blossom again.

Oliver Cromwell died in September, 1658, being succeeded as Protector by his inept son, Richard ('Tumbledown Dick'), who

Charles II by John Riley. (The portrait is the property of The Blues and Royals Serving Officers' Trust)

dissolved Parliament and resigned the headship of state in 1659. General George Monck, who had conquered Scotland for Oliver, saw that the vacancy could only rationally be filled by England's hereditary heir. Monck duly marched his army from the Tweed at Coldstream to London, where, in January, 1660, he declared his intention to the weak Rump parliament; and, accordingly, opened negotiations with the exiled Prince. In April came the Declaration of Breda, Lord Chancellor Clarendon's design for the Restoration. On May 25 the new King landed at Dover; and, escorted by Lord Gerard at the head of the King's Own Troop of Life Guards, drove to London via Canterbury, entering the capital on the 29th. Monck was created Duke of Albermarle and Knight of the Garter.

The Life Guards numbers had swollen to about 600, 400 of whom had been sent to strengthen the (2nd) Duke of York's Troop at the now Royalist garrison of Dunkirk, the nucleus of which was this and a regiment of Foot Guards under Lord Wentworth.

ORIGIN OF THE BLUES

At the time of the Restoration there were still some 60,000 soldiers of the Republican New Model Army camped around London, symbols of the Commonwealth's tyranny. One of Charles II's first tasks was to pay off

and disband most of that unpopular force and to appoint Royalist officers to such regiments as he saved. Among those former Cromwellian units was one of cavalry which Charles adopted as 'His Owne'. 'That the souldiers may see the affection that His Sacred Majesty hath for the Army,' the *Mercurius Publicus* told its readers that summer, 'he hath been pleased to do them so much Honour as to take that Regiment that was lately Colonel Unton Crook's for His Owne, which is now styled the Royal Regiment of Horse.'

But there was no way the ultra Royalist Convention Parliament of 1660 would consent to a continuation of the New Model army in any shape – quite apart from the fact that the nation was desperately short of money. So, by Royal Assent in September Charles reluctantly signed the order for its disbandment, including Colonel Unton Crook's old Ironsides, now under command of Daniel O'Neale, one of Charles's Grooms of the Bedchamber. These were paraded at Bath, paid off and summarily dismissed.

FIFTH MONARCHIST REVOLT

Charles was now left with no land forces at home other than his Life Guards, Albermarle's Foot, the city garrisons and the so called trained bands. During the later

The Horse Guards at the time of Monmouth's Lord Generalcy of the army. His father, Charles II, is the central figure at the head of the throng to the right of the picture. (Artist unknown)

autumn of 1660, however, England was so rife with republican plots and rumours of plots that Parliament sanctioned the raising of a new Royal Regiment of Foot (later the Grenadier Guards) composed of 12 companies under Colonel John Russell's command. Charles was eager, for the security of himself and the nation, to build such forces as he had into a comprehensive standing army, provided it could be something controlled by him and not by Parliament. His chance came soon enough.

On Sunday, January 6, 1661, while the King was at Portsmouth, a wine cooper named Thomas Venner, recently returned from New England, urged a congregation of Fifth Monarchist zealots to take to the streets, denounce the King and his government, shout for 'King Jesus' and seize the Kingdom. Having caused much death and havoc Venner and his rebels were cornered in Ken Wood, north London, by the Guards, horse and foot, along with Albermarle's and the city militia. Many of the rioters who escaped began making trouble three days later until all were either killed, or captured and hanged.

ENGLANDS FIRST STANDING ARMY

This rising thoroughly alarmed the Government, whose fears were well founded when reports came in of old Commonwealth men, Quakers and other Dissenters committing similar violence in the provinces. The Venner riots gave Charles the excuse he wanted.

Even The Life Guards had not been recognised by Parliament as soldiery, but merely as unofficial protectors of the King and his brothers.[2] However, after Venner, on January 26, the order was signed for the permanent establishment of 'His Majestie's Owne Troope of Guards and His Grace The Duke of Albermarle His Troope of Guards.' A fourth Troop was raised in Scotland on April 2. The King's Own Regiment of Foot Guards (subsequently the Grenadiers) also passed under the order of January 26.

By the regulations for the disbandment procedure all the units of the New Model Army must be seen to be broken up. Therefore on February 14, 1661, Albermarle's regiment of Foot was drawn up on Tower Hill, disbanded by the commissioners, then promptly re-engaged in the King's

service as the Duke of Albermarle's Regiment of Foot Guards (afterwards the Coldstream).

Meanwhile the Royal Warrant of January 26 was extended to the Royal Regiment of Horse, formerly Unton Crook's. On February 16 that regiment, consisting of eight troops – 'One Troope of 80 souldiers besides officers to be His Majestie's and seven Troopes of 60 soldiers each,' as it was phrased – and wearing their old Ironside tunics of dark blue,[3] were mustered on Tothill Fields, on the south side of Westminster under the Colonelcy of Aubrey de Vere, Earl of Oxford[4] and the immediate command of Daniel O'Neale. Such was the origin of what would be the Royal Horse Guards. By November the regiment was referred to as the King's Regiment of Horse Guards and will be called henceforward, in this book, 'The Blues'. In a letter penned on the same day as the Royal Warrant one cavalier gossiped to another:

> These four lords were all with the King yesterday contesting for a troope in the Earl of Oxford's Regiment - my Lords Mandervil, Windsor, R Butler and Falkland. The King answered one of them that, if he had a troope in this Regiment he must not think to stay here to play at Hombre [a fashionable card game] but to lie and quarter abroad in the country there to attend his service'.[5]

What King and Parliament had in mind for England's first standing army was a resplendent force, based on the model of the French that would not only protect the

Aubrey de Vere 20th Earl of Oxford, The Royal Horse Guards' first Colonel

King, his brother and the realm in general and present itself colourfully and in a well drilled fashion on State occasions, but also act as police and be ready to form a trained cadre for rapid expansion in war. Gunners, sappers and other auxiliaries were civilian.

That summer of 1661 English envoys sailed to Portugal to negotiate the King's marriage to Princess Catherine of Braganza, who was at this time incarcerated in a nunnery. For the bride's dowry the Portuguese government gave England their colonial port of Bombay, and also Tangier on the Moroccan, or Barbary, coast, a fortified trading post hotly contested for ownership by the neighbouring Moors. As part of the run-down of Dunkirk[6] two foot regiments were transferred from there and two more raised in England for the Tangier garrison. To provide those battalions with cavalry support the Earl of Peterborough, the colony's first Governor, raised a troop which, on October 21, 1661, mustered for the first time in St George's Fields, Southwark. This little unit, known as the Tangier Horse, would one day expand and evolve, as the Royal Dragoons, to be absorbed eventually into the Household Cavalry. But that

regimental precedent, in the 17th and 18th centuries, was the preserve of The Life Guards.

There were precursors to The Life Guards. The Corps of Yeomen of the Guard was formed under Henry VII in 1485. Some 25 years later his son, Henry VIII, established the Honourable Band of Gentlemen Pensioners, which became the Corps of Gentlemen-at-Arms. Both had been obliged to keep horses. But London had never before witnessed anything so splendid or so stirring as these new Household troops, The Life Guards, as they appeared for Charles II's Coronation. Early on the morning of St George's day, April 23, 1661, the King and his brother, the Duke of York, took the Royal barge from Whitehall steps to the Tower, and from there rode in their coaches in triumphant procession through the City to Westminster for the crowning ceremony:

Upon Tower Hill the King's Horse Guard, all well mounted, having Buffe coates and white armour, their Horses furnished Hooses (being a short ffoot cloth) with Red Scarfes and Plumes of Red and White feathers commanded by the gallant Lord Charles Gerard of Brandon fell into the Reare, and at

Impression of a 17th century member of The Royal Regiment of Horse Guards, by Colonel Clifford Walton, of the RUSI, from his book, *The British Standing Army*

Algate his Grace the Duke of Albermarle's guard, commanded by Sir Philip Howard, Brother to the Earle of Carlisle fell into the Reare of them... The van of all was led by the Guards of His Royal Highnesse the Duke of York commanded by S. Charles Berkeley, all having black armour, red, white and black feathers, Red Scarfes with belts of His Highness's livery...[7]

The Life Guards' strength at this time was 500 'private gentlemen' deployed in three troops, 200 for the King's Troop, and 150 each for the Duke of York's and that of the Duke of Albermarle (the army's Lord-General). The term 'private gentlemen'[8] was significant, for they had to be men of 'good birth' and of some private means, obliged as they were to supply their own horses, swords and pistols.

Each troop was officered by its colonel, lieutenant-colonel, two majors, a quarter-master (who was, in those days, a combatant officer responsible for allotting quarters), a provost marshal, a chirurgeon (surgeon), a marshal of horse, a chaplain (who conducted divine service daily)[9], and four brigadiers or sub-brigadiers,[10] otherwise known as corporals, who were, in effect, lieutenants or second lieutenants. There were no NCOs. Although sub-brigadiers did not hold commissions they were not NCOs as such but simply on probation awaiting commissions. Officers of both The Life Guards and The Blues mostly held much higher rank in the army as a whole, as evinced by the commands to which they were appointed when the country went to war and the commissions awarded in other regiments to their private gentlemen. The Life Guards was a seminary for future officers.

During the 1660s scarlet faced with blue replaced buff for The Life Guards. But when the Lord-General, Albermarle, died in 1670 and his Troop became the 2nd (Queen's) they forsook scarlet in favour of sea-green, the livery of Braganza, while the 3rd (Duke of York's) Troop adopted yellow, the Duke's favourite colour.[11] The Blues were never to desert their dark blue.

Both Lifeguardsmen and Blues wore a metal pistol-proof skullcap (known as a 'pott') covered with a broad-brimmed leather hat with ostrich-feather plumes; buff soft-leather breeches and gauntlets and thigh-length boots; and they carried a cloak with cape attached. Each private gentleman was armed with a sword, two pistols and a short-barrelled flintlock carbine. And they wore 'a collar of bandoliers,' a shoulder belt from which were suspended a number of metal cylinders containing charges of powder and shot.

There being no barracks at this time soldiers and horses were farmed out to requisitioned accommodation. The Life Guards having the principal duties of providing Royal escorts and the sentries for Whitehall Palace and acting as London's mounted police, were quartered in the city, their principal billet being the Savoy (which was formerly a hospital built by Henry VII). When the King's sister, the Duchess of Orleans, was visiting England soon after the Restoration and staying in Tunbridge Wells, Lord Clarendon records the following dialogue taking place between the Merry Monarch and himself at the table during a meeting of the Privy Council:

King: I would willingly make a visit to my sister ... When do you think I can best spare time?

Clarendon: I suppose you will go with a light train?

King: I intend to take nothing but my night bag.

Clarendon: You will not go without forty or fifty horse?

King: I count that party of my night bag.[12]

The main tasks of the eight troops of Blues were to patrol the roads against highwaymen and other robbers, act as customs men, provide escorts, to wait in readiness to go wherever there was trouble brewing and generally keep the peace in the provinces. The Blues' troops, which were so independent that no adjutant was appointed until 1684, were deployed thus in 1670: the King's Troop (comd. Lord Hawley) at Canterbury; the Earl of Oxford's at Reading; Major Francis Wyndham's at Salisbury; Sir Edward Brett's at Hammersmith; Lord Fretchville's at York; Sir Francis Compton's at Uxbridge; Sir Henry Jones's at Highgate and Islington; and Sir Thomas Armstrong's at Farnham.

MONMOUTH'S COLONELCY

The mid-1660s saw a crisis of confidence in The Life Guards, resulting in a change of command. In particular there was a mistrust of their Colonel, Lord Gerard, as illustrated by this petition[13] from a Lifeguardsman's female relation:

Lord Gerard puts such abuses on the Guards who are all related to loyal families that it is thinned of the persons of quality who endeavoured to ride in it at the Restoration, and Lord Gerard would not find 10 men who would on occasion be commanded by him ... They are forced to give allowance to the clerk, who pretends he has great trouble to get the money ... It is now a scandal to be a Life Guardsman ... People say 'Give the King the Countess of Castlemaine and he cares not what the nation suffers.' The Guards will soon be full of tinkers, robbers and hackney coachmen, for however stout, well born, or loyal a man will be, he will not get in unless he has money to give the officers.

The clerk to the King's Troop, William Carr, absconded to France with a large sum of money advanced to him for the Troop by Sir Stephen Fox, Paymaster to the Army, while Lady Gerard had not helped her husband by casting aspersions on Lady Castlemaine, the King's mistress. Gerard, realising the fragility of his position, offered his Colonelcy for sale. The King bought it, in the context of £8,000 for his eldest illegitimate son, the handsome and person-able James Duke of Monmouth. That autumn there was a grand review in Hyde Park to mark the appointment. Samuel Pepys watched the parade:

> When I come to St James's I find the Duke of York gone with the King to see the muster of the Guards in Hyde Park; and their Colonel the Duke of Monmouth to take his command this day of the King's Life Guards by surrender of my Lord Gerard. So I took a hackney coach and saw it all: and indeed it was mighty noble, and their firing mighty fine, and the Duke of Monmouth in mighty rich clothes, but the well ordering of the men I understand not. Here, among a thousand coaches that were there ... Mr Wren hunts me out.'[14]

FIRST ACTIVE SERVICE, 1672

Four years later Monmouth and many of his soldiers were at war. Louis XIV who had accused the Republican Dutch of 'debauching my allies and soliciting my Royal cousins to enter into defensive leagues against me', announced that he was dissatisfied with the De Witt government and declared war on them, while his cousin of England found an equally high-handed and implausible excuse to join the French in their aggression. Monmouth was sent to France with a brigade of 6,000, including 50 from each troop of both The Life Guards and The Blues, elements of the Foot Guards and several newly-raised regiments, one English, two Scottish and two Irish foot and one of English cavalry.

The Anglo-French army under overall command of Louis, with both Marshals Condé and Turenne as lieutenant generals, marched to the Rhine, reduced the Rhine fortresses and blockaded Maastricht, the great fortress commanding the Meuse. The De Witt brothers were on the point of acceding to the preposterous French surrender terms when they were assassinated by the mob. The courageous, if unattractive William of Orange, the future William III of England, who was now elected Stadtholder of the United Provinces, prevented further French invasion by opening the dykes and flooding the land.

MAASTRICHT, 1673

Louis, determined to add lustre to his laurels and humiliation on the Dutch, decided that the reduction of Maastricht should be his next task. Sebastian de Vaubun, his genius engineer, had devised a new system of siege warfare (a more effective system of saps and trenches) for which Maastricht would be the first trial. Louis promoted Monmouth a lieutenant-general for the siege which opened in June, 1673. The Life Guards, who on this occasion were under command of Louis de Duras, Marquis de Blanquefort,[15] the Huguenot nephew of Turenne, were in attendance, by rotation, on their Captain-Commandant, Monmouth, who, during the sapping operations, found time to write the following to his Royal father:

> Sir Philip Howard [captain of the 2nd (Queen's) Troop of Life Guards] wrote word that your Majesty would have me write to my Lord of Rockingham to perswade him to buy the cornett's place in Sir Philip Howard's Troope for his son [Edward Watson] that is here with me, so that when Mr [Capt Francis] Watson [cousin of Edward] has taken the lieutenant's place of my Lord Marshall as your Majesty has promised him, then my Lord Rockingham's son may buy the cornett's[16] place of Mr Watson. I do

assure you, Sir, Mr Watson has had a great care of my family [as aide-de-camp Francis Watson was in charge of Monmouth's personal staff] and has put it in much better order than ever it was...'Tis such rainy weather that in the trench we are up to our knees in water, which is not very comfortable, especially when we are to stay 24 hours in the trench before we are relieved.[17]

The attack on the citadel began on the sector of the blockade commanded by Monmouth who, with great courage and personal initiative, commanded the assaults which led to its capture. Accompanying him were a number of Life Guards officers, dismounted, including Lewis and Francis Watson, Henry Slingsby, Charles Godfrey, Edward Villiers, Charles O'Brien (who died following a leg amputation) and the wily Sir Thomas Armstrong (who, at Monmouth's instigation, had been transferred from The Blues to The Life Guards), along with 12 private gentlemen of the regiment. John Churchill, the future Duke of Marlborough, also took part in the attack. Monmouth was next appointed Lord-General of the English army.

THE HORSE GRENADIERS

English foreign policy was still very much in the hands of the Monarch. Between 1674 and 1678 the fickle Charles II turned to a pro-Dutch attitude, a treaty being signed with William of Orange to oppose France, and a number of private gentlemen in both The Life Guards and Blues received commissions in regiments newly raised for active service in Flanders. It was for this campaign of 1678 that The Life Guards received an important adjunct in the form of the Horse Grenadier Guards, 80 to the King's Troop, 60 to each of the other Troops. In action, according to a contemporary *Treatise on Military Discipline*, these mounted grenadiers

> dismount, link their horses, fire, screw their daggers into the muzzles of their fusils, charge, return their daggers, fire and throw their grenades by ranks, the centre and rear ranks advancing in succession through the intervals between the file leaders. They then ground their arms, go to the right about and disperse; and, at the preparative or beating to arms they fall in with a huzza ...[18]

Sir Ralph Verney, however, was sceptical of their value, saying 'I do not understand How the Grenadeers can Doe any considerable execution with flying hand grenadoes on horseback which makes me wonder that his Majesty can have so great a ffancy for that sort of souldiering'.[19]

GOLD AND SILVER STICK

1678 was also, as described in Chapter One, the year of the innovation of Gold and Silver Stick. Monmouth, or one of his Troop Captains, was to

> attend on the King's person on foot wheresoever he walks from his rising to his going to bed immediately next to the King's own person *before all others*, carrying in his hand an ebony staff or truncheon with a gold head engraved with his Majesty's cipher and crown ... Near him also attends another principal commissioned officer with an ebony staff and silver head, who is ready to relieve the Captain on all occasions.[20]

PROTESTANT DUKE v CATHOLIC DUKE

To English Protestants Catholicism represented totalitarianism. In that respect the years 1678-79 were critical for the English constitution, being the time when the conflict between Catholic Duke (York) and Protestant Duke (Monmouth) came to a head. Under the terms of the Test Act of 1673, Catholics were not permitted in the army. In fact a great many did slip through the net when additional regiments were raised for foreign service, particularly of course in the Irish regiments. But those were regularly disbanded on the close of each campaign.

The violently anti-Catholic faction, led by Lord Shaftesbury, attempted (unsuccessfully) to prove that the King had been properly married to Monmouth's mother, the beautiful Lucy Walter, and thereby to debar York as heir to the throne. Monmouth, beloved of the populace, was tall, handsome, brave and dashing and possessed of a flair for minor tactics and regimental command; but he lacked sagacity, was morally weak and extremely vain and easily led. However, national anti-Catholic sentiment was such that the King felt obliged, in 1678, to exile his brother, the Duke of York, to Brussels.

Meanwhile, in Scotland, the Solemn League of Covenant, whose members refused to accept the Anglican liturgy, now sought total independence. On May 8, 1679, a gang of Covenanters held up the coach in which John Sharp, Archbishop of St Andrews, was travelling and murdered him, and a reign of terror swept the Lowlands. The Covenanters promised the same treatment to the unpopular Lord High Chamberlain, the Duke of Lauderdale, and put a force of 8,000 in the field. A punitive expedition under Monmouth's command defeated the Covenanters on June 21 at Bothwell Bridge, near Glasgow, where Major Theophilus Oglethorp (from the 2nd Troop of Life Guards) distinguished himself in command of the advanced guard, as did the Duke of Montrose commanding the 4th (Scottish) Troop of Life Guards.

York being absent abroad, Monmouth, commanding all the land forces in both England and Scotland, could easily have staged a Protestant coup for his candidacy since the King now fell seriously sick at Windsor. However, York, hearing of his brother's illness, hurried home to his bedside and there persuaded him to deprive Monmouth of the Lord-Generalcy and banish him to the Netherlands, which the King did. The mood of the country was such, however, that it would have been dangerous to keep York in England. So Charles dispatched him as Lord High Commissioner to Scotland, for which journey the Catholic Duke was escorted by relays of Blues troops as far as Berwick, where Montrose took over with the Scottish Life Guards. Then Monmouth, returning from Holland without the King's authority, was deprived of all his many offices (except Master of the Horse[21]). The late Lord-General's son, Christopher Duke of Albermarle, was appointed Captain-Commandant of The Life Guards.

Those developments did not put a stop to the rebellious activities of the former Household Cavalry commander, in which he was continuously encouraged by the Country Party, the Exclusionists.

When the Exclusion Bill was receiving its readings in the Commons and the Country Party activists threatened open revolt, in 1681, Charles, determined to trounce them, dissolved Parliament and called a new one to sit at Oxford that March. He regarded the army as the ultimate insurance against what he called 'going on my travels again' (ie

exile). Life Guards, Blues and Foot Guards, nearly 3,000 regulars, were deployed for his protection on the journey, in Oxford and to overawe London. Charles thus turned the tables on his and York's opponents.

Shaftesbury fled to Holland and there died, but even that did nothing to deter Monmouth's disobedience. Thought to be implicated in the Rye House Plot of 1683, whereby the King and York were to be ambushed on their return journey from Newmarket, Monmouth, being outlawed, went into hiding at the Bedfordshire home of his mistress (Baroness Wentworth of Nettlestead). But the King, wanting to reprieve him and have him back at Court, got him secretly to London. The Life Guards were the principal police in search of the plotters, but apparently their officers should have known that Charles did not wish his son's whereabouts to be discovered.

One day, Colonel Edward Griffin, of the King's Troop and acting Silver Stick, dashed to the King saying 'Sire, sire, I have seen the Duke of Monmouth!' To which Charles replied: 'Odds fish, you are a fool, James is at Brussels!' According to Monmouth's close friend, Lord Bruce, a Gentleman of the Bedchamber, Charles, who blamed Griffin for helping to destroy the reconciliation 'could, after that officiousness ... never bear the sight of [Griffin] again'.[22] The following day, Monmouth was nearly caught by some of his old Life Guards. 'I went to E and was in danger,' he wrote in his pocket-book,[23] 'of being discovered by some of Oglethorp's Men that met me recently at the Backdoor of the Garden'. Before the end of that year York tricked the King into forcing Monmouth abroad again.

Sir Thomas Armstrong, late of both The Blues and The Life Guards, who had fled to Holland following the Rye House Plot, was captured, brought home, tried for high treason and sentenced to be hanged, drawn and quartered.

DEATH OF CHARLES II

The King, now supreme, spent the brief remainder of his reign in comparative peace. The founder of the Guards, Horse and Foot, Britain's first standing army, died on February 6, 1685, the Earl of Feversham, Gold Stick, being in attendance alongside the new King, James II.

One of Charles's last acts had been to hold a military review on Putney Heath:

The Horse at their usual depth made four squadrons upon the right wing, of which the Troopes of Guards made three, and their Granadiers one. The left wing of Horse in like manner made four squadrons; whereof my Lord of Oxford's Regiment formed two and my Lord Churchill's Dragoones the other two...

BIRTH OF THE ROYALS

It is time to turn back to the 1660s to see how the Tangier Horse fared in their bleak outpost and how they grew to be 'my Lord Churchill's Dragoones'.

Henry Mordaunt, 2nd Earl of Peterborough, who had been commissioned Captain-General of Tangier on September 6, 1661, arrived there with his Tangier Horse and other reinforcements, amounting to some 3,000 men, in late January, 1662. But, failing to exercise firm command and control of the garrison he was replaced in the following year by Andrew Rutherford, Earl of Teviot, formerly Governor of Dunkirk and a soldier of strong repute, who set about strengthening Tangier's fortifications. There was some disunity between the Moorish tribes at this time. One of their leaders, however, Abd Allah Ghailan, was determined to have Tangier. Seeing Teviot's new line of forts as an effective counter to his plans of harassment, he led a full-scale attack in February, 1663.

Teviot, taking command at the main redoubt, Charles Fort, and having withstood the Arab assaults for four hours, decided to send in the Tangier Horse which had been expanded the previous autumn to three troops and who were still under command of their original Major, Tobias Bridges. He called up Captain Edward Witham of the Third Troop; and, pointing out a red standard, which appeared to be the enemy's rallying point and moral symbol, ordered him to capture it. Galloping against the Moors at the head of his cavaliers, Witham cut his way through to the flag and seized it. The superstitious Moors regarded the loss as so serious that, 'they drew off in trouble,' ran the official report, 'concluding the loss of their standard to be ominous, the like not having been done before.'

Teviot's Governorship was brief. Growing bolder, on May 4, 1664, he led out a foraging party to the colonial frontier. Ghailan's warriors intercepted and killed most of this British force, including Teviot, but the detachment of the Tangier Horse managed to escape. During the next twenty years they suffered many more scrapes and hardships.

At last, in 1683, Charles and his Parliament decided that Tangier, notwithstanding its value as a trading and refitting post, was proving too great a drain on the Exchequer, and the decision was made to evacuate the colony, which was now under the Governorship of a notorious Blues officer, Sir Piercy Kirke. The garrison had been, from time to time, a hotbed of republicanism, besides having a reputation for drunkenness and other debauchery. It had been under more or less continuous Moorish siege for over 20 years. In 1684 Lord Dartmouth was sent to evacuate and destroy the garrison. Samuel Pepys, who accompanied him as secretary, had this to record:

The Governor [Kirke] is said to have got his wife's sister with child, and that she has gone over to Spain to be brought to bed. And that while he is with his whores at his little bathing house which he has furnished with a jade a-purpose there, his wife, whom he keeps in by awe, sends for her gallants and plays the jade by herself at home ... Nothing but vice in the whole place [Tangier] of all sorts for swearing, cursing, drinking and whoring. No going by a door almost but you hear people swearing and damning, the women as much as the men... It is a place of the World I would last send a young man to but to Hell ...'

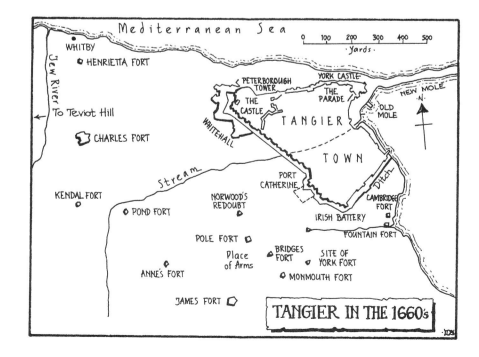

Tangier at the time of the Royals' occupation of the Colony, 1662-84

TANGIER IN THE 1660's

It was a place the dust of which the Tangier Horsemen were thankful to shake from their boots, although the battle honour of TANGIER (not granted until the 20th century) was more than well deserved. Meanwhile, in November, 1683, the King issued commissions for a new regiment to be called 'Our Own Royal Regiment of Dragoones'. The four troops returned from Tangier formed the nucleus, two more being raised in England with the mustering date May 1, 1684. It only remained for them to be trained as dragoons. The word 'dragoon' originates from the French musket known as a *dragon* which bore a carving of a dragon and was carried by Louis XIV's mounted infantry. That is how the English dragoons were to fight, riding to their battlegrounds in sections of four, three men then dismounting and advancing with their muskets while the fourth stood back holding the horses. They were uniformed and equipped like the Foot with the addition of thigh boots or gaiters. (Dragoons did not wear armour. They handed in their 'backs and breasts' on return from Tangier.) They were in effect musketeers on horseback, skirmishers, who made contact with the enemy ahead of the Foot. Their mounts were stocky ponies rather than chargers.

The Royal Dragoons, being the oldest of the cavalry of the line, were put out at being superceded by three regiments of horse raised in the following year. Those three were subsequently converted to the dragoon role. To compensate them for their loss of the *arme blanche* status they were redesignated 'dragoon guards', a status which was declared senior to dragoons.

The Royals' first Colonel, as we have seen, was John Lord Churchill. The commanding officer was old Clarendon's grandson, Edward Viscount Cornbury with John Coy as Lieutenant Colonel. The future Duke of Marlborough being, in 1684, regarded (by many people who did not perceive his potential) as a mere courtier, – notwithstanding his gallant command of a regiment of Foot under Turenne in the '70s – one wag composed these lines:

> *Let's cut our meat with spoons!*
> *The sense is as good*
> *As that Churchill should*
> *Be put to command the Dragoons.*

Anyhow, within a year, Churchill, as we shall see in the next chapter, proved those sceptics manifestly mistaken.

1. 1st Baron, created Earl of Macclesfield 1679. Brought a troop of horse to Charles I at Shrewsbury, 1641; wounded commanding a brigade at Edgehill and again at Rowton Heath. Lt-Gen under Prince Rupert in Wales. On resigning The Life Guards, 1668, became a militia commander. Owing to his support of the Exclusion Bill incurred the displeasure of the Duke of York, who, as James II, ordered his arrest at the time of the Western Rebellion. Macclesfield fled abroad. His sentence of outlawry was reversed in 1688. Died 1693.
2. Charles's second brother, Henry Duke of Gloucester, died of smallpox in September, 1660.
3. Dark blue was also, by coincidence, the livery colour of their Colonel, Lord Oxford.
4. Aubrey de Vere, 20th Earl of Oxford. Born 1627. Fought with the English regiment in the Dutch service during the 1640s. Returning to England, 1649, had his estates sequestrated. Sent to the Tower for conspiring against Cromwell, 1654, and again in 1658. Came over with Charles II, 1660. Lord-Lieutenant of Essex. KG.
5. E Gower to Sir R Leveson in Hist MSS Duke of Sutherland
6. In effect the acquisition of Tangier cancelled out the sale of Dunkirk, which the French bought, in 1662, for 5 million francs.
7. From the *Mercurius Publicus*
8. The word 'private' in this context derives from the Latin *privatus*, a man 'deprived', ie deprived of rank in contradistinction to those who possessed it.
9. ... Every officer or soldier absent from prayers shall, for every absence, lose a day's pay to his Majesty (*Article of War*, 1662)
10. From the French *brigadier de cavalerie* meaning corporal of cavalry
11. Chamberlayne, *Angliae Notitia*, Pt I, pp191-92
12. Clarendon MSS (Bodleian)
13. From the Calendar of State Papers (Domestic). The letter was received by an officer on Albermarle's staff
14. Diary, 16.9.1668
15. Soon to be Earl of Feversham and, under James II, commander-in-chief
16. From *corneta*, the Spanish for a broad pennant. Or the French *cornette*. Hence cornet of horse, the most junior officer, the second lieutenant who carried the cornet or guidon.
17. SP (France) 78, Vol 137, f112
18. There was no connection between the Horse Grenadier Guards and the Grenadier Guards of today. The latter, the 1st Foot Guards, were not referred to as Grenadiers until after the Battle of Waterloo
19. Verney, Margaret, *Memoirs of the Verney Family 1660-96* (1899)
20. Lords Journals XIII, 331. See also Chamberlayne, *Angliae Notitia*
21. The boy Duke of Richmond, a son of the King by Louise de Keroualle, became Master of the Horse in Monmouth's place, 1682
22. Ailesbury, Earl of, *Memoirs*, p 82
23. The pocket book may be seen in the British Museum. Egerton MS 1527

3 JAMES II (1685-88)

James II was escorted to his crowning on St George's Day by the three troops of Life Guards, resplendent as ever and still in their distinctive velvet and lace coats, red for the First, green for the Second and yellow for the Third, their horses festooned with taffeta bows. The Duke of Northumberland,[1] Gold Stick, was in closest attendance, while, in the Abbey, the Blues' Colonel, Oxford, carried the Sword of State and Albermarle the Sceptre.

The ease and harmony with which the new King entered his inheritance was remarkable considering his Roman Catholic tenacity and his reputation for a belief in arbitrary monarchy. Yet he was an efficient, hardworking man with a ready capacity for Kingship. He called a Parliament and promised its members that he would pattern himself on his brother's 'great clemency and tenderness for his people' and would uphold the Church of England as a Church 'for good and loyal subjects'. Most people accepting these words at their face value – rather than being uttered to lull suspicious minds (which they were) – refrained from condemning their Sovereign's religious bigotry, his papism. The Whig gentry, notwithstanding their distaste for James and their open hostility when he was Duke of York, were prepared to give him a chance. That is why the Western rebellion was probably doomed from the start. Its planners should have waited.

The Duke of Monmouth, living in the Netherlands with Lady Wentworth, was for the quiet life –'I am now so much in love with a retired life,' he wrote, 'that I am never like to be fond of making a bustle in the world again'. But, being the gullible, vain, easily swayed young man he was, his fellow Whig outlaws persuaded him, with little difficulty, to give his leadership to an invasion and his undertaking to declare his uncle a usurper and claim the throne for himself.

THE UPRISINGS OF 1685

The Scottish rebel, the Earl of Argyle, sailed from Holland on May 2 to raise his Covenanter standard at Dumbarton. Monmouth, leaving in three ships with 80 followers and a good supply of arms and ammunition a few weeks later, landed at Lyme Regis on June 11, and, within a few days, won the support of several thousand nonconformist artisans, merchants and peasants, notwithstanding that the Whig gentry, upon whose backing he had relied, turned their backs on him. Anyhow, he advanced to Taunton where he was crowned 'King Monmouth' and – his army swollen with militia deserters – he headed for Bristol, via Bridgwater. Bristol being denied him he turned east for Bath,[2] whose citizens shut their gates on him. Following a number of skirmishes he retired, on July 3, into Bridgwater, by which time hundreds had deserted him and he had heard the dismal

James II (as Duke of York)
From the portrait by
J. Huysman (National
Portrait Gallery)

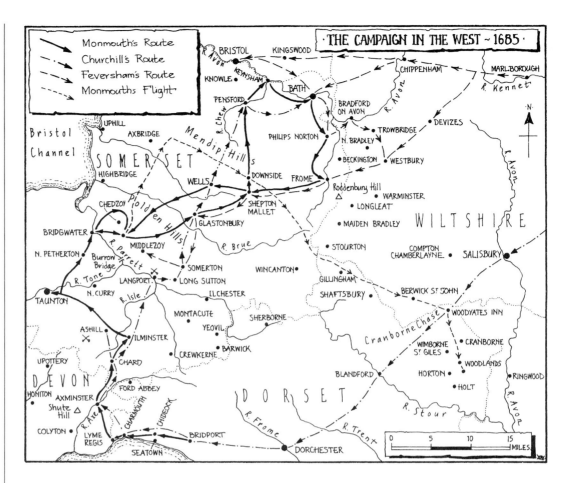

Royalist and rebel movements
during the Western Uprising,
June-July, 1685

news that Argyle's rebellion had been quelled.

The King was not slow to react. Hearing, on June 13, of the invasions he promptly dispatched two troops of the Royal Dragoons to Carlisle to patrol the Border;[3] recalled the Anglo-Dutch brigade from Holland and put Churchill, now brigadier-general, on the road to the west with four troops of The Blues, four of the Royal Dragoons[4] and five companies of the Queen Dowager's Regiment.[5] The cavalry element reached Bridport by June 17. Being hard on the heels of the rebels near Taunton on June 21, Churchill sent to harass them a patrol of The Blues whose officer, Lieutenant Monoux, was killed in a fight at Ashill.

Meanwhile Feversham, who was to be commander-in-chief of the operation, left London with 150 Life Guards and 60 of their attached Horse Grenadiers, under command of Colonel Edward Villiers, along with the First Foot Guards and Dumbarton's Regiment.[6] Those were closely followed by the guns from the Tower with an escort of The Blues led by Sir Francis Compton. Major Theophihus Oglethorp, of The Life Guards,

commanded the advanced guard. Feversham and Churchill joined forces at Norton St Philip (now Philips Norton) where, during the period June 26-28, Monmouth defended stoutly against hesitant Feversham, losing only about a dozen men as compared with the Royalists' 80 casualties.

Once he was back in Bridgwater, Monmouth, while preparing the town for siege, put it about that he was going to retire to Taunton. But his real intention was to march his army north to join the Whig dissidents in Cheshire. However, advice given him by a certain gentleman from the nearby village of Chedzoy prompted him to change his mind. William Sparke instructed a herdsman called Godfrey, who knew the ground well, to spy upon the Royalists who were encamped across the intervening stretch of dry marshland called the King's Sedgemoor, next to Weston Zoyland. Godfrey reported that Feversham's men were not only unwary and not entrenched, but that many were either carousing on, or sleeping off, the effects of the local cider. Monmouth ascertained that he outnumbered Feversham by almost two to one.

Accordingly, having climbed the tower of St Mary's church with his spyglass and surveyed the army (which he himself had once commanded), he decided on a night attack with Godfrey as guide.

THE BATTLE OF SEDGEMOOR, JULY 5-6, 1685

Unfortunately for Monmouth the Royalist camp lay behind a deep water-filled ditch, the Bussex Rhine, of which the herdsman, Godfrey, had apparently made no mention; and, despite useful moonlight, his cavalry, who were leading the column under Lord Grey of Werke, failed to find the crossing (plungeon). A Blues vedette from Compton's Troop,[7] spotting them, fired a warning shot and a trooper was sent galloping back over the plungeon to alert the camp. The tasks given to Grey of Werke had been to encircle the Royalists, open their stable doors and set their horses free. However, Grey now found himself facing trained cavalry on the Sedgemoor side of the Bussex canal. Capt Edwin Sandys, of The Blues, having relieved a badly wounded Compton, led a series of charges against the rebel cavalry, who, on their unsteady and unschooled farm horses, were sent stampeding to the rear and out of the battle.

By this time Monmouth's Foot and artillery were engaged in a fire fight across the Bussex against the First Foot Guards and Dumbarton's, who were eventually reinforced by the Queen Dowager's. But the rebel musketeers mostly fired too high. Feversham ordered Villiers up with The Life Guards and Horse Grenadiers to cross the lower (south-western) plungeon to attack the rebels' right flank, and Captain Adderley and his Blues to join Sandys against the enemy's left. Oglethorp whose Life Guardsmen had been watching in vain for rebel movement on the Bridgwater road, since hearing the shots, galloped back to camp and rode round to the upper plungeon to back up Adderley and Sandys.

Meanwhile Churchill, who had been making his presence felt everywhere, had the Royalist guns, which were guarded by the Royals, moved across from the Bridgwater road to the front of the Bussex ditch – with the timely assistance of Doctor Mews, Bishop of Winchester, a civil war veteran, who had put up for the night at the Royalist camp ('in case I could be of help'), and who lent his carriage horses for the

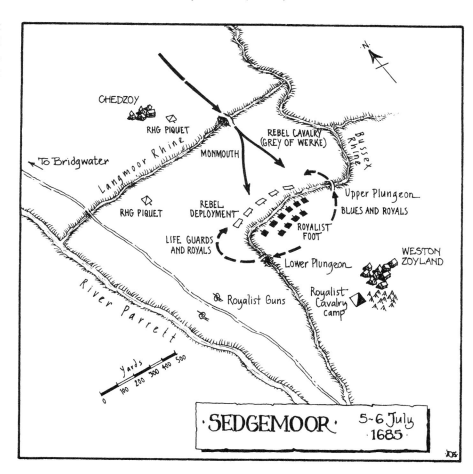

purpose. The guns now being in action the rebels' little field-pieces were soon silenced. Churchill then put himself at the head of the Royal Dragoons and galloped up behind Villiers' Life Guards.

A final concerted effort by the Royalist

Above: The Battle of Sedgemoor, July 5-6, 1685
Below: Slain at Sedgemoor: A private gentleman of The Life Guards. An impression by Colonel Clifford Walton

Horse and Foot cut down, shot or put to flight such rebels who remained in the battle, and Churchill and the Dragoons trotted on to occupy Bridgwater. Thus the Western Uprising, like Argyle's attempt, was quelled. Monmouth was captured three days later hiding in the New Forest and taken to London under guard of a troop of the Royals, and, on July 16, was beheaded on Tower Hill. Meanwhile the vindictive and vengeful King, with Judge Jeffries as his main instrument, set in motion the iniquitous cruelties of the Bloody Assize.

Oglethorp, who carried the news of the victory to James, was knighted and promoted; Feversham was made a Knight of the Garter, advanced to lieutenant-general and made Captain of the First Troop of Life Guards. Churchill for his part became a major-general, Captain Commandant of The Life Guards and Captain of the Third Troop[8]. Lord Cornbury succeeded him as Colonel of the Royal Dragoons whose eight troops were now in winter quarters in various parts of Devon.

THE WAY TO THE 'GLORIOUS REVOLUTION'

Notwithstanding his triumph of July, 1685, James was already at loggerheads with Parliament by the autumn. During the Western emergency he had not only raised a number of new regiments and infiltrated 100 Catholic officers into the army, but he declined to disband them when the threat was over, while the Fourth Troop of Life Guards remained almost entirely Catholic under the captaincy of the Catholic Lord Dover. The King imagined this troop to be composed entirely of Catholics and thereby hangs the following tale recorded for posterity by James's Lord of the Bedchamber, the Earl of Ailesbury:

> The Captain, my Lord Dover, whom the King loved, and so he was blinded – that Lord a Roman Catholic, but the other officers were half one half the other, even to subalterns. A country gentleman begged the King a place in the troop for his son. 'Why do you not go', said the King, 'to my Lord Dover?' He replied that he had been there and that Mr Mollins his secretary told him he was to give fifty guineas. 'You are a fool,' said the King, 'My Lord Dover takes no money'. Those the King loved had no faults. The poor gentleman was dashed,

and ready to sink into the ground. The King ... [perceived] that the poor gentleman was still there, and as if he had a mind to speak. 'You have something to say?' he bid him go on, on which the poor dejected gentleman took a little courage and said 'I believe your Majesty thinks the troop is filled with Roman Catholics?' 'Aye' said [the King], 'and there are no others.' To end the gentleman took courage, and told the King that above half the troops [in the 4th Troop] were French Huguenots, and it was actually so; for if a Turk had come, the fifty guineas had been acceptable to that Lord the Captain.[9]

Through the medium of his standing army James set his sights upon a personal, centralised, and absolutist style of government in England, Ireland and Scotland. Parliament's fear was that the King would soon command a massive praetorian guard, made up of men of an alien religion, divorced by their popery from the English political culture.[10] When MPs objected James prorogued Parliament, and its members were not to meet again during his reign.

The situation went from bad to worse. In June, 1686, a Catholic officer, Sir Edward Hales, was prosecuted for serving in the army in defiance of the Test Act. The verdict, after the case went to the Lord Chief Justice, was that the King being the supreme lawgiver, could legislate without any intermediary, thus setting James above the law and potentially opening the way for wholesale Catholicism of both the armed forces and the civil and judicial executive. That September the rector of London's St Giles-in-the-Fields defied the King's order that Anglican sermons were to contain no criticism of Catholicism. Henry Compton, Bishop of London, a former Blues officer and brother of the Earl of Northampton,was ordered to reprimand the vicar. When Compton declined James stripped him of his offices. Egged on by his Chief Minister, Sunderland, and his Jesuit confessor, Father Petre, the King went on to appoint Catholic lords to the Privy Council, Catholic dons to the universities and, as Lord Deputy of Ireland, the dictatorial Catholic Earl of Tyrconnel who proceeded to purge the Irish army of Protestant officers. James was also at pains to convert English army officers. One Abraham de la Pryme recorded in his diary after the Revolution of 1688 that the King had invited Captain Edwin Sandys of The Blues (whom we last met at Sedgemoor)

into his closet [and] began to talk about this and that and at last told him what he would do for him and how great a commander he should be if he would but be a Catholic. To whom the captain replied, in a big hoarse voice as he always spake 'I understand your majesty well enough. I fear God and I honour the King as I ought, but I am not a man that is given to change.' Which unexpected answer so stopped the King's mouth that he had not a word to say.

Within a few days after the captain went to the Earl of Oxford and would needs have given his commission up and gone into Holland and etc, but the Earl would not accept it, but whispered him in the ear saying 'These things will not last long', [meaning these actions of the King]. And just about a quarter of a year after the Revolution happened. Yet, for all this, when it was happening yet this good Captain got into Windsor Castle and kept for the King until he run out of [the] land.[11]

Returning to April, 1687, James issued his hated Declaration of Indulgence to both Catholics and (as a sop) to Protestant nonconformists, his aim being to suspend the Test Acts, which, despite the verdict in the Hales case, he still perceived to be the obstacle to civil rights to Catholics. These and similar moves were looked upon by the nation as a direct attack on the sacrosant Church of England. In August Lord Oxford was among those Lords Lieutenant who refused to appoint Catholics and Dissenters to military and judicial posts. He was therefore dismissed from his Colonelcy of The Blues, which went to James's illegitimate son, the Duke of Berwick[12.]

In the following spring the King ordered home the Anglo-Dutch Brigade, but, owing mostly to the persuasion of his nephew and son-in-law, William of Orange, few obeyed him except the Catholics of that force. Two months later, May, 1688, the Archbishop of Canterbury and six bishops, meeting at Lambeth Palace, agreed to petition the King against his edict that his second Declaration of Indulgence be read out in all the churches. James told them that this amounted to 'a Standard of Rebellion' and clapped them in the Tower. When, in June, they were tried

The Duke of Berwick, James II's son by Arabella Churchill (Marlborough's sister). He was Colonel of the Royal Horse Guards during his father's reign. (From a picture in the possession of the Duc d'Alba)

and acquitted James was at Hounslow in camp with the army (which had now grown to over 20,000). This news reaching the lines the soldiers gave a loud and prolonged cheer. The King asked Feversham what their jubilation was about. When told James kept muttering *tant pis pour eux*, 'so much the worse for them' [the Bishops].

On June 10 the Queen, James's second wife, Princess Maria Beatrice of Modena, gave birth to a son. It was to Colonel Edward Griffin, on duty as Silver Stick, that the physician announced 'tis a prince!' And Protestant England groaned at the prospect of a new Catholic dynasty.

Meanwhile the situation having long been intolerable, secret negotiations were in progress to bring over William of Orange and his Protestant princess, the King's elder daughter, Mary, both of whom were appalled by James's behaviour, and, in particular at the grim likelihood of an Anglo-French hegemony. Accordingly, William sailed across the Channel with a cosmopolitan invasion force of some 1,300, landing at Torbay on the Devon coast on November 5 (a date laden with Protestant significance).

James, now commanding an army over twice that size, sent a powerful field contingent to Salisbury to bar his nephew's advance, including The Blues, the Royals, Princess Anne's and Sir John Renwick's regiments of Horse. But even before Feversham, the King's lieutenant general, arrived at that vantage point, the defections began which would prove the King's downfall. Cornbury with Anthony Heyford, his lieutenant-colonel, went over to William with a party of the Royals as did Lord Colchester, Edmund Maine and Charles Godfrey[13] with some of their Life Guardsmen. Sir Francis Compton rode towards the Dutch army with his troop of Blues (in the same body as Cornbury's dragoons) but was persuaded by his major, Walter Littleton,[14] to return to Feversham's camp. Compton deserted to William later. All across England the county magnates were declaring for William.

On November 10 James left Windsor Castle to join Feversham. Churchill rode in the King's coach as Gold Stick and, according to another Life Guards officer, Sir George Hewitt, the future Duke of Marlborough intended at one point to stab or shoot the King 'being in waiting with the gold-headed stick,' as Hewitt put it. As it was, Churchill, accompanied by the Duke of Grafton and Lord Berkeley rode out of James's camp on the night of November 23 and reached the Dutch outposts by daylight. Princess Anne's husband, Prince George of Denmark, also went over to the invader, while the Princess herself was totally out of sympathy with her father.

These defections gave James a violent nose bleed which lasted for three days. He ordered Feversham to withdraw to London and, after a number of adventures, slipped across to France while Feversham, disbanding the regiments at Uxbridge, surrendered. During the King's last hours in London, the Duke of Northumberland, commanding The Life Guards Second Troop and by then Gold Stick, asked Lord Rochester what he should do next. 'Why call your Troop of Guards together', was the reply, 'and declare for the Prince of Orange!' Very soon England's late monarch with Maria Beatrice and their infant prince, were the guests of Louis XIV, who continued to recognise James as King of England. William, on his arrival in London, ordered the army to be reconstituted. An almost bloodless revolution had been effected.

1. Sir Philip Howard having died shortly before Charles II, the Duke of Northumberland – another son of the Duchess of Cleveland (formerly Lady Castlemaine) by the late King – was appointed Captain of the 2nd Troop.
2. Monmouth's change of direction was also prompted by his knowing that Feversham's army was by now close at hand
3. These were the Royals troops commanded by Captains Langston and Mackenzie. Argyle's effort was defeated before the Royals reached Carlisle
4. The Royals were employed, not as dragoons but in the conventional cavalry role throughout the campaign.
5. Commanded by Piercy Kirke, hence `Kirke's Lambs'. Afterwards the Queen's Royal Regiment (West Surrey)
6. Afterwards the Royals Scots
7. Compton also had under his command Cornbury's troop of the Royals
8. It was Albermarle's retirement to his native Devon that permitted these new Life Guards appointments, Albermarle having been Captain Commandant and Captain of the First Troop
9. Ailesbury Memoirs, p 130
10. See the pertinent comments on this situation by John Childs in *The Army, James II and the Glorious Revolution* (1980)
11. Pryme's diary was edited by Charles Jackson for the Surtees Society (1870)
12. James FitzJames, Duke of Berwick, was born to Churchill's sister, Arabella, James's mistress, in 1670. Berwick became a Marshal of France
13. Godfrey married Arabella Churchill after James abandoned her
14. Littleton, who had commanded a division of Blues at Sedgemoor, was killed later in 1688 in a duel with his brother-officer, Adderley

4 WILLIAM III (1688-1702) AND MARY II (1688-94)

William's initial promise to the Convention Parliament was that he would come to England only as 'Deliverer and Protector'. Parliament's first reaction was to offer Princess Mary the throne (in the capacity more as Regent than Queen) with William as Prince Consort. The taciturn Dutch Stadtholder, however, declined to be what he ungraciously termed 'my wife's gentleman-usher.' On January 29, 1689, the Regency was voted against in the House of Lords by 51 to 49, and a fortnight later William and Mary were jointly offered the crown. It was probably Louis XIV's support of James II and his declaration that the exiled King's infant son was the eligible Prince of Wales that tipped the balance in William's favour. The crown was what William cherished from the beginning, not for the glory of it but because he needed command of the English army, an Anglo-Dutch Protestant alliance being, as he saw it, a *sine qua non* to save his native country from the hated French aggressors.

Among William's early acts, after reconstituting James's disbanded army, was to reappoint Churchill (created Earl of Marlborough in the Coronation honours) as Captain of the Third Troop of Life Guards; award Lord Lumley[1] (created Earl of Scarbrough in the Coronation honours) with command of the First Troop in place of the now imprisoned Feversham[2] and allot the Second Troop to the Duke of Ormond,[3] vice Northumberland. As for the Catholic Fourth Troop, that was dispersed and replaced with a Dutch Troop under General Count Henry Ouwenkirk (Overkirk) of Nassau. The faithful Oxford was reinstated as Colonel of The Blues. William, however, not yet entirely trusting the English commanders, dispatched The Life Guards[4] to various stations in the Home Counties and The Blues to Northampton, while entrusting the garrisons of London to the Dutch Regiment of Blue Guards and other units which had come over with him. These were under the command of his favourite, William Bentinck (later Earl of Portland), by no means to the satisfaction of Londoners.

The Royals, who, in 1689, were at New-castle-upon-Tyne, were involved in putting down a Jacobite revolt. Their commanding officer, Anthony Heyford[5] (who, in 1688, had been a Williamite conspirator) took exception to an equestrian statue of James II

William III. After Sir Peter Lely
(National Portrait Gallery)

Mary II. After W Wissing
(National Portrait Gallery)

Irish battlefields
and sieges, 1689-92

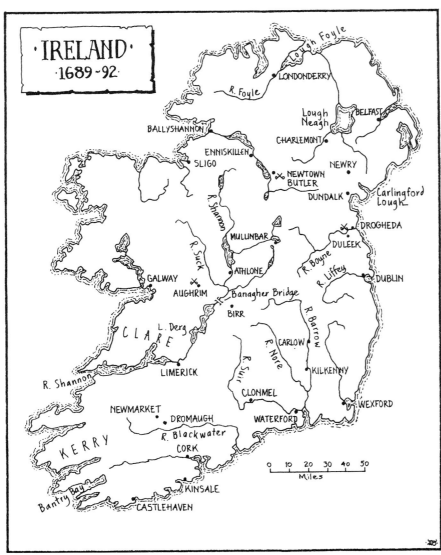

standing on the Sandhill in the centre of the city. It bore the inscription 'the statue of the first Catholic King erected by the first Catholic mayor.' Heyford had it pulled down and destroyed.

In April, 1689, The Blues and Ormond's Troop of Life Guards were among those led by Marlborough to join the Prince of Waldeck's army in Flanders. On August 25 the Allied victory of Walcourt, at which nearly 2,000 of Marshal d'Humière's troops were killed, culminated with a charge by The Life Guards and Blues with Marlborough galloping at their head.

During the month that Marlborough set sail for the Netherlands the Royals were riding north from Newcastle to Scotland to join the army of General Hugh Mackay who was intent upon defeating Viscount Dundee's Jacobite force. John Graham of Claverhouse, 'Bonnie Dundee', won a decisive victory against Mackay in the pass of Killiecrankie, in Perthshire, but was himself killed in the action. The Royals, having only proceeded a little way beyond Aberdeen by that time, missed the engagement. Anyhow, a more pressing crisis demanded their presence.

IRELAND, 1690-92

A matter of weeks before the Coronation of William and Mary – it was that good old Blue, Compton, Bishop of London, who, on April 11, 1689, placed the crowns on their heads – news arrived that James[6] had landed in Ireland with a force of 18,000, occupying Dublin, and resolved to march on London either via the Scottish or the English coast. That August William dispatched his general, the Duke of Schomberg, with an expeditionary force to Ulster. The Royals (who seem regularly to suffer rather more than their share of postings) were sent from Aberdeen to Dundalk where they went into winter quarters and a much needed rest for both the men and the horses. The strength of the Royals, as recorded for January 1, 1690, when they were quartered at Enniskillen, was given as 295 men (effective) with 68 sick and 310 horses (having lost 98).[7]

The following May they received a draft of new recruits and remounts – for whom there is a record of their daily ration for the voyage: one pound of bread, half a pound of cheese, and either two quarts of beer or a quarter of a pint of brandy for the men, and 18 pounds of hay and a peck (two-gallon dry measure) of oats for each horse.

By June The Blues, under direct command of Oxford – the Regiment was regularly referred to as the 'Oxford Blues' to distinguish them from the Dutch Blue Guards – were also in Ulster along with the First, Third and Dutch Troops of The Life Guards (the Second – joined with the Scots Troop – being assigned as bodyguard to Queen Mary). William himself now assuming command of the army in Ireland marched towards Dublin and camped on the north bank of the Boyne, close to Drogheda, where James's Franco-Irish army faced him on the south side of the river.

Next morning, July 1, 1690, William attacked. He sent the Duke of Schomberg's son, Meinhard, with a dominantly cavalry force, including the Royals (under command of Lieutenant Colonel Edward Matthews)[8] west, to cross the Boyne at Slane bridge and engage the Jacobite army on their left flank. A diversionary attack was also launched against the enemy's right. Consequently, James and his French lieutenant-general, Lauzun, depleted their centre by reinforcing their flanks. So William put in his main attack across the river against James's weakened centre, with Life Guards and Blues to the fore, and sent the Franco-Irish defenders in headlong retreat, but not before William's lieutenant-general, the Duke of Schomberg, was killed by a French bullet. Thus ended the Battle of the Boyne which is still celebrated as Ulster's national holiday.

When James reached Dublin he complained to the beautiful Countess of Tyrconnel (sister of Lady Marlborough) that 'the Irish ran away too soon'. To which she added '... and your Majesty ran still faster.' She offered him supper. 'Madam, my breakfast today has been such,' the defeated King replied, 'as to leave me no appetite for any other meal.' He hastened on to Kinsale and there, a shadow of his former self, took a French boat for Brest, while Ormond, The Life Guards Second Troop captain, rode south with a thousand Horse, including Life Guards, Blues and Royals, to occupy Dublin. In Paris the wits were soon singing

Jacques partant de Dublin
Dit a Lauzun son cousin
Avez soin de ma Couronne
J'auray soin de ma personne![9]

In August William arrived before a well-defended Limerick. Unable to storm that

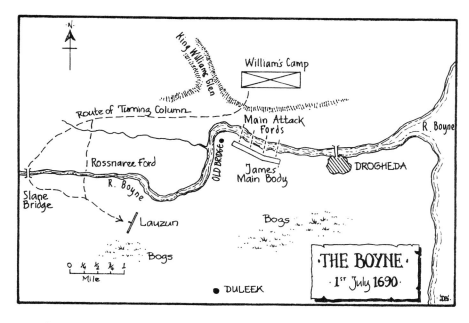

city he put his Irish army into winter quarters – under command of the Dutch Lieutenant-General van Godart Ginckel (later Earl of Athlone) – and went home, escorted by the Dutch Life Guards, to see to England's defences. The French had won a great naval battle off Beachy Head and there was an urgent fear they would follow this up with an invasion. The Royals and First Life Guards were among those regiments who hurried home with William. But, the scare being over, the Royals found themselves sailing back across St George's Channel within a couple of months, their next employment being to grapple with the freebooting gangs of Irish guerillas known as Rapparees – until October, 1691, when they were engaged in the conclusive siege of Limerick, spearheading the attack which brought about the city's surrender and the end of the Irish campaign.[10]

The Third Life Guards were posted home after the close of the 1690 Irish campaign, but The Blues stayed on, taking part in the sieges of Athlone (at the end of June 1691) and Aughrim (July 12) where they lost five officers and 45 troopers killed and 21 wounded during the final charge by Sir Francis Compton's brigade. The Rev. Mr Story, an Aughrim eyewitness, gives this account of how they forded a boggy stream, then carried the day:

Our Horse with much difficulty made good that pass. Sir Frances [sic] Compton, with my Lord of Oxford's Regiment, being one of the first that

The Battle of the Boyne, July 1, 1690

could be in a posture to engage, he fell at random in amongst the enemy, and charged them briskly with sword in hand; and, though his men were once or twice repulsed, they soon made good their party on that side though not without the loss of several, both men and horses.

The French army being finally evicted from Ireland and the Irish subdued following the capture of Limerick and then Galway, the Royals returned to England (to Leicester) in January 1692, The Blues following them in March (to London).

FLANDERS 1691-97

Each spring between 1691 and 1697 William would leave London to take command of the Allies[11] in confrontation with the French armies in Flanders while Queen Mary took over the responsibilities of government at home. When in June, 1691, William drove up to the front – attended by the Third and Fourth Life Guards troops and the Horse Grenadiers, all under Ormond's command – Marshal Boufflers had just captured Mons, a key bastion in the line of Flemish fortresses. William determined to recover Mons. Outmanoeuvred in the attempt, however, he retreated to Brussels and, handing over to the somewhat inept Prince of Waldeck, then sailed back to England taking Ormond (2LG) and Marlborough (3LG) with him. In September

John, 1st Duke of Marlborough. He was Colonel of the Royals (1683-85) and Captain-Commandant of the Corps of Life Guards and Captain of the 3rd Troop (1685-8 and 1689-92). From Sir Godfrey Kneller's portrait

Waldeck advanced to the frontier at Leuse where he was promptly attacked with a superior force by the Prince de Luxembourg. Waldeck shied away. The only troops involved in the contact at Leuse were The Life Guards – their strength in Flanders at this time was a little short of 600 – who fought the rearguard action.

Marlborough was to have commanded the English forces for the 1692 campaign. But having been caught intriguing with the Jacobites at St Germains, – by contact with his sister-in-law, Lady Tyrconnel, and his nephew, Berwick – he was dismissed from all his appointments including his Colonelcy of the Third Life Guards which passed to Lord Colchester. So our regiments were put under the Colonel of the Dutch Blue Guards, Lieutenant-General Henrik Trajenctinus Graaf van Solmes, an uncle of William's who despised the English, a sentiment thoroughly reciprocated.

That July Luxembourg occupied a position above the River Senne, 10 miles from Brussels, at Steenkirk, where William attacked him. The Life Guards and the other cavalry held their ground well and the battle, which was fought on August 3, should have resulted in an English victory, but for Solmes. When William ordered the repugnant Dutchman to send up reinforcements to support the English vanguard, instead of complying he simply watched the vanguard butchered, while being heard to shout 'let us see what sport these English bulldogs will afford us! Damn the English! Since they are so fond of fighting let them have a bellyful!' He was the personification of Parliament's complaint that William was using England and the English solely for his own ends. Solmes was formally censured in the House of Commons, who, in due course, voted to exclude all foreign officers from English commands. Anyhow Steenkirk was a devastating Allied defeat – 3,000 killed, 3,000 wounded, 1,300 taken prisoner. The Life Guards suffered more than their share of casualties.

There was, however, one significant English success in 1692. An Anglo-Dutch fleet, 80 ships strong, defeated the French navy destroying most of their ships off the Bay of La Hogue on May 19, which virtually put paid to Louis' aspiration of invading England.

The highlight of the 1693 campaign was the Battle of Neerwinden (otherwise known

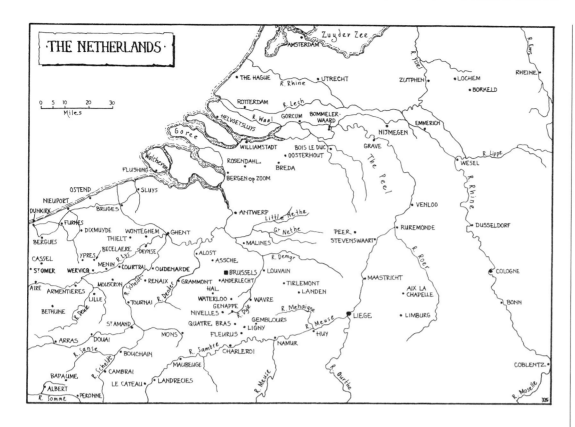

·THE NETHERLANDS·

The Netherlands

as Landen) where William III once again opposed Luxembourg and where, for the first time in their career, The Life Guards confronted their opposite numbers in the Maison du Roi. Their senior officer, Ormond, who led the cavalry charge, had his horse shot from under him, and was wounded and taken prisoner, but soon released in exchange for Berwick. The hated Solmes lost his life in this battle as, on the other side, did that great Life Guardsman, Patrick Sarsfield, Earl of Lucan. Luxembourg's capture of Charleroi put an end to the 1693 campaign, leaving the Prince de Luxembourg solidly established along the Meuse, which prompted William to ask 'Will it ever be possible to beat that nasty hunchback?' To which Luxembourg, (when this was related to him) retorted: 'hunchback? How does he know that? He has never seen me from behind'.

For 1694 Parliament voted to increase the army of the Netherlands to 83,000, which included four squadrons[12] of the Royals – who were brigaded under their own Colonel, Edward Matthews, with the 2nd Dragoons (Greys) and Fairfax's (later 3rd Hussars) – and the 1st (Scarborough), 3rd (Colchester) and 4th (Overkirk) Troops of Life Guards and the Horse Grenadiers (Cholmondeley). The 2nd

Troop followed, with The Blues, as this note from the London Gazette for April 14, 1694, tells us:

> The Second Troop of Guards commanded by his Grace the Duke of Ormond[13] and the Regt of Horse Guards Commanded by the Rt Honourable Earl of Portland, with a great number of recruit horses, are shipt in the river, and will sail this day together with the train of Artillery for Flanders.

The army was kept in the Netherlands all year round until the signing of the Peace of Ryswick in 1697, shortly after which some eighty per cent of it was disbanded, leaving only The Life Guards, Blues, Royals, the three regiments of Foot Guards and eight line regiments of infantry, a total of only 10,000 or so. The people welcomed these reductions with a sigh of relief. The nation had never previously been accustomed to bearing the tax burden imposed to raise forces on the scale needed to fight the War of the Grand Alliance. King William's army was for that reason, largely loathed and resented. And Parliament had produced the funds to fight the French only with great reluctance.

After the Treaty of Ryswick and the wholesale disbandment of the troops specifically raised for the war, the Government investigated the possibility of building a network of barracks and stables for The Life Guards and the remainder of the standing army. However a preliminary survey found that the cost of barracks and stables sufficient for a single squadron of Horse would have amounted to £542.1s.8d.[14] Aghast at the prospect of such expenditure the Privy Councillors were unanimous in voting against the projetct.

There was still the strong fear of a Jacobite rising. Sir John Fenwick, who had been an officer in the Second Life Guards and was deeply involved in the Jacobite plot to assassinate William in 1696 (a plot to be followed by a national revolt under Fenwick's leadership), was beheaded in 1697.[15]

The following extract from *The Post Boy* of November 11, 1699, gives an indication of William's affection for his Household Cavalry:

On Thursday last three troops of the Horse Guards marched into Hide Park and were drawn up under their respective commanding officers, his Grace the Duke of Ormond, the Rt Honble the Earl of Rivers and the Rt Honble the Earl of Albermarle. His Majesty rid through all the ranks on a neat Barbary Horse presented to him by the Bey of Algiers, then he ordered them to file off to the end that he might take particular notice of each gentleman and his horse as they passed before him. First His Grace the Duke of Ormond and his officers, followed by the gentlemen of his troop all mounted on black horses in their scarlet coats richly laced with white feathers in their hatts marched by the King, and then the other troops which were well mounted also in their scarlet coats, richly laced having red and green feathers in their hats, passing review ...

THE ACT OF SETTLEMENT

Meanwhile, at the close of 1694 Queen Mary, a sovereign as greatly loved in Holland as in England, had died of smallpox. There were no children of her marriage to William. The death of Princess Anne's son, the 11-year-old Duke of Gloucester, on July 30, 1700, put an end to any prospect of a continuation of the Protestant House of Stuart after Princess Anne herself. On June 12, 1701, William gave his royal assent to the Act of Settlement, which named the House of Hanover as heirs to the English crown after Anne. (It also sanctioned 'the further limitation of the Crown and better securing the rights and liberties of the subject.') As the situation stood then the Electress Sophia, granddaughter of James I, would follow Anne, who herself succeeded to the throne on the death of her brother-in-law, the unpopular King William, on March 8, 1702.

1. In 1685 Lumley raised a troop of horse to fight the Western rebels, then commanded the militia who captured Monmouth. Privy Councillor and Gentleman of the Bedchamber to William
2. Imprisoned briefly. When William paid a visit to the Queen Dowager (Catherine) shortly after the Revolution she complained that she could not enjoy her evening game of basset 'since the absence of my Chamberlain who used to keep the bank'. So William released Feversham
3. 2nd Duke. Grandson of the great Irish Viceroy
4. Two senior Life Guards officers, Theophilus Oglethorp and Edward, Lord Griffin, were arrested as Jacobite conspirators
5. Heyford succeeded Cornbury, who was dismissed from command of the Royals on account of his father, Clarendon's, refusal to swear allegiance to William
6. He was escorted by his two new Troops of Life Guards commanded, respectively, by his son, Berwick, and General Patrick Sarsfield (Earl of Lucan) who had been one of Dover's lieutenants in the Catholic 4th Troop, Life Guards, 1686-88
7. From King William's Chest, vol XIII, in SP Domestic 34
8. Heyford having died suddenly before the start of the 1690 campaign
9. *James parting from Dublin*
   Said to Lauzun his cousin
   Have care of my crown
   I will take care of myself!
10. The Jacobite garrison marched out with the 'honours of war' and escaped to France. The Irish element were the first of the 'Wild Geese,' Irish mercenaries in the service of France
11. The Grand Alliance was composed of the United Provinces, England and several of the German States
12. The line cavalry had by now changed 'troop' to 'squadron'
13. Ormond was also lieutenant general to William in this campaign
14. British Library Add MSS 38703 f52
15. Fenwick is on record as being driven to Tower Hill in a coach belonging to his brother-in-law, the Earl of Carlisle, with a detachment of The Blues for escort

5 ANNE (1702-14)

THE WAR OF THE SPANISH SUCCESSION

It was not only Jacobites who toasted 'the little gentleman in black velvet' the mole that created the mound over which Dutch William's horse, Sorrel, fell, causing his master's broken collar-bone and the shock which hastened the rider's death three weeks later, and the succession to the throne of Anne, Princess of Denmark, the second daughter of James II by his first wife, Anne Hyde. Queen Anne had disliked William as much as anyone had done and she lost no time in emphasising her contrasting Englishness. 'As I know my own heart to be entirely English,' she told Parliament (in the clear, melodious voice, which was said to be one of her chief attributes), 'I can very sincerely assure you there is not anything you can expect or desire from me which I shall not be ready to do for the happiness and prosperity of England.'

However, the jubilation and celebrations with which the nation greeted their 'entirely English Queen' tended to act as palliatives and to mask certain alarming developments and portents unfolding on the international scene during the last couple of years of William's reign. In signing the Treaty of Ryswick, in 1679, Louis XIV declared his recognition of William as King and Anne as William's heir. But, when James II died in 1701, Louis, angered by the Act of Settlement, which provided for a Hanoverian succession, supported James's son (who would be known to history as the Old Pretender) as the true claimant. By then the French King's eyes were on the properties of another deceased Catholic monarch. Spain's imbecile Charles II died in 1700, leaving, in his (second) will, his country and its vast possessions in Europe, north Africa, the Caribbean, South America and the Philippines to Louis' grandson, Philip Duke of Anjou, whose grandmother and great grandmother had both been Spanish Infantas.

Under Charles of Spain's first will, however, his throne was to go to the younger son of the Hapsburg Emperor Leopold of Austria, the Archduke Charles, who possessed a claim similar and equal to that of the Bourbons. The Protestant powers in opposition to France – England, Holland and the German States – declined to stand aside and watch the creation of a Franco-Spanish hegemony which would drastically upset the balance of power. Joining Austria they reformed in September, 1701, the Grand Alliance which had challenged Louis so successfully in the 1690s. On March 13, 1702, Marlborough was made a Knight of the Garter. Next day, in his role as Ambassador Extraordinary to the United Provinces, he left for the Hague and embarked on that part of his career which, backed by Godolphin and the Whig Government, would render him the most famous man in Europe.

Queen Anne after
Sir Godfrey Kneller's portrait.

None of the three regiments now absorbed in the Household Cavalry took a share in the glory of Marlborough's great feats: his inspired march from Flanders to the Danube, in 1704, which culminated in the victory of Blenheim and resulted in the occupation of Bavaria and the salvation of Vienna; or his defeat of the French at Ramillies, in 1706, which drove the French from the Spanish Netherlands; or, two years later, his triumph at Oudenarde, which led to the capture of Lille and left France exhausted. Of the three regiments, only the Royals were on active service during the War of the Spanish Succession. They were with Marlborough in Flanders during the two siege years, 1702-3, when the great man's initiatives were so frustratingly aborted by the Dutch Field Deputies. Then the regiment was posted to Portugal.

THE ROYALS IN THE PENINSULA, 1704-12

Joining the Grand Alliance in 1702 Portugal undertook to play her part in the drive to see the Hapsburg claimant, the Archduke Charles, onto the throne in Madrid. Consequently, Marlborough, the genius strategist, recognising the importance of the Mediterranean in the power struggle – as well as that of effectually denying the Spanish crown to the Bourbons – showed his commitment by releasing the best dragoon regiment under his command, the Royals, along with four first-rate infantry battalions for service in Portugal, where the Huguenot Marquis de Ruvigny, Earl of Galway, had just relieved Meinhard Duke of Schomberg as commander-in-chief.

The regiment set sail, without horses, from London in March 4, 1704, in the appallingly overcrowded, rat-infested, disease-ridden transports, which served in those days as troop ships, to disembark at Lisbon on March 19 – and to find there all the best horses had been allotted by the cavalry brigadier, Harvey, to his own regiment, the 2nd Dragoon Guards,[1] in defiance, as the Royals' commanding officer, Colonel Robert Killigrew, pointed out, of Charles II's edict which 'gave first post to ye Dragoons, of all those raised after them, especially Our Regiment'. In other words the Royals should have had precedence as the first cavalry regiment of the line. Harvey, having also given the most desirable billets to his own regiment, detailed the English

hospital for the Royals, whose officers 'refused to putt our well men among the sick' – and proceeded to find something more salubrious.

Much of the information regarding the Royals' long sojourn in the Peninsula comes from letters written by a number of different officers to the regimental Colonel, Lord Raby,[2] a former regular cavalryman, who had, with great gallantry, commanded a squadron of the 3rd DG at the Battle of Steenkirk and subsequently transferred to The Life Guards.

Notwithstanding that Raby was now Envoy to the Court of Berlin, he not only kept a close and devoted eye on the regiment, but was also instrumental in helping to provision and re-equip them. He was furious if officers failed to keep contact with him. Raby told Killigrew he was not pleased with Cornet Kitson: 'if he does not apply himself better to study the service than he has done to acknowledge my favours to him he need not expect to go far'. One good correspondent was Captain Jason, who wrote to Raby from Portugal '... pray God grant you may never see this hellish country, all are sick of it and everyone ill. Many say it is more unhealthy than the West Indies. They starve our horses first then us.'

The Royals made a few excursions with Galway's Corps in the direction of the frontier with Spain, where the Duke of Berwick commanded the Franco-Spanish army. But their Iberian destiny was to be less on the Atlantic side than that of the Mediterranean. Gibraltar having been seized by the Royal Navy in 1704; Marlborough having earmarked the French naval base at Toulon for capture; and the Catalonians, of all Spaniards, proving to be the most sympathetic to the Hapsburg cause, the decision was taken to open another front in the vicinity of Barcelona, capital of Catalonia. The brilliant and ingenious, if erratic, Lord Peterborough – the 3rd Baron, the Royals' Colonel in 1661 having been the 2nd Baron – was to command the expeditionary force in conjunction with Admiral Sir Cloudesley Shovell. Their ultimate objective was to place the Archduke Charles of Austria, who was with them, on the throne in Madrid as Carlos III.

Peterborough's contingent of 6,000 men containing no cavalry, he was authorised to select two regiments from Galway's command. He chose the Royals and Conyngham's Dragoons, while Ormond,

·CATALONIA & S.E. ARAGON· ·1705 ~ 13·

The Royals' theatre
of operations in Spain, 1705-13

Ireland's Lord Lieutenant, was instructed to purchase 'a thousand good squat dragoon horses' for service in Spain, with which Ormonde complied paying £10 each for them. Shovell's fleet sailed from Lisbon on July 14, 1705, and, after taking more cavalry on board at Gibraltar, were anchored off Barcelona by August 11. Peterborough besieged and stormed the fortress of Montjuich which protected Barcelona's southern side, the Royals playing their part in a dismounted role, and the city surrendering on September 27.

Peterborough would now advance on Madrid via Valencia, while Galway converged from the East. After Barcelona was captured Killigrew took over Conyngham's Dragoons,[3] James St Pierre[4] assuming command of the Royals. December, 1705, found the Royals at Tortosa, insufficiently armed. 'We are used in Catalonia entirely as Horse,' wrote Captain George Benson to Raby, 'and the sword is the weapon we have to trust to. Those we have are useless.' Benson was soon on his way home to order new clothing equipment, including serviceable swords. But Peterborough was clever in his employment of the Royals. He would, for example, send a number of detachments ahead to expose themselves to the enemy, formed up as though they led strong columns. In that way he frequently prompted his opponent, the pro-Bourbon Spaniard, Las Torres, to withdraw in alarm.

Fortunes changed from Bourbon to Hapsburg and back again. In June, 1706, Galway entered Madrid and pronounced the Archduke Charles King of Spain. But, finding the capital untenable, he marched out, and in April, 1707, got trounced at Almanza by the Duke of Berwick who then marched up the coast towards Barcelona. The Royals (with their new swords) were dispatched north to the valley of the Ebro and on patrol duty along its tributary the Cinca. 'The enemy made many motions to pass the river,' Raby was told, 'which kept us always, and chiefly in the night, upon our guard and ready to mount'. That November Cornet John Cope (to be famous as General Sir John in the 1740s) joined the regiment, of whom St Pierre declared that he had never met 'a more sober, judicious young man'. St Pierre retired in June, 1709, handing over to Captain Edward Montagu from the 2nd DG.

The Bourbons, with the Duke of Orleans now commanding for Philip of Anjou, captured Lerida and Tortosa in 1708, while the Hapsburgs occupied Sardinia and Minorca. But the period 1708-9 was relatively quiet for the Allies in Spain. Since Marlborough's victories at Ramillies and Oudenarde Louis had been withdrawing troops in large numbers from Orleans' contingent. On July 4, 1710, Stanhope, the Allied cavalry brigade commander, was writing to Raby that 'your regiment is now the fullest both in man and horses in the field and in every other respect in good order, which till now could not be said of it since it

Field Marshal
The Duke of Argyle and
(2nd) Earl of Greenwich.
From an engraving.
He was Colonel of the
4th (Scottish) Troop of
Life Guards (1696-1703)

was in this country. This change is owing to Colonel Benson and Major Killigrew [Henry, nephew of the former commanding officer] who are both very deserving officers'.

1710 was the most crucial year for the Hapsburg cause in Spain. The Austrian general Guido von Stahremberg, who had been the Archduke's commander-in-chief

since 1708, went onto the offensive in June, 1710. Crossing the rivers Segre and Noguera (with an army 18,000 strong) he met the Bourbons under General Villadaria on July 16 at Almanera, where a largely cavalry battle ensued. Stanhope deployed 22 squadrons in two lines. The enemy fielded 42. However Stanhope led a charge of such elan and ferocity that the Bourbon Horse was quickly broken and scattered, whereupon their nine battalions 'fled without waiting to be charged.' Though dusk was falling the Royals continued to press the fugitives. 'Colonel Montagu pursued them at full gallop ... to the very ditches of Lerida,' Raby was told. The Bourbon army lost '1,250 men, several guns and all its baggage.' Captain James Crofts,[5] the Royals officer whom Stanhope entrusted with the despatches for the Queen was rewarded with £500 '... for coming express from Spain with news of the victory over the Duke of Anjou's forces.'

Stanhope's cavalry now pushed out into Aragon obliging Philip of Anjou's forces to hasten north-east along the Ebro valley to prevent a rupture of their communications with Saragossa. There on August 9, the two armies met once again and Stahremberg scored another decisive victory, the Royals who were posted on the left flank, being in the thickest of the battle and suffering 11 men killed and 25 badly wounded, not to mention the loss of 55 horses. Stahremberg turned for Madrid on August 16, and, the Royals leading, entered the city (with the Archduke Charles), unopposed, on September 10.

That autumn, however, the Hapsburg fortunes in Spain changed for the worse. Louis sent Marshal Vendôme to command Philip's army. Vendôme, determined to redeem his defeat at Oudenarde, acted with great energy, speed and skill. Putting a force astride the Tagus at Talavera, he cut off the Allies' contact with Portugal. In November, Stahremberg moved his army out of Madrid to the more easily defended Cinchon. While all Castile rose in support of the Bourbons, and the Archduke Charles withdrew to Barcelona, Stahremberg determined to transfer to more friendly territory. On November 25 Stanhope led his column, including the Royals, into the old Moorish fortress of Brihuega where, two days later, he found himself surrounded by 9,000 enemy and Vendôme's artillery pounding the town's walls.

The Battle of Saragossa,
August 9, 1710

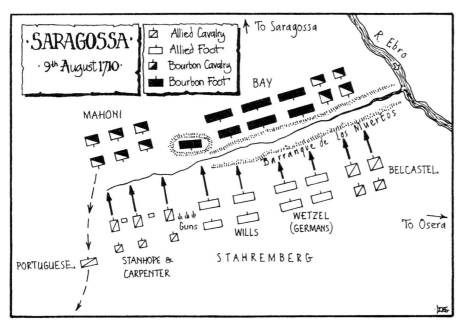

On November 28, following a most gallant defence, with hand-to-hand fighting continuing well into the night, Stanhope surrendered. The Royals suffered another 40 killed or died of wounds at Brihuega, the remainder becoming Vendôme's prisoners. Stahremberg, who had been hurrying to relieve the town, managed to repulse Vendôme at Villa Viciosa, then withdraw into Catalonia. There was little more to be said of the campaign in the Peninsula.

The Royals were not too badly treated in captivity. Those who survived, being released in August, 1712, took ship from Bayonne to England where the regiment was posted to Doncaster. The Royals had spent eight years in the Peninsula. They had played a gallant part in several significant victories. But whereas the regiments that accompanied Marlborough were festooned with battle honours, those in the Peninsula gained none. For, albeit the War of the Spanish Succession was an Allied triumph, the Spanish campaign itself was ultimately a disaster for the Hapsburg cause.

With the end of the war over half the regiments of Foot were disbanded, along with three of horse and most of the dragoons.

HOME DUTIES 1702-14

During those victorious years of Queen Anne's reign, which left France crippled and ended with the Peace of Utrecht, in 1713, the Peace which marked Great Britain's emergence as a world power, there had been imperative contingency tasks for The Life Guards and The Blues. For although the Treaty obliged Louis to recognise Anne's position as Queen and the Hanoverian settlement; and although he duly expelled the Pretender (the Chevalier St George as the French called him) from Paris to Lorraine, the Sun King soon went back on his word. Moreover even Anne herself and many of her Tory ministers were strongly suspected of wishing to bring over her half-brother in preference to the Electress (or as it turned out, the Elector) of Hanover. And the threat of a French invasion, coupled with the Jacobite risings, became increasingly dangerous following the Act of Union (of England and Scotland) in 1707. As a result of that Union, incidentally, the 4th (Scots) Troops of Life Guards and Horse Grenadiers were moved from Edinburgh to Kingston-on-Thames, and were now clothed,

armed and accoutred like their English comrades.

Despite Marlborough's vast requirements and those of the commanders in the Peninsula, a very substantial force of the best trained troops – particularly cavalry which could be rapidly deployed to threatened locations – were held in readiness at home. The first of those contingents were, of course, The Life Guards and The Blues; and it must have been frustrating for them to lose many of their most promising officers, and soldiers, too, who were wanted in regimental and subordinate commands under Marlborough.

Notwithstanding that the Palace of Whitehall (with the exception of the Banqueting Hall) was burned to the ground in 1698, The Life Guards continued to mount guard at the adjacent Horse Guards, 'the gateway to Royal London', as the Household Cavalry have continued to do ever since, although rather more in earnest then than now. For then they were police as well as soldiers. The Life Guards with their Horse Grenadier Guards were still deployed in three semi-independent Troops. And, although each Life Guards Troop was under command of a captain, that officer still held the rank of general or colonel in the army at large, just as all junior officers of The Life Guards held a higher rank outside that corps.

The Queen, by contrast with her predecessor, was a lover of pomp and ceremonial, and The Life Guards were naturally very prominent on such great State occasions as her coronation on St George's day, 1702, and the celebrations and thanksgivings for each of Marlborough's victories, not to mention the funeral in November, 1708, of the Queen's beloved consort, Prince George of Denmark, Duke of Cumberland, who died that year on October 28.

The Life Guards and The Blues were stood by to march at an hour or so's notice on many an occasion when it looked as if French ships might be sailing for British shores. And the aborted attempt by the Pretender to land in Scotland in March, 1708, saw the 1st and 2nd Life Guards, along with their Horse Grenadiers and The Blues, riding with all speed up the Great North Road and riding back with a bevy of Scottish prisoners.

A typical example of The Life Guards in a police role was the occasion of their use for riot control. In 1710, a large bulk of the populace rose angrily in support of Doctor Sacheverell, the Jacobite zealot who (at the instigation it seems of the Lord Mayor) preached a sermon in St Paul's Cathedral amounting to a thinly veiled attack upon the Government and the Act of Hanoverian Succession. The fanatic doctor was impeached; and, while he stood trial in Westminster Hall and the mob roared and heckled at those doors, The Life Guards strove to prevent the sacking of meeting houses and the homes of Bishops and Dissenters and to clear the streets.

On July 31, 1713, the Queen held a grand review of all her Life Guards and Horse Grenadiers, six troops of The Blues and seven regiments of Foot. In recent years she had been mostly carried in a sedan, or at best walked very slowly with the assistance of a cane and a courtier's arm. By the end of that year she was seriously ill; and, on August 1, 1714, to the nation's profound grief, she died, the last of the Stuart monarchs. And, the Electress of Hanover having predeceased Anne, that old Dowager's son – 54-year-old George Louis, great-grandson of James I and grandson of Elizabeth of Bohemia, the 'Winter Queen' – was duly proclaimed King of England.

King George arrived at Gravesend in a thick fog on September 17 and landed next morning, to be received by the Duke of Northumberland,[6] Captain-Commandant of the Household Cavalry and Gold Stick, with an escort of 100 Lifeguardsmen and 50 Horse Grenadiers waiting on the quayside. The remainder of the regiment were camped in Hyde Park on alert to meet any Jacobite attempt that might erupt, for a great body of the nation was still persuaded that the more attractive figure of the Pretender might change his religion and were ready to rise in his cause, as were thousands more who would have welcomed him as a Catholic King.

For the drive from Gravesend to the City Northumberland travelled in the Royal coach with King George and his son, the Prince of Wales. The conversation was in French, for the new King spoke not a word of English. He was scarcely to speak a sentence of it to his dying day.

A week before the advent of England's first Hanoverian Monarch in London the Earl of Mar had raised the Jacobite Standard at Braemar declaring 'James the Eighth' (of Scotland) and 'the Third' (of England) to be 'our rightful and natural King by the Grace of God.' That was on September 9.

1. Afterwards the Bays
2. Thomas Wentworth, Lord Raby, had recently succeeded his cousin the 2nd Earl of Strafford in the barony when he followed Edward Matthews in the Colonelcy of the Royals in 1697
3. Afterwards the 8th Hussars
4. One of the most effective and colourful of the Royals officers St Pierre was originally gazetted cornet on September 1, 1685.
5. This was a son of the Duke of Monmouth by his mistress Eleanor Needham, Crofts having been the name adopted for Monmouth before Charles II made him James Scott, Duke of Monmouth and Buccleuch. James Crofts, who transferred to the Royals from the KDG in 1695, went on to become a major-general. His daughter, Maria, married James Wentworth Smyth Stuart, Monmouth's son by Baroness Wentworth, as Smyth Stuart's second wife. Crofts was appointed Lieutenant Colonel of Rich's Dragoons, then, in 1719, of the 9th Dragoons (9th Lancers)
6. George Fitzroy, Duke of Northumberland (born Dec 28, 1665) third son of the Duchess of Cleveland by Charles the Second, had been appointed, aged 19, captain of the 2nd Troop of Life Guards within a week of the accession of James II.

6 GEORGE I (1714-27)

'He was born with all the attributes of a country gentleman,' said Marshal von der Schulenberg of George I, 'but he is devoid of those of a monarch'. This son of a prince of Hanover and a princess of Bohemia was not an attractive man either in looks, manner or culture, as reflected in Princess Anne's (as she then was) unhesitating rejection of him as a suitor in 1680. He married, two years later, the Princess Sophia Dorothea of Celle who became the mother of the Prince of Wales (George II). But the marriage lasted no more than twelve years, for she indulged in an affair with the Swedish adventurer, Count Königsmark, who disappeared (and was almost certainly murdered) being last seen leaving her apartments when her husband was absent in Berlin in 1694. A divorce was promptly arranged for George, while Sophia Dorothea was imprisoned by her father-in-law in Ahlden Castle, where she spent the rest of her life.

George I had been a professional soldier in his youth, serving under his father in the Imperial army against the Turks in Hungary and Austria. Displaying great qualities of leadership and an habitual disregard for his own safety, he went on to be present at the capture of Buda and fought at the Battle of Neerwinden. So perhaps the chief asset he brought with him when he came into his English inheritance was that valuable experience coupled with a great enthusiasm for military life. And it must have been with considerable pride that he listened to reports of the army, of which he was newly commander-in-chief, going to defeat the Pretender's supporters in 1715.

His government acted promptly that autumn of his accession, arresting leading Jacobites and, among other military measures, sending the Royal Dragoons to Newcastle to join General Carpenter's command which was to march to Scotland. Learning that a rebel force of Scots was making for Cumberland, Carpenter raced eastwards across the Lowlands in pursuit. At the same time more of King George's forces were advancing north from Manchester. That contingent joined hands with Carpenter's on the Ribble where the rebels were hemmed in at Preston. So the Royals were among those to receive their surrender. On that same day, November 13, the Jacobite army under the inept Lord Mar was driven off its position at Sheriffmuir, if not over-whelmed, by the Duke of Argyll (who was to be rewarded for his services with the Colonelcy of The Blues). So there was little for which the Pretender[1] could hope when he landed at Peterhead on December 22. The remainder of his adherents retreated north to disperse in the mountains, while, in February, 1716 he sailed home to France.

The circumstance in which the Royals lost their Colonel, Lord Raby – Earl of Strafford, too, since 1711 – was indirectly coupled with those of the '15 rebellion. After Berlin, Strafford was appointed Ambassador Extra-ordinary to Holland. As such he was indicted

George I.
From the portrait by
Sir Godfrey Kneller.
(In possession of Count
Kielmansegg)

(along with the pro-Jacobite Tories, Oxford, Bolingbroke and Ormonde,[2] who were also impeached) by the new Whig government for the part he played in negotiating the Peace of Utrecht which, they said, gave too much away to the French. Strafford's Colonelcy of the Royals passed on June 1, 1715 to Lord Cobham,[3] who, after many years' gallant active service, had reached the rank of lieutenant-general. Four months later Benson succeeded Montagu in the lieutenant-colonelcy. It was under Benson that the Royals entered Scotland in earnest once more in this reign, marching up to Fife in the spring of 1719, when Philip V of Spain dispatched a fleet in that direction in the Jacobite cause. But Philip's fleet was scattered by storms, with the exception of two ships which reached Ross-shire and whose soldiers were quickly rounded up.

As for The Life Guards – who were out on the streets in their secondary role on the occasions, among others, of the weavers' riots (1719) and the unrest over the South Sea crisis (1720) – George I re-emphasised their unique status as his Maison du Roy, his *corps d'élite*, by ordaining that they, and they alone, should pay no honours to generals except when in line with other troops, or mixed in detachments. And that they should turn out only to the commander-in-chief. Meanwhile the King's other Guards regiment of horse, The Blues, were increasingly recognised as being in effect, if not in fact, the second regiment of Household Cavalry.

Our first Hanoverian monarch initiated many improvements, too, in the army as a whole, particularly in the spheres of false musters, abuses of civilians by the military, officer absenteeism, the manner in which commissions were purchased (a practice of which he was in favour of stopping altogether), uniform patterns of drill and the stamping out of sedition. In 1716 he decreed that every regiment should be inspected annually by a general officer. (Thus for example, when the Royals were encamped at Hornby, in Lancashire, in 1723, they were reviewed by Brigadier-General Honywood, who gave them an excellent report, their 'cloathing' being 'good', their camp necessaries 'compleat', their accounts cleared and their arms and accoutrements in very favourable order.)

'Whenever the hand of King George the First can be traced in the administration of the Army,' wrote Sir John Fortescue in his exhaustive history,[4] 'it is found working for integrity, economy and discipline; and it is sufficiently evident that when he gave decided orders the very officials at the War Office knew better than to disregard them.

1. By this time the Chevalier de St George could expect no support from France, his best friend there, Louis XIV, having died on September 1. The Regent, the Duke of Orleans, was not prepared to help him
2. Henry St John, Viscount Bolingbroke, fled to St Germains in April, 1715, and was soon followed by James Butler, Duke of Ormonde. Robert Harley, Earl of Oxford was sent to the Tower
3. Cobham was followed in the Colonelcy of the Royals, in 1721, by Sir Charles Hotham, who died two years later and was succeeded by General Humphrey Gore
4. In Volume II of *A History of The British Army* by the Hon Sir J W Fortescue

7 GEORGE II (1727-60)

As George I had abhorred and despised the son who became George II, so George II (himself the son of divorced parents) detested his eldest son Frederick Prince of Wales, the heir who was never to be King. And the second King George was joined, at least as vehemently, in that hatred by his powerful consort, Queen Caroline, who not only ruled George's heart and mind, but exercised, too, a great influence over his first minister, Sir Robert Walpole. It is not so much Prince Frederick, however, as his young brother, Prince William Augustus, Duke of Cumberland, who is to feature more prominently in this chapter. Cumberland, like his father and grandfather, displayed the mentality of a drill sergeant, a brave and cunning drill sergeant with a passion for dates and data. The Hanoverians' abiding interest (in England) was the army, particularly the regiments of Guards, and, above all, those soldiers who were ever closest to them, The Life Guards.

George II may too often have displayed a blinkered mind, but he was by no means devoid of imagination. It was he who, in 1739, established the first military training camps, and he who ordained that greater emphasis be placed upon regimental distinction, which he saw as being the foundation of the British army's esprit de corps. Perhaps the principal drawback of this King was that, like his father, he valued the interests of Hanover more than those of England. Kings still ruled England in an active

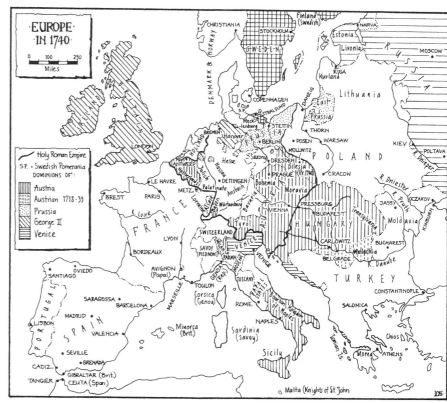

Far Left; George II.
From the portrait by
Thomas Hudson
(National Portrait Gallery)

Below; Europe in 1740

sense and in foreign affairs George was more or less the final arbiter. Anyhow this was another reign in which English men and women rightly perceived England's needs to be subordinated to Hanover's.

The first fifteen years of George II's reign was a quiet time for the army. The Life Guards carried out their duties in London and The Blues helped to keep the peace in the home counties, while the Royals were mostly in the north of England employed on the 18th-century cavalry's ceaseless peacetime pursuits of bringing highwaymen, smugglers and other lawbreakers to book and keeping order in the towns. Then, early in the 1740s, England went to war again.

THE WAR OF THE AUSTRIAN SUCCESSION

In 1740 the Emperor Charles VI of Austria

and the Holy Roman Empire died, to be succeeded by his daughter the Princess Maria Theresa. The Elector of Bavaria's counter-claim to the Empire, albeit a tenuous one, was supported by France, Spain, Prussia and Saxony. King George, as Elector of Hanover, was pledged to support Maria Theresa, while the English Parliament saw in Bavaria's staunchly backed bid for the Imperial throne both a fresh threat to the balance of power in Europe and to England's trade and growing colonial interest. The Dutch, feeling ever more threatened, promptly joined the Anglo-Austrian alliance although as usual they were reluctant to commit their forces to foreign lands. In 1741 France advanced against Austria and Hanover, and Frederick of Prussia occupied the state of Silesia. The English Parliament voted £800,000 and 16,000 men to mount an expeditionary force in support of Maria Theresa, the man chosen to lead it being the old Earl of Stair, a veteran of Marlborough's wars. In the summer of 1742 The Blues and the Royals left with the expeditionary force for Flanders; and three months later, the 3rd and 4th Troops of The Life Guards with the 2nd Troop of the Horse Grenadiers, joined them.

When, in April, 1743, Stair led his army eastwards into Germany to seek out the French he left The Life Guards and Blues behind at Brussels, the former anticipating the arrival of the King,[1] the latter to provide the escort for the state entry of Archduchess Maria Theresa and her husband, the Prince of Lorraine, into the city from the Austrian Netherlands. By mid-May, Stair – with the Pragmatick Army, as the Anglo-Austrian force was called – was established a few miles south-east of Frankfurt on the west bank of the river Main, on the north side of Aschaffenburg. Stair would have crossed the river in an attempt to bring the French Marshal de Noailles and his 70,000 men to battle, but the English commander's jealous and quarrelsome Austrian colleague, the Duc d'Aremburg, sent a message to King George persuading him to prohibit that, which the King did (because, as he put it, he was 'not officially at war with France'). The result was that the Pragmatick Army not only lost a golden opportunity of victory but also of gaining essential food and forage supplies. In fact George II did little to endear himself to the British element of the army. Accompanied by his second son, the Duke of

The campaign of 1743

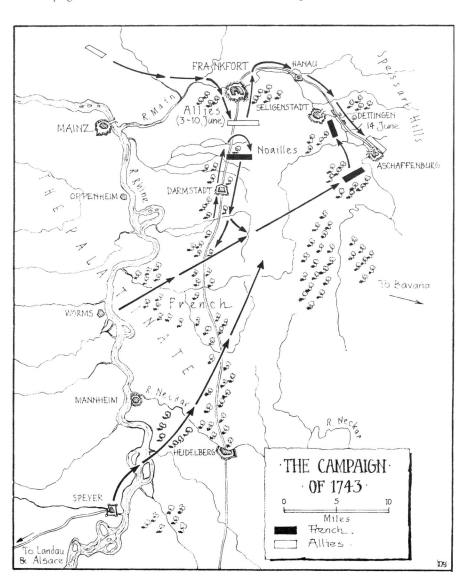

THE CAMPAIGN OF 1743

0   5   10

Miles

■ French.
□ Allies.

Cumberland, his chief minister, Lord Carteret and the Gold Stick in Waiting, Lord Crauford[2] and escorted by his Life Guards the King reached the Pragmatick encampment to take command on June 19.[3] He celebrated his arrival with a grand review of the troops; and, says his biographer:

> ... the men belonging to the British regiments must have presented a sorry sight, for they were ill-clad and ill-shod, and had been on short rations for days; and they were fiercely resentful because the Hanoverians claimed privileges which were denied them. The discontent spread to the officers. From the moment of his arrival in the camp the King studiously ignored Stair, preferring the company of the Hanoverian staff officers; and in this way he managed to leave upon the minds of his British subjects the impression that he was callously indifferent to their interests.[4]

THE BATTLE OF DETTINGEN, JUNE 27,[5] 1743

A week after his arrival the King, as Stair had foreseen, ordered a retreat northwest, to Hanau, to obtain forage. De Noailles saw his chance of locking the Pragmatick Army into what he called 'my mousetrap'. For the road to Hanau, close alongside the Main, being hemmed in on the west by thickly wooded hills, gave a frontage for deployment of less than a mile. The French marshal determined to lock King George into that corridor by occupying the village to the south, Aschaffenburg, and thus barring the road to Bavaria; and also by sending his nephew the Comte de Grammont, with 28,000 including the Maison du Roy, to establish a position behind a marshy stream on the west side of Dettingen, while subjecting the marching Allies to a bombardment by three batteries of 18-pounders from across the river. The Pragmatick Army started their march in the early hours of June 27, the King with his Life Guards being on the left, close to the river. Kendal, a private gentleman in the 3rd Troop (Albemarle's[6]) takes up the story in a letter to his wife from the previous afternoon (June 26):

> The same day I mounted the King's guard and in the afternoon the K's baggage and all the Generals were packed up ... We who were upon the King's Guard, which were 36, were ordered to have our horses already bridled, to go out with the King that night ... He had not rode above a mile ... but they began to fire at him from a battery of 12 pieces of cannon but as God would have it they levelled too high. I saw several balls go within half

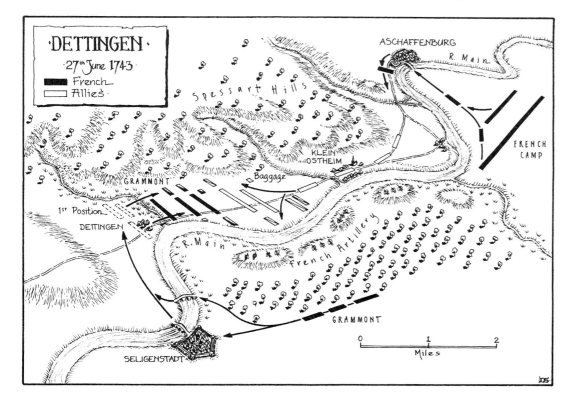

The Battle of Dettingen, June 27, 1743

a yd of his head. I was in the first rank next the King; our Capt had his hat shot off, the man on my right had his horse shot and the man on my left was shot in the shoulder and the next to him shot dead. Then they fired from three batteries upon the horse and the balls flew thick as hail. All this time the King was not at all concerned; the duc d'Aremberg desired him to go out of danger: He made answer, Don't tell me of danger. I'll be even with them. He is certainly the boldest man I ever saw...[7]

Certainly, too, it looked as though the Pragmatick Army was doomed to annihilation, until the Comte de Grammont, in his impetuosity to commit his force to battle, crossed the miry stream which would have rendered him excellent protection. His blunder was to prove the salvation of the Anglo-Austrian force. Stair, so often frustrated in his military judgement by both the King and d'Aremberg, now, as he put it, 'thought it my duty to meddle'. As de Grammont's troops marched towards him he reformed his column into two extended lines, while The Blues, the Greys and two regiments of dragoon guards covered this redeployment at the riverside and got heavily bombarded from across the Main for their pains. The King, dismounting and handing his charger to his Life Guards orderly, took his place at the head of the second line of Foot, exhorting them to 'fight for the honour of England'.

George, here there and everywhere to encourage his soldiers in the fight, never showing the least trace of fear and, at one point, working the gun of a Hanoverian battery with his own hands, went a long way to redeem his churlishness in camp. Meanwhile, the following passage from a letter written by a Blues subaltern to his brother a fortnight after the battle shows how that regiment fared:

When we were ordered to the Banks of the Main to cover the Infantry while they were forming, as I told you in my last we sustained the severest cannonade that ever happened in any action from three large batteries, and though we had several men and horses killed and wounded in this post and fully expected to be all tore in pieces we stood firm and immovable like a senseless bastion to be battered for

upwards of two hours.[8]

De Grammont, who made a rather faltering and disconcerted infantry attack against the Pragmatick centre, then came under the withering and disciplined fire of the British and Hanoverian Foot. His own foot soldiers having been halted with devastating losses, he sent in his cavalry which received similar punishment. It was now that the Black Musketeers, one of Louis XV's Household Cavalry regiments, composed largely of high-born youths, swerved to their left in face of another devastating volley of Allied musketry and found themselves confronted by the Royals who put in a fiercely galloping charge and routed them. It was in those minutes that a Royals sergeant snatched the Musketeers' standard, a square of white satin embroidered in gold and silver with a bunch of nine arrows in crimson and bearing the motto *Alterius Jovis Altera Tela*. (It was from that epic encounter against the Black Musketeers that the Royals adopted the black elements of their insignia, embellishments worn to this day by The Blues and Royals.)

De Noailles rushed across reinforcements to his beleaguered nephew, but it was too late. The bulk of de Grammont's corps was already in headlong retreat. Only those two famous regiments of Foot, the *Gardes Suisses* and the *Gardes Françaises,* stood their ground. Stair sent an ADC to Crauford to say that it was now The Life Guards' turn for offensive action. Crauford, an outstandingly gallant and resolute commander, told his men to forget their pistols and trust simply in their swords. His trumpeter (on his own initiative) sounded the call *Britons strike home!,* and the determined knee-to-knee rush of the tall hot-blooded men and their heavy horses carried all before them. ('Our men and horses could stand it no longer,' wrote a Life Guardsman in a letter home, 'for in three days they had but one feed of corn and neither Hay nor Water: However we took the French Life Guards' standard; we charged them sword in hand when they stood nine file deep and drove them out of the field with the devil to them.')

The Life Guards pursued the French and Swiss Foot guards to the water's edge, and the whole army would have followed up de Noailles's and de Grammont's retreat had not the King restrained them, repeating 'I am not at war with France!' He would not even wait to have the wounded brought on to the new encampment at Hanau, but left them to the mercy of the French. Stair resigned his command in disgust. George Wade – famous as a builder of roads and bridges, but less able as a general – taking over from him. Anyhow DETTINGEN is registered as the first battle honour of both The Life Guards and The Blues. The army was back in Flanders in the autumn.

1744-45

Those elements of what now constitutes the Household Cavalry, who had fought at Dettingen, languished in Flanders until 1745. Both the Dutch and the Austrians had, by this time, lost a good deal of heart. On March 25, 1744, France at last declared war on England, but her marshals, being now sick of Germany, turned their aggressive eyes on the Netherlands. Since neither the Dutch nor the Austrians were prepared to send their armies out in true tactical defence of their territories, France's brilliant Marshal Saxe and his 80,000-strong army proceeded to assault and take the frontier towns while encountering little opposition. May, 1744, found the Allies with 92 squadrons and 40 battalions at Ath, to cover Brussels. But when the Austrians invaded Alsace, Saxe was obliged to detach a large measure of his army to the upper Rhine while going on the defensive in the Netherlands.

However, neither Maurice of Nassau commanding the Dutch nor the awkward Austrian d'Aremberg were willing to go on the offensive – until they were eventually persuaded by Wade that such an advance would prove the best way of saving the Netherlands. Albeit the Dutch still refused to commit their siege guns, the Allies duly marched south to the vicinity of Lille where they spent much of their time foraging, which resulted in some skirmishes with French outlying piquets. In September, 1744, they withdrew again. During the following spring the King's second son, the 24-year-old Duke of Cumberland who had conducted himself well at Dettingen, was sent out by his father to replace Wade, while the Austrians recalled d'Aremberg and filled his place with Marshal Konigsegg, both of which appointments made for greater harmony at command level. Saxe's numerically superior army was now busy investing Tournai on the River Scheldt. Cumberland,

eager for battle, led the Allies to Maulbray, a couple of miles southeast of Tournai, with the objective of forcing Saxe to raise the siege.

THE BATTLE OF FONTENOY, APRIL 30, 1745

For the impending battle the French fielded 56,000 against the Allies' 46,000. Hearing of Cumberland's approach Saxe, while continuing to invest Tournai, adopted a powerful position on a forward slope with his right wing protected by the Scheldt. In order to clear the immediate front and flanks, the Prince of Waldeck, commanding the Dutch and Hanoverians on the Allied left was to assault the enemy outposts in and between the villages of Anthoing and Fontenoy while, on the right, Brigadier-General Ingoldsby was to advance his brigade through the Bois de Barri, and clear the woods and the redoubts next to them. On April 29 the French piquets and light troops were duly dislodged from the foreground.

Next day the cavalry, including the Royals, led by Lieutenant Colonel Naizon, and Crauford's brigade of Life Guards now with The Blues under command, covered the advance of the British infantry (under Sir John Ligonier the formidable 65-year-old lieutenant-general of Foot); and, having seen them past the French redoubts, turned to the rear, but not before a French cannon had taken the life of Sir James Campbell commanding the Allied Horse. Ligonier's regiments, though exposed to a terrible flanking fire, now marched, line abreast, towards the enemy's centre until, when well within range, they halted to unleash the deadly musket volleys for which they were now celebrated throughout Europe. As their comrades fell they closed ranks and fired again, inflicting the most severe damage on Saxe's strength.

But almost everything else went wrong for the Allies. Richard Ingoldsby's brigade failed to press on strongly enough through the Bois de Barri, leaving the French redoubts, as we have seen, free to pour their enfilade fire on that brigade.[9] The Dutch, refusing to attack with the least resolution, made little effort to take their objectives. ('They [the Dutch] remained idle spectators of our exertions,' said an English eyewitness.) The cavalry, being leaderless since Campbell's death,

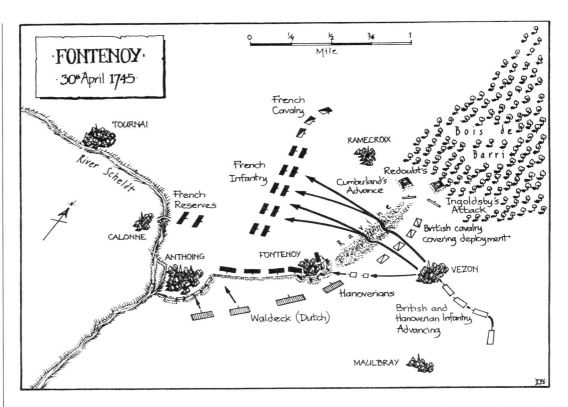

The Battle of Fontenoy,
April 30, 1745

received no orders to come in behind
Ligonier's infantrymen who, despite their
extraordinary courage, were now being
subjected to crippling counter-attacks by
Saxe's reserves.

By the time Crauford assumed command
of all the cavalry, victory had virtually
gone to the French. All Crauford's cavaliers
could do was to cover the withdrawal
of the gallant British infantry. There was
a charge, in which two squadrons of
The Blues got farthest forward and
engaged the enemy – 'the behaviour of
the Blue Guards is highly to be commended,'
a 1745 issue of *The Gentleman's Magazine*
was to record, 'the lieutenant-colonel
[Beake] and the major [Jenkinson]
distinguishing themselves particularly on
the occasion'[10] – but the rest of the Horse
were mostly stopped in their tracks by
fleeing Austrians as well as Dutchmen.
Crauford, having rallied his men, attempted
to gallop them up the slope again only
to be impeded by the cowardly fleeing
Dutch and Austrians ('... another body of
runaways came upon us and broke us
anew,' recalled Crauford). However,
sufficient cavalry, including the Royals,
got into action to check the French
pursuit and to induce Saxe to halt his
victorious troops and return them to the
siege of Tournai. Thus ended the Battle of
Fontenoy, a defeat owed principally to the
chicken-heartedness of the Dutch.

THE '45 JACOBITE REBELLION

The Allies retreated under the protection
of the artillery to Ath; then, with Saxe's
army on the march again, and subduing the
greater part of the Austrian Netherlands,
Cumberland ordered a further retirement,
hastening to cover Antwerp, the mouth of
the Scheldt and the Dutch province of
Zeeland.

In July, 1745, while the Allies remained
in these desperate straits in the
Netherlands, the Pretender's son, Prince
Charles Edward, landed in Scotland; and, on
August 19, with over 2,000 Highlanders
behind him, he unfurled his standard at
Glenfinnan. On September 17 he entered
Edinburgh and, four days later, routed
King George's army – commanded by that
staunch old Royal Dragoon, Johnny
Cope – at the Battle of Prestonpans. By
November 28 the 'Young Pretender' was
at Manchester and on December 4 at
Derby. Meanwhile the King had recalled
Cumberland and the bulk of the British
regiments from the Netherlands. Cumber-
land was put in command of a new
force to repel the invader, which he did,
eventually crushing him at Culloden in
April, 1746.

The Marquis of Granby. From the portrait by Sir Joshua Reynolds. He was Colonel of the Royal Horse Guards Blue (1758-70). (By Gracious Permission of Her Majesty The Queen)

Neither Life Guards, Blues nor Royals were home in time to take part in that campaign but were held in the south of England as a contingency against the threat of a French invasion in support of the Jacobites. The Peace of Aix la Chapelle – a treaty almost wholly to the advantage of France – being signed on April 30, 1748, there was a fresh dis-bandment, or reduction, of British regiments. The Blues and the Royals were unaffected by that, but eighteen months previously The Life Guards had lost their 3rd and 4th Troops.[11] That regiment's only really noteworthy duty during the late 1740s appears to have been to stand guard at the execution of the gallant Jacobite, Lord Lovat, in January, 1747.

In 1756 for the first time non-commissioned officers were appointed in The Life Guards. The four 'right-hand men' of each troop became warrant officers with the title of quartermaster, while the four juniors were named corporals-of-horse, the equivalent to sergeants of the line.

THE HORSE GUARDS, WHITEHALL

In 1750 the Horse Guards, the buildings now occupied by the headquarters of the Household Division, the Household Cavalry and the Queen's Life Guard, were rebuilt according to William Kent's plan, George II driving through the famous archway for the first time in 1751.

Also in 1750 two successive Blues Colonels

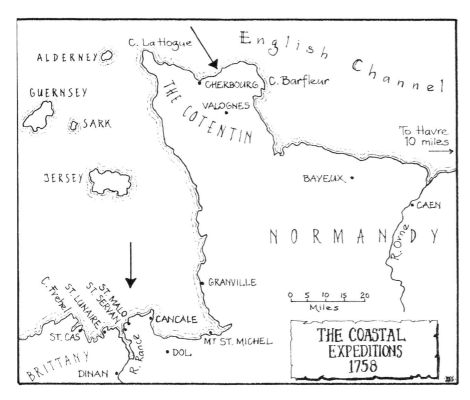

THE COASTAL
EXPEDITIONS
1758

The Royals' coastal expeditions,
July-August, 1758

died, the Dukes of Somerset and Richmond, the latter being followed in the appointment by the greatest British general of the recent wars, Sir John Ligonier. He was succeeded five years later by one of the most dearly loved of Blues Colonels, the Marquis of Granby, of whom more later in this chapter. (The Colonelcy of The Blues had been described by Walpole as 'the most agreeable post in the army'.)

THE SEVEN YEARS WAR 1756-63

In 1756 France, having sent an army into Hanover, threatened to encircle Prussia, whose ruler King Frederick, 'the Great' (George II's nephew) responded by invading Saxony, and thus began the Seven Years War. On May 18 England declared war on France again. Most importantly for England this was the conflict which rendered the Royal Navy virtually supreme, in which British arms prevailed over those of France in Canada, the West Indies, West Africa and India, in which William Pitt (Lord Chatham), a former Blues officer, was to win his fame as a war leader.

By the spring of 1758, Prince Ferdinand of Brunswick, commanding (in succession to Cumberland) what was known as the Army of Observation, had driven the French westwards from the Elbe to the Rhine, which

he now proposed to cross. But he was seriously under strength. In late summer that year, therefore, Pitt sent him 12,000 men, under command of the (3rd) Duke of Marlborough, with Lord George Sackville as second-in-command and the cavalry, including The Blues, led by their Colonel, Lord Granby. This force linked up with Ferdinand's army near Munster on August 21.

THE ROYALS IN COASTAL RAIDS, 1758

In 1755 all regiments of dragoons (by now conventional cavalry) were each ordered to raise a light troop having the original dragoon role, which is to say mounted infantry. Along with those of eight other dragoon regiments the Royals' light troop (under command of Captain-Lieutenant George Warrender) formed a composite regiment which took part, in July-August, 1758, in three successive raids on the French coast, two near St Malo and one on the Cherbourg peninsula, with the object of diverting the enemy's attention from the campaign in Germany. In the most notable of these three expeditions the composite light dragoon regiment occupied Cherbourg and captured 20 ships and 200 cannon.

THE CAMPAIGN OF MINDEN, 1759

Pitt, one of whose mottos was 'I will win America for us in Germany,' was determined to keep the French occupied in as large numbers and as busy as possible in that country, where the seat of war lay between the Rhine to the west, the Weser to the east, the Main to the south and the sea coast to the north. In 1759, while Frederick the Great was occupied on three fronts, Prince Ferdinand of Brunswick was intent upon the defence of Hanover, Brunswick and Hesse-Cassel. It looked, in particular, as though the French, now under command of Marshal Contades, were resolved to commit their vastly superior forces to the subjugation of Hanover.

Following the death of the (3rd) Duke of Marlborough, Lord George Sackville assumed command of the British expeditionary force with the Marquis of Granby as his second-in-command and commander of the cavalry, which were led by The Blues. Ferdinand responding to the threat to his main Westphalian base, Munster, marched his

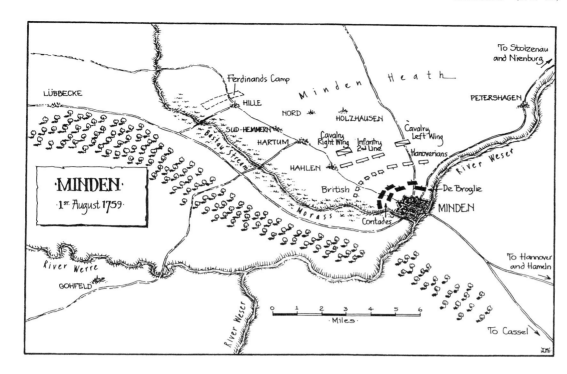

·MINDEN·
·1ˢᵗ August 1759·

The Battle of Minden,
August 1, 1759

army to Hanover. Contades, however, outwitted him and captured Minden, thus cutting the Allies off from Munster. The struggle was now exclusively for Hanover, and the two armies clashed on August 1 at Minden, which proved another triumphant day for the infantry, but - as at Fontenoy - not for the cavalry.

THE BLUES FRUSTRATED AT MINDEN, AUGUST 1, 1759

Six British and three Hanoverian regiments, along with a detachment of Hessians, marched against a force of both Horse and Foot four times as large and made them turn tail and flee at Minden, but the Allies could not render this a rout without cavalry support. Prince Ferdinand sent three ADCs at different times during the battle ordering Sackville to send in the cavalry, but all were ignored until Sackville sauntered up to the Prince to enquire what exactly he wanted. Ferdinand eyed him coldly with the words 'my lord, the opportunity has now passed'. Sackville, on returning to the British lines, was met by The Blues adjutant Lieutenant John Walsh, with a message from the latter's commanding officer, Lieutenant Colonel James Johnston, to say 'the second line is now advancing, my lord, might The Blues follow?' The answer was 'no!' and Walsh was sent to halt the second line.

Granby, however, on receiving an order direct from Ferdinand, who saw that something might still be done, now put in a pursuit. But, although that was too late, and Ferdinand was thus robbed by Sackville of an overwhelming victory, while the Allied infantry continued to press the fleeing enemy the British artillery, under command of the dashing Major Phillips, did sterling work against the scattered remnants of the French, whose losses were 8,000 men and 40 guns, not to mention their marshal's baggage train. Ferdinand recaptured Munster with ease.

On August 29 Granby was writing to the Duke of Newcastle: 'Your Grace will excuse me if I remind your Grace of my friend and Lieutenant-Colonel [Johnston, of the Blues]; it was unhappy for him that The Blues had not an opportunity of showing the pains he had for so many years been at in disciplining them was not thrown away ...'

As a result of Sackville's court martial that general was judged 'unfit to serve His Majesty in any military capacity whatever... neither high birth nor great employments can shelter offences of such a nature'.

At the other extreme of awards King George visited Prince Ferdinand's camp at Kroffdorf in the autumn of 1759, dubbed him a Knight of the Garter and handed him £20,000 for his services, The Blues being in close attendance at this ceremony.

1759 was also the year of Wolfe's scaling the Heights of Abraham and his capture of Quebec.

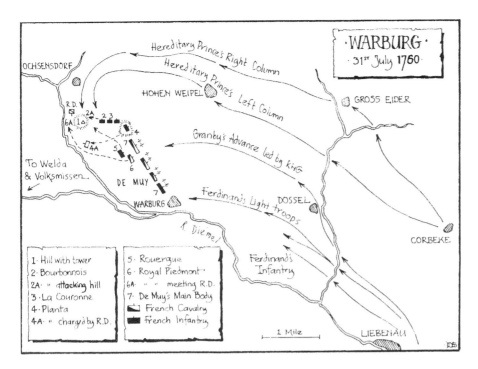

- 1· Hill with tower
- 2· Bourbonnois
- 2A· " attacking hill
- 3· La Couronne
- 4· Planta
- 4A· " charged by R.D.
- 5· Rouergue
- 6· Royal Piedmont·
- 6A· " meeting R.D.
- 7· De Muy's Main Body
- ◰ French Cavalry
- ◼ French Infantry

The Battle of Warburg,
July 31, 1760

BLUES AND ROYALS TRIUMPHANT AT WARBURG

During the years 1758 and 1759 the Royals, with the exception of their light troop, had shifted between various quarters in the south of England with little to mention save at command level. Their colonel, the abrasive and stubborn General Hawley, died in March 1759 to be succeeded by Lieutenant General Henry Conway. In the same month James Johnston, who was to be referred to as 'Irish Johnston' to distinguish him from the Blues' commanding officer of the same name, replaced John Toovey in the lieutenant colonelcy. And, early in 1760, the regiment was earmarked for active service again. For, as soon as the Marquis of Granby followed Sackville in command of the British expeditonary force in Germany, he applied to the commander-in-chief at home, Lord Ligonier, for reinforcements.

Apart from substantial infantry and artillery, the Royals (by now at Sudbury, in Suffolk) along with the 7th and 11th Dragoons, followed by the Bays, the Irish Carabiniers and Brigadier General Eliott's newly-raised 15th Light Dragoons were duly detailed to make ready for embarkation. By May 20 'the Glorious Reinforcement,' as this was known, was complete in the army's new encampment near Detmold, Hesse, where they were reviewed by Prince Ferdinand. He complimented the Royals on their turnout and more particularly on the condition of

their horses, which, said Brigadier General the Earl of Pembroke,[12] 'excelled the others very much, when there are no flies stirring which make them mad and the Cadogan tail [the then fashionable docked tail] can't defend them'. The Royals were now brigaded with Mordaunt's (the 10th) and the Inniskilling Dragoons under Brigadier-General Eliott.[13]

By the spring of 1760 Prince Ferdinand's army was divided into two corps, the other one being in adjacent Westphalia. The French, who were again vastly superior in numbers, were also in two camps, one with the Comte de St Germain on the Lower Rhine and the other with Marshal de Broglie by the banks of the Main. Early in the summer the French united their armies at Corbach. Prince Ferdinand, achieving the same effect, sent his nephew, the Hereditary Prince of Brunswick with a cavalry detachment to prevent Marshal De Broglie getting between the Allies and Westphalia. The Hereditary Prince surprised and scattered a much larger enemy at Emsdorf, a battle which ended with a brilliant pursuit over 20 miles by the 15th Light Dragoons, their baptism of fire. ('Time hence it will never be believed,' wrote Lord Pembroke, 'that one regiment of young Light Dragoons … after having almost by itself in a manner defeated a whole army, alone made about 1600 prisoners.')

But that success could not prevent Marshal De Broglie from occupying his old base, Cassel. Ferdinand, however, seized the opportunity, on July 31, to fall with great speed and surprise on a detached French corps of 20,000 men, which was drawn up under command of General De Muy (successor to St Germain) between the villages of Ochsendorf and Warburg by the river Diemel. Ferdinand's tactics, having crossed the Diemel by night, were as follows. His nephew, the Hereditary Prince, having formed up in two columns (largely composed of grenadier companies) at Corbeke, was to head round the enemy's left flank and rear, assulting through Ochsendorf and the hillock (which De Muy had failed to occupy) behind the village. Each column was to be led by a regiment of British dragoons, the Royals with the left, Cope's with the right. While Ferdinand himself would assault through Warburg against the French right wing, Granby, with 22 squadrons and Major Phillips' guns under command, would advance through Dossel against De Muy's centre.

The Allies' approach march of some ten miles was largely concealed by fog, De Muy not being aware of their presence until nearly midday. The Hereditary Prince's left-hand column reached their objectives first with the Royals foremost in the fight. As Colonel Beckwith, commanding the British infantry, occupied the hill De Muy sent his Royal Piedmont regiment to counter-attack. The Royals met them head-on and drove them back in dissarray. The Hereditary Prince's other column with Cope's Dragoons in the lead, was in the mêlée now and a savage struggle ensued, De Muy committing all his reserve to that flank. Ferdinand's main body of infantry, weary from their night march and now almost stifled with the heat of the July day, could only be induced to advance at a stumbling, if dogged, pace. But the British cavalry – the 22 squadrons in two lines, with the Blues riding immediately behind their Colonel, Lord Granby – had set off, with five miles to traverse, at a spanking trot through Dossel, Phillips and his guns keeping the same good pace.

Granby swinging left-handed and losing both hat and wig in the process – hence his shining pate and the birth of the expression 'going bald-headed for it' – gave the order to charge. In galloped his cavaliers with blood-curdling huzzas and lines of glinting forward-pointing swords to smash the French centre and to send the bulk of its men fleeing over the Diemel. Only three of De Muy's squadrons refused to turn tail with the rest. Granby – before himself leading the final pursuit – detached Colonel Johnston to break those last remaining squadrons with his Blues, and that was quickly accomplished. Ferdinand's infantry were in the thick of it now, and the remnants of De Muy's corps, having both flanks driven in, rushed headlong for the Diemel and its fords, while Phillips' guns played upon them from across the water. The Swiss regiment of Planta turned in an attempt to cover the retreat, but the Royals galloped straight through them.

The result of the victory of WARBURG, one of the most glorious days in the annals of The Blues and Royals – the formers' second battle honour, the latters' third – was that Prince Ferdinand's communications with West-phalia were at last free and the threat to Hanover greatly reduced. Ferdinand wrote to King George saying '*my lord Granby a*

infiniment contribué, avec la cavallerie anglaise au succès de cette action'.

CLOSTERCAMP – ANOTHER FIGHT FOR THE ROYALS, OCTOBER 16, 1760

Yet the situation was, for Ferdinand, still precarious, the French, notwithstanding Warburg, having occupied Cassel and Göttingen. The Allies were short both of men and provisions while good water was described as being 'as precious as wine'. Granby appealed to Ligonier for further reinforcements, but England having massive commitments elsewhere overseas, none was available. Nevertheless, in September, Ferdinand dispatched the Hereditary Prince to seize Wesel on the Lower Rhine with a force which included the Royals (still in Eliott's brigade).

Wesel was guarded by a contingent under command of General de Castries positioned by a canal running westward from the Rhine near Rheinburg. The Hereditary Prince believed he could roll up de Castries' force from its left flank by crossing the canal bridge near the village of Clostercamp under cover of darkness, and this he attempted, with the Royals in the lead. But surprise was not complete, the French piquets raised the alarm and their infantry had the better of the Allies on this occasion. However, as soon as it was light enough, Eliott's brigade swept onto the enemy's flank, the Royals coming face-to-face with the Piedmont Horse again (or what was left of them after Warburg) and giving them another good thrashing. The result of the Battle of Clostercamp was a draw. The Royals lost eight men and 50 horses killed, four soldiers seriously wounded (including Colonel Johnston) and three officers and 25 other ranks captured.

Five days after Clostercamp George II, attended by his Life Guards, held a review in Hyde Park; five days after that (October 25) he died at Kensington Palace – at a most triumphant moment in the life of the nation. For, apart from Warburg and the salvation of Hanover, news had recently come through of the capture of Montreal by Lord Amherst, and the French surrender of Canada. North America was British from the Polar ice to Cape Florida; the one little French settlement on the Gulf of Mexico, Louisana, had lost all importance. It could scarcely have been a more propitious moment for the end of the reign.

'What an enviable death!' wrote young Horace Walpole. 'In the greatest period of the glory of this country and of his reign, in perfect tranquillity at home, at seventy-seven growing blind and deaf, without a pang !...' The Blues Colonel, Lord Granby, gave another epitaph: 'no King ever lived more beloved, or died more sincerely regretted'. And we have it from Richard Cannon[14] that

'a Gold Stick order was immediately issued for the officers of the Life and Horse Grenadier Guards to provide themselves with a suit of scarlet cloth: the coat to be lapelled and turned up with black, trimmed with black buttons, and to have the button-holes trimmed with black; the hat to be plain with crape round the crown; the sword belt to be trimmed with black; and the sash to be covered with black crape...'

On the death, in 1751, of George II's eldest son the late King's eldest grandson had been created Prince of Wales and was now, aged 22, King George III.

1. The King paid his annual visit to Hanover in May-June, 1743. Although his chief minister, Carteret, who accompanied him, made a fleeting visit to the Hague, there is no evidence that the King was in the Netherlands that summer. My conclusion (at variance with other regimental historians) is that The Life Guards rode from Flanders to Hanover to meet him in June.
2. John Lindsay, 20th Earl (1702-49) Colonel of the 4th Troop, an officer with a long and distinguished military career behind him.
3. The King's 'baggage train' is on record as being composed of 660 horses, 13 coaches, 35 wagons and 54 carts.
4. Davies, p 208
5. Atkinson gives the date of Dettingen as June 16, and Col Hills, in his brief histories of the three regiments, repeats the error.
6. William Anne Keppel, 2nd Earl, succeeded 1718. His godmother was Queen Anne, hence his second name. Albermarle had his horse killed under him at Dettingen and was badly wounded
7. This letter was published in a 1743 issue of *The Gentleman's Magazine*
8. Quoted from Arthur, I, 391
9. Brigadier-General Ingoldsby was court-martialled after the battle, found guilty of disobedience to orders and suspended from the Army
10. Beake having been wounded Jenkinson commanded The Blues for most of the battle
11. The two Troops of Horse Grenadiers were retained notwithstanding the fact that the army had dispensed with the hand grenade.
12. Henry Herbert, born 1734, succeeded as 10th Earl, 1750
13. Founder of the 15th Light Dragoons (later Hussars), Eliott became the 1st Baron Heathfield and was famous for his defence of Gibraltar, 1779-82
14. Historical Records (1837) p 155

8 GEORGE III (1760-1820)

Although he was twenty-two years of age when he came to the throne George III was then mentally and emotionally little more than a boy. He was 11 before he could read and, at 20, still wrote like a child. He was easily influenced by mediocre men like Bute (his early father-figure) and North, while disliking men of reater substance, such as Pitt, Pelham, Rockingham and Burke. George – whose reign was to last in theory (if not in practice towards the end of it) for sixty years – thought, in the spirit of some of his Stuart predecessors, in terms of Divine Right and of the sacred obligation of sovereigns.

He imagined, for example, that to compromise over such issues as the rebelliousness of John Wilkes or the revolt in America ('the Colonists must be reduced at all costs to absolute obedience') would be a betrayal of God's trust. He was stupid and obstinate and subject to fits of insanity, an affliction by which he was to be entirely possessed during the last decade of his life. On the credit side, he was scrupulously honest, clean living, hardworking, thrifty, and a faithful family man, who was the first Hanoverian to be truly British (in spirit if not in blood). He gloried in being a Briton born and bred.

Having wanted to marry the love of his life, the Duke of Richmond's pretty daughter, Lady Sarah Lennox, and being dissuaded from doing so by Lord Bute, he chose for a wife a woman widely regarded as one of the ugliest and dullest princesses in Europe. Charlotte Sophia of Mecklenburg-Strelitz, who was to bear him fifteen children, of whom the princes were all highly eccentric and what the Duke of Wellington called 'the damndest millstones ever to be hung round the neck of a Government'.

CORONATION, SEPTEMBER 22, 1761

George and his Queen were married on September 8, 1761. A fortnight later nearly 3,000 soldiers were on parade for the coronation, the organisation of which was presided over by The Blues' former Colonel, Field Marshal Lord Ligonier, who, on the great day, positioned himself in a tent in Old Palace Yard, on the flank of a raised platform which ran from Westminster Hall to the west door of the Abbey. The Life Guards – apart from supplying 100 men to line the staircase and hall at St James's Palace - carried out their customary duties to the satisfaction of most, if not quite to everyone's. In the 1761 *Annual Register* a journalist writes that outside the Abbey were stationed, at proper distances, several parties of Horse Guards, whose horses somewhat

George III.
From the portrait by
John Zoffany

incommoded the people that pressed incessantly upon them though I did not hear of any great mischief being done ... I must confess it gave me pain to see the soldiers, horse and foot, obliged unmercifully to belabour the heads of the mob with their broad swords and muskets; but it was not unpleasant to observe several tipping the horse soldiers slily from time to time (some with halfpence, and some with silver as they could muster up the cash) to let them pass between the horses to get near the platform, after which these unconscionable gentry drove them back again ...

Most enterprising of all were the young bloods who dressed themselves up as officers in order to get onto the processional route. They walked up and down the platform arm-in-arm with their officer friends and successfully blocked the view for countless less fortunate bystanders.

END OF THE SEVEN YEARS WAR

Meanwhile The Blues and the Royals remained on active service in Germany where the French, occupying the greater part of Hesse, threatened Hanover again. The French fielded 150,000 against the Allies' 92,000. Of the latter a high proportion were sick, and so were their horses. Of Britain's 20,000, little more than half

were really fit for duty notwithstanding Granby's reputation for making every endeavour to alleviate the suffering of his soldiers and to see them restored to health. And there were few reinforcements available, for Britain was committed at this time to providing field forces or defensive garrisons in India, Cuba, Africa, both the West and the East Indies, Gibraltar, America and Ireland, not to mention the defence of Britain. The French mustered a menacing army of 45,000 on the Channel coast a threat for which due contingency must be made at home; and when Spain came into the war on the side of France, in January, 1761, England sent an expeditionary force of 6,000 to support her old ally, Portugal. Besides which there were few willing volunteers for Westphalia. *High Germany*, a popular song of the time, ends with the lines *They pressed young Harry from me/Likewise my brothers three/And sent them to the cruel wars/In High Germanee...*

The mounted arm did not figure prominently in the 1761 campaign. The nearest The Blues (brigaded with the Carabiniers and Honywood's Dragoons) and the Royals (with Mordaunt's and the Inniskillings) got to grips with the enemy was at the Allied victory, on July 16, at Vellinghausen where Ferdinand's army was deployed between the rivers Aese and Lippe to defend Ham – when the

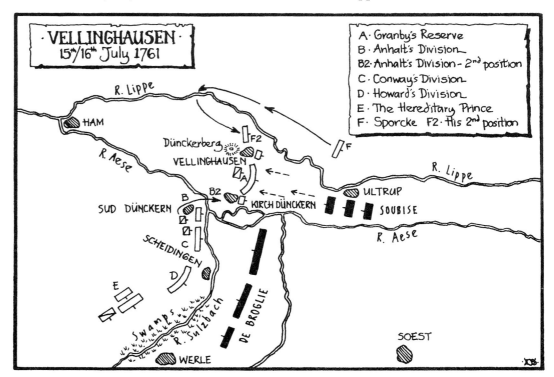

The Battle of Vellinghausen, July 15-16, 1761

cavalry might have been used in a pursuit role, except that the maze of enclosures and woods prevented such action. The gallant and recently wounded Colonel Johnston, of the Royals, still rode at the head of his regiment having pleaded with Granby to be excused an appointment to a staff job. 'I took the liberty of declining,' he was to write, 'preferring the honour of commanding the Royal Dragoons to any other while my health will permit, as long as His Majesty pleases to continue me to them.'[1] By the end of that season's campaigning the Royals were reduced to 245 rank and file, the weakest in numbers of any of Granby's cavalry regiments.

WILHELMSTAHL 1762

In 1762 Ferdinand determined to clear Hesse-Cassel of the French. And he largely offset his opponents' vast numerical superiority by skilful strategy. While sending the Hereditary Prince to keep an eye on General Conde's corps on the Rhine, Ferdinand advanced south with his main army from Paderborn with the objective of cutting the enemy's communications between Frankfurt and Cassel. Forming two columns he converged on France's new Commander-in-Chief, Marshal Soubise, just north of Cassel at Wilhelmstahl. The main body of them escaped; but, in the confused manoeuvres, Granby's British came upon the French rearguard (commanded by General de Stainville), surrounded them and forced them to surrender, 2,700 prisoners being taken.

Granby then set off to surprise an isolated corps (under General de Rochambeau) at nearby Homburg. The French, seeing themselves attacked on two sides, began to pull out. This was the moment when The Blues (under Lieutenant Colonel Harvey) and the 15th Light Dragoons charged against the enemy's tail; and, in a six-mile pursuit, cut them down 'by the hundreds'. (Ligonier, after studying the result of Wilhelmstahl, wrote to the Prime Minister, the Duke of Newcastle,[2] that 'Granby did the whole business, than whom no man acted with more courage, or more like a commanding officer than in cutting off De Stainville's Corps from the French army ...' [There was a slight check but] 'Granby soon recovered it and his Blues did almost beyond what was ever done by a Regiment of Cavalry...' And yet the Battle of Wilhelmstahl never found its

way onto The Blues' list of battle honours. Anyhow, it was the Royals' turn next in that famous combat. They came in at the head of the 5th Fusiliers (who led Lord Waldegrave's brigade) and fell upon de Stainville's rear, 'pouring in a fire so destructive and effective that it ended the fight'.[3]

Prince Ferdinand of Brunswick entered Cassel in considerable triumph. With that operation and the capture of Cuba and a foiled French counteroffensive in Canada, 1762 was indeed another glorious year for British arms. The Peace of Paris was signed in February 1763 and so ended the Seven Years War. Britain had won an empire, the campaign in Westphalia being a sine qua non to that end. For which one is entitled to ask: would not 'Westphalia 1756-1763' be a most suitable battle honour for the Blues and Royals?

BLUES AND ROYALS UNHONOURED, 1763

Granby being seriously ill it was Conway, the Royals' Colonel, who led the army back to England in the spring of 1763 – an army about to be drastically reduced. Lord Bute, the new Prime Minister, ordered the disbandment of all infantry below the 70th Regiment and all cavalry regiments junior to the 18th Light Dragoons. The Blues, who marched home 518 strong, were brought down to under 300, while the Royals who mustered some 330 soldiers at the end of the war were now almost halved in number. Neither regiment received much credit for their remarkable campaigning. The Royals were dispatched to the north of England, then Scotland, then the Southern counties, moving almost every year during the next three decades. The Blues, also denied a part in the victory celebrations, were posted to the east Midlands. It is on record that those Blues who were discharged were allowed nine day's pay, were permitted to sell their horses and to keep the proceeds and to retain their clothes, in gratitude for their services.

The King dismissed Conway from the Colonelcy of the Royals in 1764 – for the offence of voting against the Government on the legality of 'general warrants', a subject which arose following the arrest of the turbulent John Wilkes whom George hated. Conway's successor was that grand old cavalry commander, the Earl of Pembroke. Both The Blues and the Royals proved

Henry, 10th Earl of Pembroke.
From the painting by
Sir Joshua Reynolds.
A general in the Army he
was Colonel of the Royal
Dragoons (1764-94)

Henry, 10th Earl of Pembroke.
From the painting by
Sir Joshua Reynolds.
A general in the Army he
was Colonel of the Royal
Dragoons (1764-94)

pioneers in horsemastership and equestrianism at this time. Lord Pembroke, author of the widely esteemed *Military Equitation*, determined to improve standards in his new regiment, arranged to have the riding master of the 15th Light Dragoons, the exceptionally able Lieutenant Floyd, attached to the Royals for a year. Pembroke was also instrumental in the abolition of the docked ('Cadogan') tail, cruel both in the act of amputation and in the deprivation of a horse's means to rid its quarters of flies. The Blues, meanwhile, had a riding school built for themselves at their garrison at Nottingham, the first of its kind in the army.

DEATH OF LORD GRANBY, 1770

Lord Granby succeeded Lord Ligonier as Commander-in-Chief in 1766, but, in 1770, he resigned from that post, while retaining command of The Blues. Later that year, to the great sorrow of the regiment, he died.[4] Ironically the officer who followed him at the head of The Blues was Conway, who had lost the Colonelcy of the Royals six years previously. ('To Lieutenant General Conway,' wrote the King that October, 'I choose to acquaint you that I have directed Lord Barrington to notify you as Colonel of the Royal Regt of Horse Guards. I shall therefore expect to receive you in that capacity on Wednesday.') But Conway was also to receive more Royal frowns in 1772, by remarks he made about the Royal Marriage Act[5] and again in 1776 by showing sympathy with the American colonists. In May that year the

King, after reviewing The Blues, had a dig at Conway by finding fault with the officers. 'I wish I could see the Blues behave as well as as they used to do!' he told him. To which Conway replied: 'I regret that your Majesty should lay blame on the officers merely to mortify the Colonel'.[6]

TWO REGIMENTS OF LIFE GUARDS, 1788

1788 was a milestone year for The Life Guards, who, until then, were essentially the 'Horse Guards' with four troops and two of Horse Grenadier Guards. They were beginning to get a bad reputation (as they had in Lord Gerard's time during the 1660s), their recruitment depending too much upon the size of the recruit candidate's purse and too little on his merit. In July that year at a time of one of the King's most serious illnesses, his second son (and the best of them), Frederick, Duke of York, wrote to Lord Cornwallis:[7]

... I have no doubt your Lordship will not regret the reduction of the four Troops of Horse Guards and Horse Grenadiers as they were the most useless and the most unmilitary Troops that ever were seen. I confess that I was a little sorry for the Horse Grenadiers[8] because they were to a degree soldiers, but the Horse Guards were nothing but a collection of London Tradespeople.

The 'reduction' to which HRH refers was the recomposition of the corps during the previous month. The two troops of Horse Grenadiers were redesignated First and Second Regiments of Life Guards, their strengths being completed largely from the best of the disbanded four troops of Horse Guards. The Gold Sticks were General Lord Amherst (2nd Regiment) and Lieutenant General the Marquis of Lothian (1st Regiment); but Lothian was deprived of the Gold Stick in March of the following year having incurred the King's displeasure by backing the Prince of Wales and voting in favour of the Regency Bill (following another of the King's ilnesses), the new Colonel of the First Regiment being Lord Dover. It was the Duke of York himself who was largely responsible for seeing that the new Regiments were smart and efficient.

The most meticulous directions were issued as to dress. Here is an example apropos officers' hair:

... to be queued, the queues of the same

length and size as ordered for the men; the Hair Ribbon to be kept as black as possible and to be tied at the top with a short ribbon instead of a Rosette, the loops and ends of the bow knot to be three inches long and always kept free from powder, the Tupee to be combed back and dressed as Officers please so that it is dressed: the side locks to be dressed or curled so as to cover the ear but at no time to be lower than the ear ...

GROWING STATUS OF THE BLUES, 1788

A sidelight on the increased status of The Blues – moving them ever further towards recognition as Household Cavalry – is reflected, during the same year, in this opening sentence from a letter addressed to the Judge Advocate General by the King's private secretary. The letter goes on to set out the cost of commissions for officers of all three regiments [dated July 3]:

I am to signifiy to you the King's pleasure that you do summon the General Officers commanding the two Regiments of Life Guards and the Royal Regt of Horseguards; and lay before them the enclosed papers, stating the prices of commissions in the Horse Guards, Horse Grenadier Guards,[9] and Horse [ie The Blues] ...

THE FRENCH REPUBLIC

Apres moi le déluge! exclaimed Louis XV

shortly before he died in 1774. And so it was. For the reign of his successor and grandson, Louis XVI, was to become engulfed in the Revolution within 15 years of that. Following the storming of the Bastille on July 14, 1789, the National Assembly abolished all feudal privileges and promulgated a new constitution. The Revolution quickly developed into a movement of Republican aggrandisement and expansionism, starting with war against the Austrian empire, which was ruled by the family of the hated French Queen, Marie Antoinette. In April, 1792, the French invaded the Austrian Netherlands, albeit the French army was in extremely poor shape. The ill-success of French arms at the outset of the campaign infuriated the Paris mob, who, on August 10, 1792, stormed the Tuileries, slaughtered the Swiss Guards[10] and overthrew the monarchy. 'France, having wasted her own substance,' says Fortescue, 'was to live by the plunder of her neighbours.'[11]

ENGLAND AT WAR WITH REVOLUTIONARY FRANCE

The greatest horror and indignation having been expressed in England at the guillotining of Louis XVI in January, 1793, the new French Convention (responding in part to that very small English minority who applauded the Revolution) declared war on her on February 1. Chatham's son, William Pitt the Younger, Prime Minister in his mid-20s, being intent upon reducing the national debt and restoring the country's revenue, had been determined not to become involved in the conflict until such a course was unavoidable. At the same time it had long been a cardinal principle of British policy that the Low Countries – and, in particular their North Sea harbours – should not be permitted to fall into the hands of a power hostile to England. By that spring, the French military threat was acute.

As for the British army, now amounting to only 40,000 men, it had never reached such a low ebb. Since the Seven Years War discipline and training had been sadly neglected; there were no uniform drills, either for cavalry or infantry; the method of selecting officers was totally unsatisfactory; drunkenness and absence without leave were rife, while a dire shortage of arms and equipment prevailed.[12] However, in the spring of 1793, a field force of some 7,000

Field Marshal Jeffery Amherst 1st Lord Amherst. From the portrait by Sir Joshua Reynolds. He was Colonel of the 2nd Regiment of Life Guards (1788-97)

under command of the 28-year-old Duke of York, went to join the Austrian Prince of Coburg's army (the 'First Coalition'). The state of the French army was now even worse than the British. Such was the indiscipline and disorder of both the remnants of their old Royalist forces and the Revolutionary levies that, if Coburg had marched on Paris, there would have been little of consequence standing in his way. Instead he confined himself to largely useless siege warfare in the Netherlands.

The main British cavalry force, under General William Erskine, joined the Duke of York's contingent in June, The Blues and the Royals being with the 3rd Dragoon Guards, and each providing two service squadrons in Mansel's brigade.[13] However, considering the siege operations which preoccupied Coburg, there was little employment for cavalry other than reconnaissance and piquet duty, except for one lively action on the river Marque at Pont-a-Tressin which helped force the French to evacuate Menin and raise their siege of Nieuport. On November 9 the Duke led his Corps into winter quarters near Ghent. The Royals' highly respected Lord Pembroke died, aged 60, the following January being succeeded by Major-General Goldsworthy, a Royal of 35 years standing. The regiment was

led on this campaign by Lieutenant-Colonel Thomas Garth.

The Emperor Francis of Austria arrived from Vienna in April and the Allies, on pretence to the French of being absorbed in preparations for a grand review, marched south on the 16th against the enemy positions spread out between the Scheldt and the Sambre. On April 17 an attack was launched with eight small separate columns. ('It is impossible to bring the Austrians to act otherwise than in small corps,' wrote the Duke's chief of staff, Colonel Craig; 'we shall some day be the victims of their folly and ignorance.') The Blues and Royals, in Mansel's brigade, were with Erskine's column, their objectives being at Premont and Bohain. Although Erskine forced the French to bolt, darkness fell before he could engage them, and Mansel was blamed for the delay.

Brigadier General Mansel was guilty again a week later, when the Duke ordered the Austrian General Otto northwest to engage the considerable French forces now on the march from Caesar's Camp. Mansel, who should have been in close support, was left behind, and Otto found himself confronted by a vastly superior force at Villers-en-Cauchies. Nothing daunted, and expecting

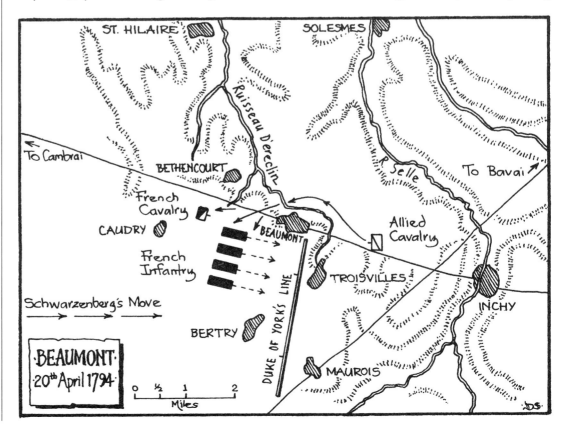

The Battle of Beaumont,
April 20, 1794

Mansel to be close behind, Otto sent the 15th Light Dragoons and the Leopold Hussars – amounting to 300 sabres – into the attack. Astonishingly, this light cavalry force rode straight at and over some 3,000 French bayonets and routed them. Mansel, arriving late, got his brigade entangled in an enfilading fusillade from which his regiments, covered by a Royals squadron, quickly withdrew.

Having lost much faith and duly covered with shame from his two blunders, Mansel determined not to emerge alive from the next encounter which proved to be astride the Cambrai-Le Cateau road at Beaumont, the Duke of York being entrenched south of the village. There, on April 26, the French General Picheru took the offensive with an army of 28,000 men. The Duke, learning that the enemy's left flank was uncovered, sent the cavalry of his right wing, under Prince Schwarzenberg, to circle around the village. This division amounted to 18 squadrons (six Austrian Cuirassiers and 12 British). Mansel's brigade was broken up, The Blues being in the front rank, the 3rd Dragoon Guards in the second and the Royals in the third (which was led by Schwarzenberg himself). The cavalry took advantage in their approach march of a thick fog, so that when the French advanced to assault the Duke's entrenched positions they found themselves suddenly attacked on their left flank by those 18 squadrons who had formed up for their attack in a dip just short of Bethencourt. Mansel, leading the front rank, true to his promise, was quickly cut down and killed; The Blues behind him rode straight through the enemy; and, by the time Schwarzenberg – with the Royals and third rank of Cuirassiers – entered the mêlée, the bulk of the French army was in headlong flight. The cavalry pursued vigorously until (as Atkinson phrases it) 'they wearied of the slaughter and their horses could gallop no longer'. BEAUMONT was added to the laurels of both Blues and Royals as was the next engagement, WILLEMS.

Unfortunately things were not going so well for the Allies elsewhere in Flanders. A corps under the Austrian general Clairfayt had been seriously defeated on April 28 near Tournai, on the Scheldt, towards which town the Duke of York now hastened in torrential rain; and, the baggage wagons having been left behind, no change of clothes was available for the men on arrival. Anyhow,

next day the Duke entrenched his infantry on the west side of Tournai, where Pichegru, with 30,000 men under command, was to advance against him in three columns on May 10. The Duke dispatched Erskine with the British heavy cavalry in an endeavour to turn the enemy's right flank (the brigade including the Blues and Royals being now commanded by Ralph Dundas[14]). The French, determined not to be rolled up from the flank as they were at Beaumont, formed resolute squares around the villages of Baisieux and Camphin and beat off several charges by the Allied Horse, which was much handicapped by the rain-sodden heavy arable ground which they crossed. The French muskektry was not, however, very effective, the Allied squadrons suffering more from the enemy cannon posted next to the River Marque at Gruzon. Anyhow Pichegru was forced to retreat north of the Lille-Tournai road.

But the British guns had by now unlimbered not far from his tail, and as he withdrew, his forces were subjected to such a pounding that his squares began to waver. One by one they were split asunder. Then, as Harry Calvert, an ADC, wrote, 'Dundas's brigade broke in upon them with great execution'.[15] The French – with Blues', Royals' and 3rd Dragoon Guards' sabres

The Battle of Willems, May 10, 1794

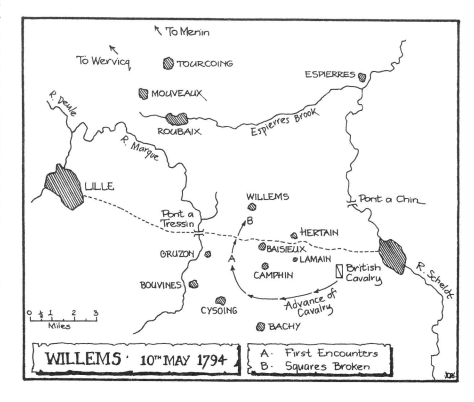

flashing around them – scattered in headlong retreat, at least a thousand of their number being cut down,[16] and 400 taken prisoner. (59 years later (1852), a very old Blues veteran, Joseph White, was telling many an admiring listener of how he had fought a duel with a French officer at Willems, having run his sword through the Frenchman's body, took from him two watches, a purse and a pocket book – all of which, to colour his story, he proudly displayed.) The Blues suffered 12 casualties, the Royals only one. Thus ended the Battle of Willems.

HANOVER, 1795

Owing to the failure of the Austrian commanders to coordinate their plans with the British, coupled with the irresolution of either themselves or the Dutch to defend their territories and the treachery of the Prussians (who, under the Treaty terms, were pledged to come to the assistance of the Austrians), the allies evacuated the Austrian Netherlands that autumn. The Duke of York was ordered to besiege and capture Dunkirk, a nigh impossible task with the forces available; and, in November the King summoned him home, the British troops then coming under command of Lieutenant General Harcourt, and the foreign troops in British pay under the Austrian Lieutenant General Walmoden. During the bitterly cold January of 1795 they withdrew across the waterways of Holland, eventually retiring to Germany, the Austrians to the vicinity of Munster, the British to Osnabruck, with the enemy only ceasing to press them at the river Ems. The French not being prepared to pursue another campaigning season at this juncture, the Peace of Basle was signed on April 5, and the British repaired to Hanover, which was just as well considering the hospitals were full and morale dreadfully low.

The British infantry, being wanted by the Government to assist the French Royalist resistance in Brittany and La Vendée, were called home (much to the annoyance of the Prussians). But, since the King had no wish to see Hanover denuded altogether of British troops, the cavalry were left behind. The Blues and Royals enjoyed at least one advantage during this sojourn – they were exercised regularly by their energetic brigade commander, Ralph Dundas, one of the leading exponents of cavalry tactics and battle drills.

However the Treaty of Basle had insisted that no foreign troops should remain on German soil. At last King George relented and, in October, the cavalry sailed home, The Blues[17] proceeding to Northampton, the Royals first to Epsom, and then, in January, 1796, to join the regiment's home service troops at their new barracks at Dorchester.

SEASIDE ROYALS ESCORT FOR KING GEORGE

During May, 1794, two of those Royals' home-service troops which had been under orders to join the army in the Netherlands, had proceeded to Croydon ready to embark from Lewisham and Camberwell, which they did, but in such stormy weather that their transports were driven back. Their orders were then reversed: they were to return to Dorset. They had no sooner arrived at their barracks than they were detailed to form an escort (70 men under their Colonel, General Goldsworthy) for the King who had gone to bathe at Weymouth. The supposed danger was that 'one of the smugglers' row-gallies ... in the constant practice of running cargoes between St Alban's Head and Weymouth may land on the north side of Weymouth bay and carry the King away at night'.

JOHN ELLEY

One young Blues trooper who received his baptism of fire in the War of the French Revolution, John Elley, was to enjoy a most remarkable career. Born in Leeds to a father who kept an eating house, young Elley, having first been articled to a London solicitor, decided to 'go for a soldier' and joined The Blues in November 1789. In the following year his father bought him a troop quartermastership in the regiment. Having fought at Beaumont and Willems John Elley was a cornet before the end of 1793. And we shall meet him again, for he rose to be the regiment's lieutenant-colonel in 1808. He was a staff officer during the Peninsular Campaign, Adjutant-General of Cavalry at Waterloo, then KCB and lieutenant-general, and, finally, Tory MP for Windsor.

THE DUKE OF YORK, COMMANDER-IN-CHIEF

In 1795 the King promoted the Duke of York field marshal to succeed, as commander-in-chief, Lord Amherst who, notwithstanding his reputation as a competent commander in America, had proved ineffectual in the top job. The Duke had studied the military arts – as approved by Frederick the Great – in Germany, between 1781 and 1787, before going as General commanding the British contingent in the Netherlands, for the failure of which he was unfairly blamed, but where he learned much about leadership and the conditions of the soldiery and their needs. The young Duke was ardently keen to improve standards throughout the army; and, having the King for his father, he was not to be obstructed or denied.

Among countless other beneficial measures, he laid down uniform battle drills; he ordained regimental training days and rest days; ordered annual inspections, training camps and brigade manoeuvres; did much to reduce the army's endemic vices of drunkenness and absenteeism; instituted the annual submission of reports on officers, and was himself assiduous in his rounds of reviews and inspections. British partici-pation in the Napoleonic wars was fast approaching, and these were the years – the late 1790s and the early 1800s – when the army underwent some of its most important adaptations and reforms. Light cavalry and light infantry were relatively new on the battlefield, horse artillery was being streamlined; the new rifle corps, with its sniper and scouting roles, was emerging, while formation staffs were expanding and being professionalised. In 1800 the energetic Duke established the Royal Military College at Woolwich. He was fortunate, too, to have such men of vision as John Le Marchant, founder of the military school at High Wycombe (the parent of Sandhurst) and John Moore, the great trainer of infantry, to assist him in piecing together all these innovations and developments, and galvanising the army for war.

EXPANSION OF THE LIFE GUARDS

As shown earlier in this chapter the reorganisation of The Life Guards into two regiments was largely based on the Horse Grenadiers (a fact ever since commemorated by the grenade fasteners on the officers' cloak collars and by the flask cords threaded through the pouch crossbelts). From 1788 each regiment was organised in four troops of fifty men each. Before Monarchs were able to travel by railway the Household Cavalry spent a good deal of time providing escorts in the provinces. To give just one example

the King required a Sovereign's escort when he travelled to Portsmouth in 1794 to greet Lord Howe and the Fleet, following the Royal Navy's 'Glorious First of June' victory off Ushant. And, of course, the Prince of Wales and his six brothers were all entitled to escorts for their official functions. In addition The Life Guards were out daily on what amounted to police duty. Anyhow, since they were undermanned, the King added a fifth troop to each regiment in 1793 and a sixth a few years later. At this time, too, a veterinary officer was taken on the establishment of each. At the turn of the century the King's Life Guard was composed of three officers, a quartermaster, a trumpeter, two corporals-of-horse, 49 privates and 55 horses, plus an attachment of five mounted light dragoons.

By the last decade or so of the 18th century, London barracks were in embryo. The Regiments of Life Guards had their headquarters, stables and parade grounds at Knightsbridge, Charing Cross (which were to pass to the Foot Guards) and King Street, Portman Square. But there were still no quarters for the men, whose pay included lodging allowance, and who were required to live within trumpet call of their barracks. To many people these new accommodations represented little less than power bases for government suppression. One MP com-plained of 'Praetorian camps in the capital' while the *Pilot* newspaper objected that

We have frequently of late had occasion to express our sentiments on the subject of Barracks, and in a constitutional point of view we cannot cease to regard them otherwise than with an eye of jealousy, considering them capable of being ... converted to so many fortresses of the Crown, formidable to the freedom of the People. The new Barracks for the Life Guards in Mary-le-Bone have been particularly objected to...

The *Pilot* went on to say that

We notice the malignity with which a paper strives to fasten on [the Duke of York] the unpopularity attached to the erection of these expensive Barracks as if he, the Commander-in-Chief, had forced the Minister into this measure! Now it so happens the Commander-in-Chief has very little to do with the building of Barracks - merely to give the formal sanction of his name in certain stages; and even this is not done in the case of the Life Guards, who are regarded as Household troops of the Crown, and left out of the general arrangement and control of the Army.

Since the Household Cavalry had not been to war since the 1740s it was natural that people should look upon them either as mounted policemen (or as a mere adornment). But, following the resumption of hostilities with France in 1803, it will not be long before we find The Life Guards on active service once more.

THE BLUES' WINDSOR CAREER BEGINS

The Blues, who had been in the habit of camping in Windsor Great Park during the late 1790s and early 1800s, went into

The Royal Horse Guards Blue in 1808.

As depicted by J A Atkinson

quarters near the town in 1804 until 1812 when it was time for more campaigning. The Royal Horse Guards Blue was the King's favourite Regiment; before his final insanity possessed him in 1810 he was often to be seen dressed as a Blues officer, and he made frequent impromptu visits to the officers mess thus attired. Early on the morning of the Garter Ceremony in 1805 he presented the Regiment with a pair of silver kettle drums. The escort commander on this occasion was the aforementioned (Major) John Elley.

Increasingly the Regiment was coupled with The Life Guards, and it was a matter of great significance for the future of The Blues that, in 1807, they were instructed to draw their Standards from the Lord Chamberlain's department as The Life Guards were privileged to do.

THE ROYALS FOR PORTUGAL

After returning with The Blues from Germany in 1795 the Royals made their customary changes of stations in the provinces – on anti-smuggling patrol, highway surveillance, riot control and other work which would one day be taken over by the constabulary - until 1807 when they were posted to Ireland. As with other cavalry regiments they were augmented at this time with a veterinary officer, a second surgeon, a saddler sergeant, an armourer sergeant and a sergeant paymaster. It is also interesting to note that they continued to share with The Life Guards, Blues and King's Dragoon Guards the tradition of being mounted on black horses.[18]

One of the Royals subalterns, Ralph Heathcote, left some vivid vignettes of regimental life in letters to his mother in Germany at the turn of the 18th century, his first station being

> ... a mile from Edinburgh, very near the sea and in a most delightful situation; [his brother officers] are perfectly well bred, polite and gentlemanly men, some indeed far superior to most people I have seen. The style in which we live is very elegant, though not expensive'. [The day starts with a dismounted parade at 9.00 am when] 'The different troops being formed before the stable doors, march towards the centre of the barrack-yard, and, after having been formed in a line, are examined by the Major [viz their dress and arms

inspected]. A Sergeant's guard having been mounted the Sergeant-Major takes over and exercises the Regiment, the officers retiring to breakfast, after which the subalterns repair to the Riding School at 11.00 am for an hour, followed by another hour's foot drill. Four days a week a Field-Day allows the subalterns to escape riding school and foot drill. By Field-Day is meant exercising the whole Regiment on Horse Back. As we exercise on the sands of the sea shore we must regulate our time according to the tides of the ocean, and I leave you to judge how fine it must be riding on the hard sand, having a most beautiful sea-view before you, adorned by the shores of Fife ... the Royal Regiment of Dragoons is far above any foreign Regiment of Cavalry I ever saw... I have seen a good many foreign troops, but can positively assure you it would be impossible for any to resist the charge of our cavalry...[19]

The Royals were in Ireland during the period 1807-9. In 1808 Deputies from the Junta of northern Spain's Asturias came to London pleading for British help against the French invasion and the occupation of the Spanish throne by Napoleon's brother, Joseph. An expeditionary force was duly dispatched under command of Lieutenant-General the Hon Sir Arthur Wellesley, but its endeavour ended with the unhappy retreat, in January, 1809, of the army to Corunna, and the death there of its gallant subsequent commander, Sir John Moore.

Wellesley was short of troops. Castlereagh wrote to him, saying 'if you very much want another regiment you may have the Royal Dragoons'. The news from Corunna however, forestalled the departure of the Royals from Cork to Lisbon that spring. The regiment then marched to Clonmel and there awaited orders. After some uncertainty, the decision was taken to keep a British presence in Portugal notwithstanding the Corunna disaster. But it was not until September 2 that eight troops, under command of Lieutenant-Colonel the Hon George de Grey, embarked at Cork, arriving at Lisbon on the 12th and 13th of the month. Lord Wellington (as Wellesley now was) had a view of them and wrote as follows to Lieutenant-General Payne commanding the cavalry:

My dear General,
I arrived here [Lisbon] yesterday, and I saw the Royal Dragoons in the streets,

An officer of the Royal Dragoons in 1808. From a drawing at Windsor Castle by Robert Dighton. (By Gracious permission of Her Majesty The Queen)

and I think that in my life I never saw a finer regiment. They are very strong, the horses in very good condition, and the regiment apparently in 'high order'.[20]

It was an auspicious start to a long campaign in which Life Guards, Blues and Royals were all to be most honourably involved.

1. Johnston was to rise to the rank of Major-General in 1770
2. Bute succeeded Newcastle as Premier later in that year
3. Wilhelmstahl, fought piecemeal, was an extraordinarily confused battle giving rise to several different versions of it. My account of the sequence of events may not be precisely accurate. I feel that to attempt a timescale might prove misleading.
4. Granby was probably the most popular general since Marlborough. Owing to the large number of pubs set up by him for old soldiers and named 'Marquis of Granby' he would never be forgotten. The first such sign appeared over a pub kept by an ex-Blues trooper at Hounslow.

5. Passed in 1772, whereby no descendant of George II ('other than the issue of princesses who married into Royal families') might lawfully marry without the consent of the Sovereign.

6. Quoted by Horace Walpole in his *Reign of George the Third*

7. Charles Earl Cornwallis (1738-1805) became 1st Marquis. Had been ADC to Granby in Germany. Distinguished himself as a commander during the American War of Independence. Was then Governor-General, India; later Lord Lieutenant, Ireland.

8. York had been Colonel of the Horse Grenadiers' 2nd Troop, 1782-84

9. The name Grenadier Guards, later to be bestowed on the 1st Foot Guards, was, until June, 1788, only applied to the Horse Grenadiers. But it is strange that reference should still be made to Horse Guards and Horse Grenadiers since both were disbanded in the previous month.

10. Among the witnesses to this was a lieutenant of artillery called Napoleon Bonaparte

11. Fortescue, 4i,51

12. For a detailed account of these facts the reader is referred to Richard Glover's excellent *Peninsular Preparation*

13. Both Arthur and Fortescue have The Blues brigaded with the 1st, 2nd and 3rd DG for the 1793 campaign and the Royals with the Greys and the Inniskillings. I have followed Atkinson whose evidence appears to be more sound. Arthur concurs with Atkinson for 1794

14. Atkinson states the new brigade commander to be David Dundas. But, according to Fortescue, Ralph is correct, brother David being in command of another cavalry brigade. Neither should be confused with Henry Dundas, 1st Viscount Melville, the War Minister

15. Sir Harry Calvert, *Journals and Correspondence*

16. Atkinson. Arthur says 3,000

17. Arthur, along with the earlier Blues historians, appears to assume that the Regiment returned home from the Netherlands late in 1795. It is clear, however, that they had withdrawn with the rest of the cavalry to Germany in the spring of that year.

18. Throughout Europe black had long been the favoured colour for war horses. It was supposed to be the colour that would most instil fear in the enemy. The Household Cavalry have been mounted on black horses since their inception.

19. Heathcote's letters to his mother were privately published by one of his granddaughters under the title, *Ralph Heathcote, Letters of a young Diplomatist and Soldier during the Time of Napoleon*

20. Quoted in de Ainslie, p110

9 GEORGE IV (REGENT, 1811-20 KING, 1820-30)

Although George III was nominally King until 1820, owing to the malady which was now to grip him until his death, his reign effectively ended on February 6, 1811, when his eldest son took his oath of office as Prince Regent. George Augustus Frederick, Prince of Wales, then not quite fifty, was an intelligent man, of charm and stylish demeanour, but he was also excessively vain, recklessly extravagant and incurably indolent, with a total lack of inhibition (except in the matter of his corpulence, which inhibited both physical exercise and application to business). Owing to those characteristics, coupled with his ill-treatment of his wife, he was far from popular with the people. Fortunately England was to have such men as the competent, if uninspiring, Spencer Perceval, then Lord Liverpool and Lord Castlereagh at the head of affairs, the conscientious Duke of York at the head of the army at home, and Sir Arthur Wellesley, afterwards Duke of Wellington, to lead her forces against the French aggressor.

Following the tragedy of Corunna there had been a strong mood in England of cutting losses and leaving Portugal and Spain to their fate. Sir John Moore had pronounced Portugal to be indefensible; Wellington thought otherwise. It was Wellington who urged the Government to send another force to Lisbon with the mission of 'expelling the intruder from the Peninsula'. He had already envisaged the Lines of Torres Vedras, that series of entrenchments that were to keep some 10,000 Portuguese peasants at work during the winter of 1809-10, the fortifications that would supplement the rocky hills beyond the capital as a defensive barrier, as a *ne plus ultra* that would render Lisbon nigh impregnable, that would be the bastion from which Wellington would take the offensive.

The French were vastly superior in numbers. Napoleon having expelled Moore's army – and, more recently (July, 1809) trounced the Austrians at Wagram – released another 100,000 men for the Peninsula (making nearly 300,000). The enemy now threatened Portugal by way of Andulusia and Extremadura, along the valley of the Guadiana in the south and Old Castile and the passes at Ciudad Rodrigo in the north – with forces at least three times the size of the Allies, the British, the Spanish (who proved almost totally unreliable, except as guerillas) and Portuguese (who were hastily trained and armed by the British). Marshal Massena, Prince of Essling, the French commander-in-chief, chose the 'northern corridor' for his

George IV. From the painting by Sir Thomas Lawrence at Windsor Castle.
(By Gracious permission of Her Majesty the Queen)

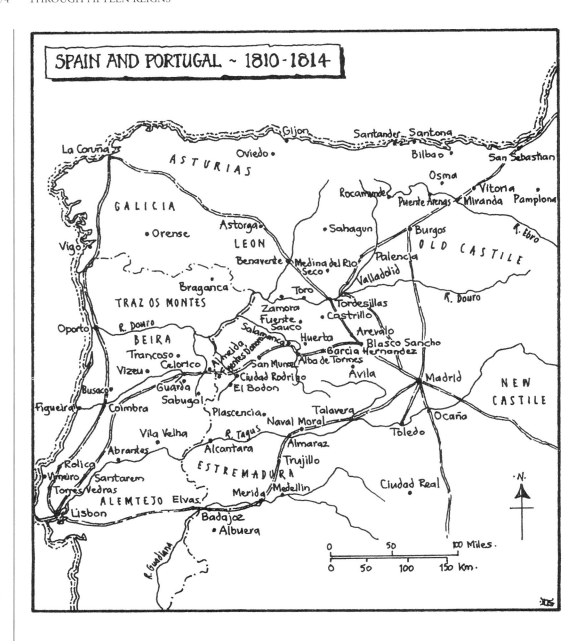

offensive against Lisbon. Lord Wellington having encountered him at Ciudad Rodrigo, conducted, step-by-step, a skilful withdrawal to the Torres Vedras – laying waste the land and soundly defeating the French army at Busaco on the way. Massena's nervous staff excused itself for its omission to report to him upon the lines by explaining apologetically that 'Lord Wellington made them'. *Que diable*, snapped the great marshal, *Wellington n'a pas construit ces montagnes!*

THE ROYALS, 1810-12

April 1810 had found the Royals in the 'southern corridor' where General Hill's[1] division defended the Guadiana valley; but when Massena's march through Ciudad Rodrigo got underway the regiment was sent north via Belmonte where Col de Grey, promoted to a brigade, handed over command to Colonel Wyndham (who, at the end of July, had the misfortune to ride into a French vedette, command then devolving upon Major Jervoise). The regiment, deployed in the brigade led by Colonel Slade (himself a former Royal, who had transferred from the 10th Dragoons in 1798), had their first encounter in August when Major Phillip Dorville galloped two squadrons into an attack against vastly superior infantry and cavalry, prompting Wellington to speak of 'that gallant and successful charge'. By October 10 the Allies were behind the Lines of Torres Vedras with Massena's men and horses starving in front of them.

British reinforcements reaching Lisbon early in the spring of 1811, the thwarted French began their weary journey back to Spain with the Anglo-Portuguese army close on their tail. Traversing ground which had received the 'scorched earth' treatment from Massena, Wellington's regiments were mostly dependent upon re-supply from Lisbon, and that necessitated good regimental commissaries. The Royals were afflicted with a rogue called House, as reflected in the captains' and subalterns' *Club Book*,[2] (a most illuminating and often satirical document now held in the Household Cavalry museum:

When the regiment had been marching and fighting all day, and at night fall had put up in a wet camp, about half an hour afterwards Mr House would make his appearance, pitch his tent (and as, of course, no commissary since the campaigns of great Julius Caesar up to the present day ever knew what the pangs of comfort were) he had his dinner cook'd, and after dinner in company with old Mason and Ryding would drink hot rum and water until comfortable. It was in vain that every night the poor officers and men look'd to the rear, and at every jingling of the mules bells thought that surely at last rations were arriv'd; but alas! vain hopes! mules would pass by with rum and corn and biscuit for Bull's artillery and the 14th[3], but nothing for the poor Royals. When spoken to upon the subject he would take off his hat scratch his bald head and assert that no one living was more sorry for it than he was ... One night near Sabugal[4] as House had pitch'd his tent as usual of a sudden the men driven to dispair ... sent such a volley of stones at the tent that House thought himself very lucky to escape with an whole skin ... it was no wonder that the horses were at death's door, the wonder is how they lived at all... As the regiment was filing over Santarem bridge 'in the previous spring' Lord Wellington and his staff pass'd by and was particularly struck with the excellent condition of the horses, their coats so jet black and shining. In fact it is not too much to say that there were not such grooms in the world as the Royals were in those days. This was the

The conquests of Napoleon Buonaparte

first week in March; in one short month, from that period this truly beautiful regiment might be said to exist no more. The number of men and horses indeed was not much diminish'd; but the latter exhibited but very sorrowful remains of their once boasted condition; one half of the beasts were lame and soreback'd: and the whole in perfect dog condition. Their coats were long and brown and a parchment skin seem'd every instant to break and leave the ribs bare: while the eyes of the wretched beasts were deeply sunken in their heads... The causes were numerous; the two principal ones were first the excessive hardships and fatigues; roads almost impassable, long marches, cold and wet bivouacs: and second Mr House the Commissary!...

Nevertheless the Royals, who were soon close to the Spanish frontier, had rounded up a great many prisoners. On May 1 Massena advanced westward from Ciudad Rodrigo and attacked the British garrison at Fuentes D'Onoro, an attack well resisted by the infantry. On May 5 it was the cavalry's turn. The *Club Book* takes up the story:

The fifth of May at half past three in the morning an heavy firing began on the

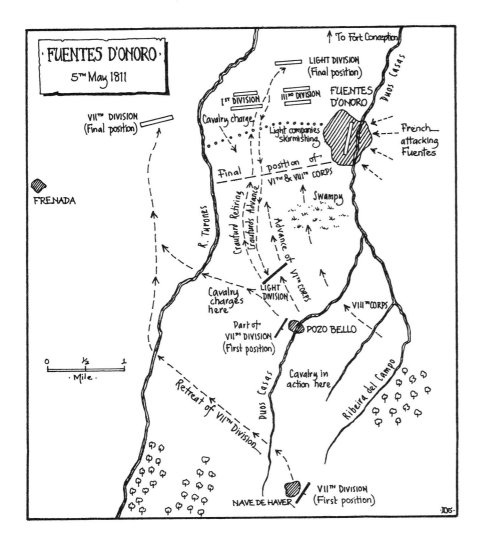

The Battle of Fuentes
d'Onoro, May 5, 1811

right of the line ... the piquets were driven in with considerable loss on the part of the infantry ... Edmund Trafford[5] much distinguished himself by a charge ... about 12 o'clock the cannonade became extremely heavy, to which the regiment was exposed for nearly four hours, altho' most fortunately nearly every ball went over the heads of the men. Several gallant charges were made during the course of the day, in one of which a Col. Latour was taken prisoner and surrendered his sword to Gubbins (nickname of Lieut Gunning). Steward the adjutant general had the impudence to declare that it was he who took the French Colonel. The secretary [of the *Club*] takes this opportunity of correcting the false assertion of Gen Steward, and begs it may be known that the frenchman was knocked off his horse in a charge with the Royals and taken prisoner individually by the

Warrior Gubbins. Slade [brigade commander] behav'd very well during the whole day, except the mistake he made in ordering Bull [artillery commander] to fire on the Brunswick corps, which mistake was corrected by his acting aide de camp Methuen...

'We had nearly three to one against us engaged,' wrote Wellington of his victory at Fuentes; 'above four to one of cavalry; and moreover our cavalry had not a gallop in them; while some of that of the enemy were fresh and in excellent order. If Boney had been there we should have been beaten'. Anyhow, such were the privations of this campaign, that cavalrymen had become somewhat inured to the risks of battle, the Royals singing the cavalryman's song – 'when squadron square we'll all be there to meet the French in the morning' – with the best of them.

Massena's defeat at Fuentes sent him reeling back to Ciudad Rodrigo and a lull in the fighting saw the Royals pulled into reserve. ('After eight days constant duty,' says the *Club Book*, 'no thing could be more delightful'.) In late May Napoleon, having punished Massena with dismissal for having failed to hold Portugal, the Allies now faced Marshal Marmont, who decided to join forces with Soult in the southern sector at Badajoz – in which direction Slade's brigade were now sent. Having captured Ciudad Rodrigo in January, 1812, Wellington (who received an earldom from the Prince Regent) turned his attention to Badajoz close to which the Royals were camped among the olive groves where, in the early hours of May 18, says the *Club Book*:

the French made a sudden attack on Trafford's piquet at Leira, supriz'd the videt and rode in upon the piquet. The night being extremely dark and the road very winding and broken, the piquet altho' smartly pursued effect'd its escape with the loss of four or five men. The ruler (the commanding officer, Col Clifton[6]) afterwards tried to bring forth evidence that Trafford had rode off in his shirt and his rump bare; but as he [Trafford] never was known to have more than one pair of overalls covered with black leather during the whole of the peninsular campaigns and, as he had all his accoutrements on when visited by Hulton[7], the Ruler failed in his amiable wishes; although considerable blame was attach'd to him for not attending to the report a Spaniard gave the preceding night of the advance of the French ... On the 20th of May the regiment turned out in marching order and formed a square in the olive wood near the town [Badajoz] for the purpose of witnessing a very severe flogging upon seven men...

Their crime was this. A picquet composed of Corporal Granger and six troopers, having got drunk, waylaid a Spanish mule train and stole 'a sufficient quantity of liquor to render them insensibly drunk', which was how they were found by the orderly officer. Granger was reduced to private and awarded 600 lashes, the others to 400 lashes each.[8]

Following Soult's evacuation of Andalusia and the raising of the French siege of Cadiz the Royals made the 160-mile march with General Hill to Madrid, while Wellington – after defeating Marmont at Salamanca in July – besieged Burgos; but, finding himself surrounded by the united French armies, he withdrew to Portugal again. Madrid proving untenable Hill, too, withdrew. This is how the *Book* describes the Royals' march back to Portugal:

> The roads, or more properly speaking the beaten foot paths soon became a perfect bog; each step which horse or man took was as in a quagmire. The army very soon became disorganised, so great were the privations, and so necessary was it to make long and forc'd marches that stragglers from the infantry, some ill and unable to move others drunk, were hardly regarded and for the most part fell into the hands of the enemy... What few stores ever reached the regiment consisted [only] of biscuits and rice, thus the horses in whom nature was exhausted, died daily in great numbers, others, unable to proceed were obliged to be shot. So entirely destitute were the officers of any food or baggage or comfort of any sort that even the Ruler [Col Clifton] and his chum Harold France [who had replaced House as commissary] were reduced to the same helpless plight as the rest ... [But] upon all occasions, however hard the times might be [Clifton] never omitted shaving. During the 30 days retreat altho' it rained day and night the ruler on parade was always clean shav'd... A retreating army is avowedly the greatest scourge to the villages that are situat'd on the line of march. It need'd but one short half hour to strip a village of every article save the bare brick walls, and if by chance a beam of timber remained the succeeding division would accomplish the work of destruction...

Wellington was furious with his army, complaining that the indiscipline was due to 'the habitual inattention of the Officers of the regiment to their duty'.[9] It must be said for the Royals, however, that, although almost half made the retreat on foot, there was not a straggler among them. The regiment came to rest for the winter of 1812-13 in the valley of the Tagus close to the Portuguese frontier 'in a miserable village', says the *Book*, but 'this was a paradise after the excessive hardships of the retreat as it very fortunately contained quantities of long forage, and before long the miserable skeletons of horses began to get the famine out of them'. (It was during that winter, too, that the Royals' cocked hats were replaced by brass helmets adorned with long black horse-hair plumes.)

However disheartening this retreat to Portugal may have been for regimental soldiers, the prospect for the commander-in-chief was far from gloomy. Marmont's army, greatly reduced in strength and numbers, was confined to the north of Spain, King Joseph had been (effectively if not in name) knocked off his throne, while Napoleon, whose Grande Armée was broken by Borodino, Beresina and the Russian winter, could do nothing more to bolster his Peninsular army. Wellington, on the other hand, was receiving substantial reinforcements from England. Those included The Life Guards and The Blues.

A HOUSEHOLD CAVALRY BRIGADE FOR SPAIN

In the autumn of 1812 the two Regiments of Life Guards were each increased from eight troops to ten for the purposes of active service, for which, like the Royals, their cocked hats were replaced by metal helmets with long trailing horsehair plumes. The Blues, being brigaded with The Life Guards, were also augmented by a couple of extra troops (from six to eight). Thus six squadrons, two from each regiment (comprising over 1,000 men per regiment all ranks) sailed from Portsmouth to Lisbon in

November. They were led by Major-General Rebow (2 LG) until January, 1813, when Sir Robert Hill, of The Blues, took command (handing over the regiment to Captain Robert Packe). Command of the Household Cavalry Brigade was to change again in September when Colonel O'Loghlin (1 LG) took over and Hill returned to the head of The Blues. In mid-January the Brigade was moved up country to Thomar and, in May, they joined the Allied camp near the Spanish frontier.

WELLINGTON, COLONEL OF THE BLUES

Durng the winter of 1812-13 the Marquess of Wellington received further honours. The Spaniards at last recognised him as their commander-in-chief; the Portuguese made him Duke of Victoria, while the Prince Regent endowed him with the Colonelcy of The Blues.[10] The Blues' previous Colonel, the Duke of Northumberland, had a polite, if fierce, dispute with the Duke of York, in attempting to insist that only he, Northumberland, was gifted with the power to appoint officers to his regiment and that Blues officers had the right to be promoted within the regiment, if they so desired, and none could be foisted on them from outside. The Duke of York wrote:

> In looking back to the Royal Regiment of Horse Guards, since its original formation, I confidently believe that no grounds will be found upon which that Corps can assert privileges unknown to any other of His Majesty's regiments of Guards, and your Grace must be aware that even the Life Guards, who are possessed of the highest and most peculiar privileges, have ever been accustomed to have Officers brought or promoted from other regiments into them according to the discretion of the Sovereign.

Northumberland, losing the argument, resigned, and The Blues felt as honoured to have the great Wellington as their Colonel as Wellington felt honoured to be elected to that most coveted of posts. At this time Guards regiments were still obliged only to do honour to Guards officers. Wellington, on receiving a salute from a detachment of the Foot Guards, shortly after his appointment to The Blues, was heard to exclaim 'Thank God – I have got a "present" out of the Guards at last!'

OVER THE PYRENEES AND HOME

The Allied commander-in-chief was now intent upon two immediate objectives: that of employing General Graham's division to turn King Joseph's left flank and thus cut off the enemy's road of withdrawal to Bayonne; and, having secured command of Spain's north coast, of moving his supply base from Lisbon to the much closer Santander. Wellington began his advance on May 21; and, as he rode over the frontier into Spain, he looked behind him and raised his hat with the words 'farewell Portugal, I shall never see you again!' (And he never did.) To divert the enemy's attention from his flanking movement he now advanced in strength on a broad front towards Salamanca with the Household Cavalry Brigade not far behind him.

The Brigade having spent the last week of May in Salamanca, in monasteries which the French had adopted as barracks, crossed the Douro on June 4 and, by the evening of the 12th, were within sight of the spires of Burgos. A few days later Santander was in Allied hands, and Wellington pointed his army towards Vittoria on the north side of the Ebro. His victory over King Joseph and his lieutenant, Jourdan, at Vittoria, on June 21, virtually decided the eventual fate of Napoleon's Peninsular enterprise.[11] The French left a vast amount of military equipment and loot behind (including the marshal's baton of Comte Jourdan, which Wellington sent as a gift to the Prince Regent, who, in his turn, had a field marshal's baton designed and dispatched to Wellington.[12]) The 1st Life Guards led the entry into the town; a member of the 'Seconds', Corporal Sammons, who was a favourite model of the historical painter Benjamin Jaydon, also took a share according to the artist, who says that Sammons was

> ... a soldier in every sense of the word. He would have brought a million safe and sound from Portsmouth to the King's mint, but he pushed his hand into King Joseph's coach at Vittoria and brought away a silver pepper box. He was an old satyr, very like Socrates in face, faithful to me, his Colonel and his King; but let a pretty girl come in the way and the Lord have mercy on her.

With the Allies heading into the foothills of the Pyrenees and their wooded mountain passes there was not much scope for cavalry work, the fighting being largely monopolised by the infantry and artillery. The Royals, who had marched up from the Tagus – in Fane's brigade (Slade had been removed from the command) – with Hill's division, took little part in the Battle of Vittoria but suffered a casualty, as described in the *Club Book*: 'A trumpeter in Phipps' troop of the name of Wright had his horse killed and his foot carried off by a cannon ball, of which wound he died about three weeks afterwards of a lock'd jaw'.

The Household Brigade (whose brigade major was a Royals officer, Lieut Webb) were now sent into reserve by the banks of the Ebro where they remained until March, 1814. On the 13th of that month William Dobson, a troop quartermaster of the 1st Life Guards, wrote to his wife in Bloomsbury:

> I've got plenty of work, seven or eight hours on horse back every day, and ever since March came in never had a fine day... I've never been in bed since I left old England ... We live very well. We have tea or chocolate for breakfast, and the Allowance of Meat and Bread, Spirits, etc, as much as ever we can get through – The Troop is served with rum, but I can draw either brandy, wine or what I chuse ... I long to hear all the news at the old Detachment. There is a great many of them gets there [sic] wives with child all the way from Spain to England. Taylor Smith's wife is one: the Burning Buty they used to call her.[13]

The Royals, too, were left by the banks of the Ebro until the spring of 1814:

> The out troops were quartered in two villages close by [Villa Franca]. The squadron under Purvis [he had succeeded Dorville as squadron leader] was at Fumes and that of Stisted [club secretary] at Marilla ... Duty there was none and therefore the four months spent in these towns might safely be call'd the best and most agreeable of any during the Peninsular war. The regiment had not long been quartered here before the remount arrived from England consisting of 60 horses and four officers...

Meanwhile Napoleon had recalled his brother Joseph, ex-King of Spain, replacing him with Soult, who fought a well-conducted rearguard action as he withdrew across the Pyrenees, while Wellington's men pushed him, little by little, back into France. The

Household Cavalry Brigade rode over the mountains in mid-March. On leaving Bayonne they were billeted at Pau for a week and were present in reserve at the final battle for Toulouse (April 10-12), as were the Royals behind Hill's infantry.

It was at Toulouse that Napoleon's abdication was reported to Wellington. The Peninsular war was over and Louis XVIII was on the French throne. By arrangement with the restored Bourbon government the British cavalry were to ride across France to the Channel ports. On July 17 the Royals embarked for Dover from Calais; a week later the Household Brigade crossed from Boulogne. For what was to follow, in 1815, The Life Guards and Blues were to be very thankful for the hardening experience of those eighteen months. The Royals, who endured nearly as long in the Peninsula as their regimental predecessors during Queen Anne's reign, perhaps had too much of it. The last campaign comment in the *Club Book* summarises the sentiments of many Royals in the summer of 1814:

> The regiment left Cork in 1809 and landed at Dover in 1814 making a period of rather more than five years. Many is the change that had tak'n place in that short time, and how few remain that first went out with the regiment! Some of the officers are promot'd in other regiments, some exchang'd, others resign'd, and others'... heads now lie low in some obscure and now forgotten spot in Spain and Portugal. Cold shivering agues, fevers, fluxes, Rheumatisms, starvation, the weary listlessness of many a long night's march, wet Bivouacs, the privation of Baggage, the want of sleep, the intolerable heat of an Estremadura's sun are Peninsula miseries now at an end. The events are pass'd and gone, and all is like a dream!

BRIEF RESPITE

The end of June, 1814 found the 1st Life Guards comfortably ensconsed at Knightsbridge, the 'Seconds' in the King Street barracks and the Royal Regiment of Horse Guards Blue at Windsor. And, while each was reduced to a peacetime strength of 200, their soldiers fully expected to remain in those stations for the remainder of their careers.

The Royals, who moved into the West Country from their depot at Newbury, were

Captain Alexander McInnis, 2nd Life Guards. He retired in the rank of captain in 1814, but rejoined later in the year, as a cornet, to take part in the Waterloo campaign

Europe at the Congress of Vienna

In December, to the abject despair of one and all, the Royals were ordered to make ready to sail for Canada. As for the indomitable Phill Dorville:

'the silent tear of Agony ... perceiv'd to trickle down his veteran cheek,' observes the *Book*, 'wonders whether it will be his lot to finish in a black wood and perhaps to find the arrow of some damn'd copper coloured Indian sticking in one's arse?'

But the order was reversed and, instead, peacetime soldiering continued and already began to pall:

'A Barrack life ... is the same, uniformly dull and uninteresting. It is precisely the same thing whether one is quarter'd at Exeter, Ipswich or Canterbury or Birmingham or where you please in the United Kingdom the same routine of duty invariably takes place. The Barrack chaplain regularly attends the riding school on a Sunday at 12 o'clock. Riding school and squad parade at 4 pm on a Monday. Tuesday a parade under arms, every man off duty to attend A parade in Marching Order and inspection of necessaries the other two days of the week...

anyhow understrength and simply completed their reduction by dismissing their sick, elderly and undesirables. According to the *Club Book* Provost Sergeant Else, who was one such man, '... went to Birmingham, connected himself with a gang of thiefs, committ'd a daring burglary, was convict'd, condemn'd to death and execute'd within the short space of three months after his quitting the Royal Dragoons!'

Wellington was in session at the Congress

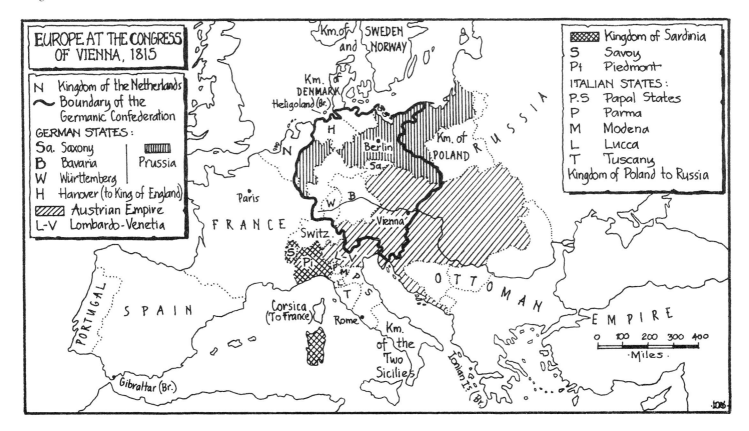

EUROPE AT THE CONGRESS OF VIENNA, 1815

N   Kingdom of the Netherlands
～   Boundary of the Germanic Confederation
GERMAN STATES:
Sa.   Saxony
B   Bavaria
W   Württemberg
H   Hanover (to King of England)
▨   Austrian Empire
L-V   Lombardo-Venetia

Prussia

Kingdom of Sardinia
S   Savoy
Pt   Piedmont
ITALIAN STATES:
P.S   Papal States
P   Parma
M   Modena
L   Lucca
T   Tuscany
Kingdom of Poland to Russia

of Vienna in March, 1815, when news came through of Napoleon's escape from Elba to which he had been exiled after his abdication. *Il ira droit a Paris!* predicted the Austrian statesman, Prince Metternich. And so it was. Louis XVIII fled to Ghent, while Napoleon's veterans of the Grande Armée, disgusted with *Le Gros Cochon*, as they called Louis, flocked to their old chief's standard. By early June Napoleon boasted a command of 100,000 men. But to retain his power – having been rebuffed in his bid for friends abroad and declared an outlaw by the Congress of Vienna – he must defeat the Allies then assembling in Belgium under Wellington.

Of those 70,000 Allies, 30,000 were largely unreliable Dutch and Belgians and raw Hanoverians, while most of the Duke's Peninsular battalions were in America.[14] Wellington considered this army to be the worst of which he had ever taken command.

Britain mobilised for service in the Netherlands in the third week of April. Clifton ('the Ruler') having still received no orders by the end of the fourth week, thought the Royals had been forgotten. He wrote to the Adjutant-General, who replied by return that the regiment was needed for defence in the West country. A few days later, however, the Colonel was ordered to march his regiment to Canterbury and prepare for immediate embarkation. The two leading squadrons left Ramsgate for Ostend, under Major Phipps, on May 13. By the 17th the whole regiment was at Ghent. At Ninove they were grouped with the Inniskillings and the Royal Scots Greys in the 2nd (Union)[15] Cavalry Brigade under Sir William Ponsonby.

Early in April the commanding officers of both the two regiments of Life Guards and The Blues were ordered to bring their strengths up to 589 each; and, on April 17, they were each told to organise two field squadrons and to 'hold themselves in readiness for foreign service'.[16] The order was 'received with unfeigned joy by the officers and men, all of whom were eager to draw the sword in the hope of gaining glory and distinction'.[17] The long black horsehair plumes of the Peninsula were replaced by red and blue crests worn on a new style helmet. The Regiments were at Ostend on May 3, assembling as the Household Cavalry Brigade three days later, with the rest of the cavalry at Ninove, where, says a contemporary:

the appearance of Lifeguardsmen lounging about the street and before the houses, these people so intimately associated in one's mind with London, the Park and the Horse guards, produced a curious sensation, nor was the contrast between their tall full figures and rosy complexions, and the gaunt awkward figures and sallow complexions of the Flemish peasantry, the tight smart fitting scarlet or blue jackets of the one with the coarse, homely garbs and dingy coloured smock-frocks of the other less curious.[18]

To bring the 'Householders' up to strength[19] the four squadrons of the King's Dragoon Guards were attached for the campaign, making a brigade total of 1,349 sabres – under overall command of Major-General Lord Edward Somerset. Wellington's cavalry as a whole (seven brigades, 48 squadrons) [20] were led by Lieutenant General the Earl of Uxbridge who was also the Duke of Wellington's second-in-command. The Duke reviewed this magnificent force of cavaliers at Ninove on May 29.

THE WATERLOO CAMPAIGN

On June 13 Wellington heard that Napoleon's army had crossed the Belgian frontier. He was at the Duchess of Richmond's ball in Brussels two evenings later when he learned that the French army was concentrated around Charleroi with their advance guard heading for Quatre Bras. It was this intelligence which prompted his exclamation 'Buonaparte has humbugged me!' Wellington promptly ordered his army forward to Quatre Bras. But, turning to his staff, he added 'we shall not stop him there ...' He pointed to the map, to the ridge south of the village of Waterloo, the centre of whose crest is marked by Mont St Jean. 'I shall fight him – *there!*'

By noon on the 16th he was with his Prussian ally Prince Blucher, at Ligny, where that Marshal's regiments were deployed to meet the French on an exposed slope; and, within three or four hours of that, the Prussians were, as Wellington had predicted, 'damnably mauled', the septuagenarian Blucher himself being thrown from his horse and severely trampled on. The Prussians retired 18 miles to Warre. By 2.30 pm Wellington was back at Quatre Bras, where Marshal Ney put in some very heavy and wild attacks against the Allies, all of which were repulsed with severe losses on both sides. The heavy cavalry brigades were not involved. Captain Clark, one of the Royals' squadron leaders, recalled that his regiment 'bivouaced for the night in an open field a little in rear of the houses of Quatre Bras, the horses being linked in column, saddled and bridled, the officers and men lying or standing by them. The night was fine and warm'.

That fair weather was to break with a vengeance next day. Meanwhile – quite apart from his resolution to keep his main battle for those slopes to the south side of Waterloo – Wellington felt obliged to withdraw because his Prussian allies had done so. He spent that night of the 16th on the ground by the town of Genappe which lies a little way behind the Quatre Bras crossroads. While the infantry marched northwards a cavalry rearguard action took place there on the 17th. Somerset's brigade was on the right, Ponsonby's on the left, while the light cavalry maintained contact with the French. When two of the enemy's lancer regiments got the better of the 7th Hussars,[21] Uxbridge ordered the 23rd to take their place. But '... his address to the Light Dragoons not being received with all the enthusiasm he expected he ordered them to clear off the *chausée,* exclaiming, "The Life Guards shall have this honour!"'[22]

Accordingly the two squadrons of the 1st Life Guards, led by Major Kelly (accompanied by Colonel Sir John Elley of The Blues) put in '... a magnificent charge; its rapid rush into the enemy's mass was as destructive in effect as it was terrific in appearance; for, although the French met the attack with firmness, they were utterly unable to hold their ground and in a single moment were overthrown with great slaughter ...'[23] Capt John Kincaid, of the 95th Rifles, wrote 'it did one's heart good to see how cordially the life-guards went at their work ... and sent their opponents flying in all directions'.[24]

It was during the next withdrawal, to the Waterloo position, that the thunderstorm which drenched both antagonists, broke, as described by the secretary of the Royals young officers' club:

Up to 11 o'clock on the 17th of June the weather had been remarkably fine ... It was not until half past six in the afternoon when the last cavalry regiment had filed through Genappe that the heaven began to open its torrents.

The rain ... together with the necessity of manoeuvring among the high standing wheat render'd all idea of cloking perfectly useless. Forster, who had provid'd himself with a double oil skin and had tak'n every precaution, was alike wet to the skin with every one else in two minutes ... For not one moment did the rain cease the whole of that night until 5 o'clock the next morning.[25]

Wellington's forces were positioned over a sodden front of more than two miles, his right being hinged on the château and farm of Hougoumont, which was defended by battalions of the Foot Guards, and his left on the hamlet of Papelotte, in the vicinity of which Blucher was expected to join him. Indeed, although Wellington determined to retreat no farther, it was essentially on condition the Prussians came to his support. The two brigades of heavy cavalry were drawn up behind the crest of the ridge, astride the Charleroi-Brussels road, which is to say half a mile back from the château and farm of La Haye Sainte, the central feature of the battleground. The Union Brigade were on the left of the road, the Householders to the right. Of the Union regiments the Inniskillings were on the left, the Royals to their right with the Greys in support. Of Somerset's regiments the KDGs occupied the central position with the 2nd Life Guards to their left, the 1st on their right, and The Blues forming the second line. The journal of Major Radclyffe, of the Royals, tells us that

We found ourselves in our place in close column behind the second line of infantry, fetlock deep in mud; no baggage for the officers, and neither provision nor water for the men,though some stray cattle had been killed and eaten, and a small supply of spirits had a short time before been found on the road so that we might be said to go 'coolly'into action, for every man was wet to the skin.[26]

Moi je vous dis que Wellington est un mauvais général, Napoleon told Marshal Soult that morning, *que les Anglais sont de mauvaises troupes, et que ce sera l'affaire d'un déjeuner.* Soult replied glumly, *je le souhaite.* Napoleon then promised his marshals that they would sleep that night in Brussels. Viewing the field from the inn of La Belle Alliance, two miles south of Waterloo, he deployed Comte Reille's corps to his left, Comte d'Erlon's to his right. He began by

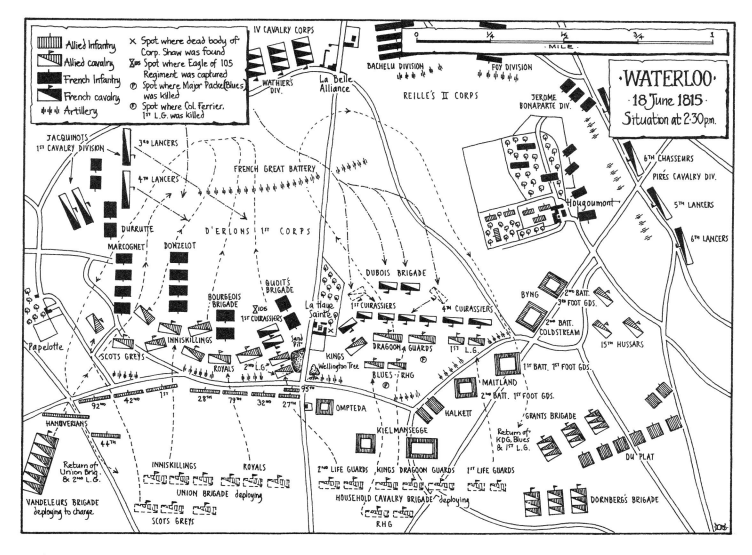

The Battle of Waterloo,
June 18, 1815

sending Reille against Hougoumont (which was destined to hold out all day), then ordered a massive artillery barrage from eighty 12-pounders, under Ney's direction, against the Allied left and centre, followed quickly with the advance of the best part of d'Erlon's command. Napoleon, having given his men and the ground a few hours to dry out, it was well past mid-morning before these offensives commenced.

The ominous roll of the French drums, accompanied by shouts of *vive l'Empereur!* were scarcely drowned even by the intense cannonade. General Picton's redcoats (who had suffered terribly at Quatre Bras), now lying on the reverse slope, were relatively safe. (But poor Picton was among those killed at this juncture.) When d'Erlon's close-packed columns, supported by Dubois' cavalry, swarmed through La Haye Sainte and began to mount the slopes of the British position, Uxbridge decided to send in the heavy cavalry. He put himself next to Somerset, at the head of the Household Brigade (which was a great error on his part since it meant there would now be no commander to coordinate the operation, to rally the survivors or to call up reserves).

Anyhow the Duke, riding behind at that moment, shouted 'now Life Guards, for the honour of the Household Brigade!' They trotted across the sunken east-west road. Then Somerset's Life Guards' trumpeter, 16-year-old John Edwards, sounded the 'charge'; the Union Brigade advanced level with the Householders. Thus their engagement began; and, in Crofton's words, 'the lines came together with a crash, but the superiority of weight of the Life Guards, men and horses, together with the slight downhill impetus they had gathered, completely swept away the oncoming French...'[27] That applied evenly to all seven regiments of 'Heavies'. As one

An artist's impression of Captain Clark, Royals, taking the Eagle of the French 105th Regiment at Waterloo

eyewitness said: 'intoxicated with slaughter and inciting each other to kill, they pierced and cut down the miserable mass with glee'. With the result that they galloped on, uncontrolled – the Second Life Guards farthest – as far as the French artillery emplacements, their horses by then exhausted.

Napoleon, having foreseen this turn of events, now dispatched two of his lancer regiments to finish off the isolated 'Heavies'. However, one of the other cavalry brigade commanders, Vandeleur, went to the rescue with his light dragoons, who covered the surviving, retreating heavy cavalrymen back to their squadron lines. So the mêlées continued. And Wellington was there again to say 'I thank you, Life Guards!' It was in these charges that the Union Brigade commander, Major-General Ponsonby, Colonel Ferrier (1LG), Captain Fitzgerald (2LG), Major Packe (RHG) and Captain Windsor (Royals), among more than 230 others of the Heavy Brigades, were killed, and at least that number seriously wounded. There were over 600 casualties among the horses.

It was during those charges, too, that Corporal Shaw (2LG), a name famous in England as a heavyweight boxing champion ('the milling lifeguardsman') accounted for more than a dozen cuirassiers until his sword broke and he was toppled from his saddle and slain. His squadron comrade, Private Godley, having a shiny bald pate, was

nicknamed 'Marquis of Granby'. When Godley's horse was killed he got up and slew the cuirassier who attempted to run him through, mounted the Frenchman's horse and galloped back to his squadron ranks amid cries of 'well done, Marquis!' Lieut George Story (1LG), who had been captured by the French in the Peninsula, was about to cut down an enemy officer when the latter shouted *'monsieur, ne me tuez pas, je vous connais de Verdun!'* Sparing the cuirassier Story sent him back, a prisoner of war.

The 'Eagle' standards were the objects most cherished and revered by the French regiments. To them they were as 'holy' emblems. So the greatest single triumph of the Heavies was, perhaps, the capture by Captain Clark and Corporal Styles,[28] of the Royal Dragoons, of the Eagle of the 105th Regiment, which was to be adopted as the Royals' crest. Clark reported afterwards as follows:

When my squadron, the centre one of the Royal Dragoons, had advanc'd about two or three hundred yards beyond the second hedge on the British left, and the heads of the columns of the French infantry had been brok'n by our charge, I perceiv'd a little to my left an enemy's Eagle, with which the bearer was making away with the intention to carry it off to the rear. I immediately rode to the place, calling out to secure the colour, and, at the instant I reach'd the spot, ran my sword into the officer's right side who carri'd the Eagle. He stagger'd and fell forward. But I do not think that he, at this time, reach'd the ground, on account of the pressure of his companions. I call'd out a second time 'Secure the colour! It belongs to me!' This was addressed to some men close behind me at the time. The officer was in the act of falling, and, as he fell with the Eagle... I was not able to catch the Standard so as to hold it. Corporal Styles and some other men rushed to my assistance, and the Eagle was secured, it falling across his horse's neck ... I immediately order'd the Corporal to carry it to the rear, and I remain'd, although wounded, in charge of my squadron.[29]

Clifton having taken Ponsonby's place at the head of the Union Brigade, command of the Royals devolved upon Dorville, who, with the help of Clark, formed up the remnants of the regiment behind Vandeleur's light dragoons. Napoleon then conducted a fresh assault on La Haye Sainte, employing most of the remainder of his cavalry reserves (unsupported by infantry), riding stirrup to stirrup and closing ranks as they were mown down by Captain Mercer's artillery. As for the Duke of Wellington, he had no more reserves to call upon. So it was as well that Zeiten's Prussian corps appeared on the Allied flank just then, which was about 6.30 pm.

But Napoleon had not yet finished. He hurled his Imperial Guard against the right of the Allied line where General Maitland and his Foot Guards were waiting behind the crest. As Napoleon's veteran columns surged up out of the smoke towards the ridge, Wellington called out 'now Maitland, now's your time!' And so the cream of the French infantry, the Old Guard, met the musketry of the scarlet-coated British guardsmen, followed by their bayonets – in a devastating massacre.

On the left of the line, the Prussians undertook the pursuit. And so Napoleon's ragged remnants tramped the road to Paris with Blucher's hussars hacking at their backs, while Wellington's men bivouaced on the gory field of battle. The following morning they, too, were en route for Paris.

The word 'Waterloo' would now be borne upon the standards, guidons and colours of all those regiments that participated in the great fight while the men who were there would eventually receive the Waterloo medal, the first of its kind.[30]

DEATH OF TWO MONARCHS

The cavalry proceeded from Waterloo to the French town of Nanterre, seven miles from Paris, the regiments being with the army of occupation until the end of 1815. They returned to England early in 1816, The Life Guards to London, The Blues to Windsor and the Royals to Ipswich. In July 1815 The Life Guards learned that 'the Prince Regent, as a mark of his high appreciation of the distinguished bravery and good conduct of his First and Second Life Guards at the Battle of Waterloo, on the 18th ultimo, is pleased to declare himself Colonel-in-Chief of both regiments of Life Guards'. (At which, according to that gossipy captain of Foot Guards, Count Gronow, Wellington was heard to remark 'his Royal Highness can do what he pleases, but this I will say – that the cavalry of other European armies have won

The Eagle
of the 105th Regiment

victories for their generals; mine have always got me into scrapes. It is true, though, that they have always fought gallantly, and have generally got themselvs out of difficulties by sheer pluck'.)

The first twenty years of the 19th century formed a long twilight to the reign of poor George III. That reign had seen the sudden and startling growth of a new empire, coupled with victories over France and Napoleon, which rendered Britain the supremacy of the world. But now a new world was blossoming, based on industrial power, and a new society with which the old King would never be identified. The popular, mad George died on January 29, 1820, and the unpopular Prince Regent (who was no more associated with the new world than his father) became George IV. Within a month of that the new King incorporated The Blues in the Household Cavalry, his brother, the Duke of York, commander-in-chief, writing to the Duke of Wellington, Colonel of the Blues:

I have received the King's Commission to acquaint your Grace that, taking into consideration the distinguished conduct of the Royal Regiment of Horse Guards Blue, and being fully aware of the partiality which his late Majesty ever entertained for that Corps, His Majesty conceives that he is only fulfilling the intention of his late Majesty in granting to that Regiment the same honours and privileges in every respect as are possessed by the two Regiments of Life Guards, and in consequence of which it is His Majesty's intention that your

Grace should roll with, and take your share of duty as Gold Stick with the Colonels of those two regiments; and also that the Field Officers of the Horse Guards should take their share of the duty of Silver Stick.

So The Blues had an equal share with The Life Guards in the ceremonies of the Coronation, on July 19, 1821, for which the King ordained that the Household Cavalry should wear cuirasses and grenadier bearskins adorned with white-feather plumes.

When the Duke of York died in 1827 his brother, the Duke of Cumberland[31] was appointed Colonel of The Blues, Wellington now being no longer eligible as commander-in-chief. Within three years of that there was another death, that of George IV and the accession of another brother, the Duke of Clarence, as William IV.

1. Sir Rowland Hill, later Lord Hill, not to be confused with Sir Robert Hill of The Blues
2. After Waterloo this manuscript book, which covers the years 1811-16, came into the possession of Capt Sigismund Trafford, who appears to have been the last club secretary and who died in Paris in 1852. Subsequently, it was in the hands of one of his executors, a Mr Green. Green's son, Capt Green, of the 49th Foot, restored the book to the Royals in 1878.
3. The 14th Light Dragoons (later Hussars)
4. Sabugal had been the scene of a skirmish on April 3, 1811, with Ney's rearguard. The Royals were not involved.
5. There were two Traffords in the Royals at this time, first Edmund and second Sigismund, through whom the Club Book came into the possession of the regiment
6. Clifton, formerly of the 3rd DG, who had superseded Jervoise in command of the Royals in December, 1810, was nicknamed 'the Ruler' by the young officers
7. Capt Hulton was then president of the 'club'. He died in 1814.
8. There were few, either in the nation or in the army, who disapproved of severe corporal punishment. Since recruiting was, to a great extent, from the criminal classes the better disciplined men were particularly thankful that the example of such deterrent was available to courts martial.
9. The Quartermaster General, Col Gordon, took the blame for much of the misery, having sent the provisions along a road not used by the retreating army
10. He was gazetted on January 1, 1813
11. At Vittoria The Blues met up with their old comrade, John Elley, who was then Assistant Adjutant General of Cavalry
12. In May when the Prince Regent created him a Knight of the Garter, Wellington wrote to the Garter King of Arms saying 'I shall be very much obliged to you if you will let me know whether the riband of the Order is worn over the right or the left shoulder'.
13. The letter, which was later found in the cover of a book on a secondhand stall in Carlisle, is quoted by Hills (p 53)
14. Peace having been signed between Britain and America in December, 1814, the British troops were either in mid-ocean or about to sail home.
15. 'Union' because it was composed of regiments from England, Scotland and Ireland.
16. Regt Order Book, 2LG, 17.4.15
17. Crofton, 11
18. Mercer, Gen C. *Journal of the Waterloo Campaign*. Mercer was a captain commanding Horse Gunners at Waterloo
19. The three regiments had only managed to muster about 300 men each
20. There were five light cavalry brigades, the two 'heavies' being those of Somerset and Ponsonby. Uxbridge's command totalled over 12,400 sabres
21. Somewhat confusingly the French 7th Hussars were also involved in this action. Their commander was the dashing Col Marbot, who was Conan Doyle's model for 'Brigadier Gerard'.
22. Crofton, 29
23. Ibid, 30
24. Kincaid, Capt J, *Adventures in the Rifle Brigade*, p333
25. *Club Book*, 202-3
26. Quoted by de Ainslie, 151
27. From *Waterloo Letters*, quoted by Crofton
28. Corporal Styles was rewarded with promotion to ensign in a West Indian regiment for his part in the capture of the Eagle
29. Quoted by Clarke-Kennedy, 122
30. The Peninsular medal and clasp was not awarded to the survivors of that campaign until 1847, the authorities being then prompted to have it struck after the distribution of the Queen's medals for the Afghan and Mahratta wars
31. Prince Ernest Augustus (1771-1851), fifth son of George III, became King Ernest I of Hanover, in 1837, on the death of William IV.

10 WILLIAM IV (1830-37)

THE ROYALS DEPRIVED OF THEIR MOUSTACHES

During the reign of George IV the Royal Dragoons had divided their time between Kent and East Anglia, Scotland and Ireland. In July, 1823, riding up from Canterbury to Regent's Park Barracks they took their turn at Household Cavalry duty while The Life Guards and Blues were reviewed at Hounslow; at the same time the Royals sent a squadron to keep the ground at Hounslow.

By the end of that month they were at York; and in May, 1829, in Scotland. Their peacetime activities involved, as ever, every sort of duty in aid of the civil power. While in Edinburgh, for example, they did great work in helping to put out a devastating fire, and were then busy, for three successive nights, assisting the homeless, protecting property and maintaining order, for which they received profuse thanks from the Lord Provost, magistrates and City council.

During the new King's reign they were helping to keep the peace again in Norfolk and in Kent. In 1832, they came in for more duty at the Horse Guards,

William IV and Queen Adelaide driving to their Coronation in 1830. A detail from the painting by R B Davis (Reproduced by Gracious permission of Her Majesty The Queen). Cuirasses had been reintroduced for the Household Cavalry for the Coronation of George IV nine years before

when the Household Cavalry were out of London, while their commanding officer, Lt Col Charles Somerset (who had succeeded Clifton[1]) acted as Silver Stick. In 1835 the regiment received marching orders for Ireland once more and there they stayed until 1838. It was in Ireland that Somerset died, Major Martin then gaining the command.

To the great dismay of many Royal Dragoons, one of the first acts of William IV, after his accession, was to order the removal of moustaches from all ranks of the Royal Horse Artillery and cavalry, the only exception being the Household Cavalry and the Hussars.

THE DUKE OF CUMBERLAND'S INDIGNATION

Another of William IV's early measures was to nominate himself Colonel-in-Chief of the Household Cavalry. And it was not long before a row flared up between him and his prickly and irascible brother, the Duke of Cumberland, who, as Colonel of the Blues and Gold Stick, objected to the King's directive that the Household Cavalry should be subject to the orders of the commander-in-chief. William remaining firm, Cumberland resigned in high dudgeon. Lord Hill, of Peninsula and Waterloo fame, was then appointed Colonel of The Blues, to whom on August 13, 1832, the King presented their first Royal Standard in a ceremony that was part of the celebrations for Queen Adelaide's birthday. He also gave The Life Guards some silver kettle drums (in 1830).

ACCESSION OF QUEEN VICTORIA

William IV showed himself to be neither a statesman nor a charismatic figure. But eleven years' service with the Royal Navy, in which he had risen to the rank of rear-admiral, had helped to foster in him a strong sense of justice as well as order and discipline. Throughout his short reign, promotion by merit – which had long been the practice in the Navy – was increasingly regarded as right and proper for the army, too. William cared little for ceremonial matters, but, in the words of his biographer,

> ... he would spend long, happy hours discussing details of uniform, of drill, or of the correct precedence to be followed during manoeuvres or engagements. The Service chiefs displayed towards their eccentric sovereign a sympathy and patience which the politicians had not contrived to muster. They knew of his anxiety that they and their men should be fairly treated, well equipped and decently quartered; and, if he sometimes expressed himself a little oddly that at least was a failing which they shared.[2]

William fell seriously ill, aged 72, in May, 1837. His great wish then was to see the twenty-second anniversary of the Battle of Waterloo celebrated, which he did, and he died contented. And so it was that Princess Victoria (the only child of George III's third son, the Duke of Kent, and of Princess Victoria of Saxe-Coburg) came to the throne at the age of 18.

---

1. Clifton completed 19 years as the Royals' CO.
2. Gore Allen, 217

11 VICTORIA (1837-1901)

No other Sovereign was ever a kinder or more steadfast friend to the Household Cavalry than Queen Victoria. Their prestige and their privileges were dear to her, and she was a vigilant guardian and staunch upholder of both. In her eyes no detail of their equipment was too insignificant for her critical notice, while, in graver matters – such as those affecting the continuity of their status or the maintenance of their welfare – they could be sure of her warm sympathy and wise support.

Captain Sir George Arthur Bt,
Second Life Guards.

Few people with a close knowledge of the dialogue between The Life Guards and Blues and their Monarch in the second half of the 19th century would have disagreed with that verdict of a Victorian Household Cavalryman. And since the Queen reigned for 64 years no other Sovereign, before or since, was as close to those Regiments for so long or could have felt the glow of their loyalty and their glittering presence so strongly. Among many other initiatives, she played a considerable part in the pioneering of married quarters in London. She was also to make it plain that she did not wish her Household Cavalry to go the Crimea.

THE LONG PEACE

Thus the Household Cavalry enjoyed 67 years of continuous peacetime soldiering after Waterloo. But the three regiments, alternating between Knightsbridge, Regent's Park and the Cavalry Barracks at Windsor, were anything but idle during that time. Simply to name a few of the earlier ceremonial occasions – the Queen's Coronation (1837) and marriage to Prince Albert of Saxe-Coburg-Gotha (1840), the funerals of Queen Adelaide (1849) and the Prince Consort (1861), not to mention those

of four former Colonels of The Blues, Lord Hill (1842), the Duke of Wellington (1852), Lord Anglesey (1854) and Lord Raglan (1855), and the celebrations for the Great Exhibition (1851) – would be to underrate and to gloss over the constant activity to which Household Cavalrymen were subject in the mid-19th century.

The two regiments in London each found a daily barrack guard of 20 men and an inlying piquet of 21, while alternating in the duties of Queen's Life Guard, which amounted to a strength of two officers and 49 other ranks. Besides the part they played for State visits, reviews and other State occasions, they took their field training far more seriously than their predecessors in the 18th century had done. They continued, too, to be London's primary force of law and order, and their detachments were often to

Queen Victoria.
This photograph was published in 1887 to commemorate the Golden Jubilee of her Coronation

be found backing up the Metropolitan Police in the suburbs or on the Thames bridges. They were frequently called out, or stood by, for example, when Chartist extremists took to the streets during the 1840s (the demonstrators' principal complaint being that the Reform Acts had failed to enfranchise the working classes).

In 1847 the bearskin cap, which was introduced for all three regiments of Household Cavalry during the reign of William IV, was replaced by the helmet we know today. At about the same time the tunic replaced the coatee.

ROYALS AND RIOTERS, 1837-54

The opening of the new reign found the Royal Dragoons in Ireland. Major General Lord Vivian, who was then their Colonel, died in 1842, being succeeded by Lieutenant General Sir Arthur Clifton[1] (the commanding officer, 'the Ruler', of *Club Book* fame and after). The Chartist riots of 1838 prompted the recall of the regiment and deployment to keep the peace in Sheffield and other northern and Midland towns, with a year in Scotland in between. By the autumn of 1843 the Royals were back in Ireland and it was not long before they faced violent insurgents again, for they were there when the potato

crops failed in the late 1840s. In the face of widespread starvation the English wheat contract was a matter for bitter controversy. General de Ainslie, who transferred to the regiment as a captain in the Rifle Brigade, in 1830, and was later Colonel of the Royals, tells us that

> ... The regiment ... on the 13th of May, 1846, moved to Cork; and while on the march, in consequence of the disturbed condition of a portion of the Limerick and Tipperary districts, 1 troop was halted at Clonmel and another at Carrick-on-Suir, and were employed in convoying flour from the interior of these districts for exportation to the English markets. These disturbances, which at first threatened to be serious, were suppressed by the capture of most of the ringleaders ...[2]

ROYALS TO CRIMEA

The regiment (strength about 300) was stationed in the north of England when its commanding officer, Colonel John Yorke, received orders to mobilise for the Crimea.

The cause of Britain's participation in the Crimean war was fear of Russian imperialism. The Russians saw themselves as the patrons and protectors of those millions of Orthodox

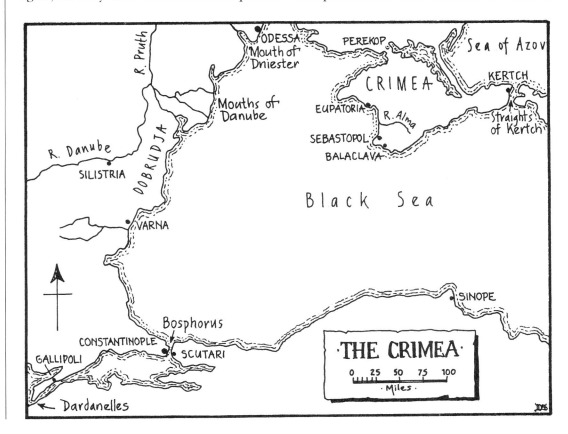

Approaches to the Crimea

Christians living under the rule of the ruthless and corrupt Turkish empire. Czar Nicholas I recognised that condition as a means of extending his country's influence in the Balkans and farther east. Realising, however, that the two strong powers of western Europe, France (champion of the Catholics living under Turkish rule), and Britain, would not tolerate independent Russian aggression, he proposed a partition of the Turkish dominions among the three of them.

Neither Britain nor the France of Napoleon III would cooperate, Britain in particular being unwilling to watch a strong European power in control of that part of the Mediterranean which lay on one of the routes to India – or indeed threatening India itself. And their sympathies were very much with Turkey. Nicholas, claiming to be the true protector of all Christians living within the Turkish orbit, but in fact being intent only on expansionism, invaded Moldavia in 1853, at which Turkey's Sultan declared war on him. Britain and France, determined to support Turkey, sent a combined fleet into the Black Sea. The Allies, being, by March, 1854, in the conflict on Turkey's side, concentrated their effort in the Crimean peninsula, upon which the Russian naval threat to Constantinople and the Turkish empire was based. But neither the French, nor to an even lesser extent, the British, army was properly prepared for war – particularly a war in such a bleak, disease-infested, far-off zone – either in terms of senior command, staff organisation, transportation, medical backing or the means and conduct of supply. Fortunately for them the Russians were little better served, although their army enjoyed the advantage of operating on more convenient lines of communication.

The British army was virtually nothing more than a conglomerate of separate regiments, each regarding itself to be second to none, and never, in peacetime, brigaded, nor thought of as part of a hierarchy, nor subject to a collective system of logistics. And although, in the wet summer of 1853, 10,000 troops of all arms were assembled on Chobham common for combined battle drills, that was little more than a token step towards closer cooperation. Anyhow, in the following year, a field force of some 27,000 was dispatched piecemeal to the Crimea and there grouped in formations for the purposes of the campaign.

A Sergeant of the Royal Dragoons in the Crimea. The artist was a French officer, Col Pajol, from whose drawings C C P Lawson took tracings

Those formations, under the overall command of the Earl of Raglan, amounted to five infantry divisions and one cavalry division. The latter, potentially amounting to about 3,000 sabres and led by the Earl of Lucan, contained two brigades, a heavy brigade, under command of Brigadier General Scarlett[3] and a light brigade (Brigadier General the Earl of Cardigan), each having a strength of 10 squadrons, which is to say in the region of 1,500 men and horses. Scarlett's command included the Royals, the Inniskilling Dragoons, the Royal Scots Greys and the 4th and 5th Dragoon Guards.

This was the time when steam was beginning to replace sail. Most of the British infantry had reached the Bosphorus straits by May, 1854, the month in which the Royals, under command of Lieutenant Colonel John Yorke,[4] embarked at Liverpool in six sailing ships, the largest of which accommodated no more than 60 men and horses. A good deal of care was taken with loading the horses. A sling was placed under their bellies and fastened to the tackling on the main yard. Then they were hoisted over the main hatchway, which was well padded, and lowered into the hold where each horse was allotted a separate stall. They were placed with their heels towards the ship's side, the heads facing each other. The mangers were fixed beneath their heads, by which they were fastened by double halters to prevent them lying down.[5]

Colonel Yorke wrote optimistically to his sister that his soldiers 'were a pattern of good behaviour and create quite a sensation in the river ... Great cheering takes place when the river steamers pass and sometimes the band plays "God Save the Queen"'.[6] He was optimistic, too, about his horses. 'My horses are beginning to discover the use of their slings and occasionally set down in them and sleep, and we have every reason to hope at this time of the year and in such a ship that nothing will go wrong'. It was in the Bay of Biscay that his regiment encountered their first disasters. Troop Sergeant-Major Cruse, writing to his wife, takes up the story:

> ... four or five of the horses in a horrible plight, loose, down under the other horses, who were all plunging dreadfully at every lurch of the ship. It took me the whole night up to 10 o'clock the next morning before I could get them all secured, some of them dreadfully bruised ... I am sure you will be grieved when I tell you that I have lost poor Fanny. I had been boasting all along how well she stood it, and how nicely she kept her legs but on the morning of the 29th just as I went down to stables she had slipped down ... she had nearly exhausted herself with plunging. We got slings under her ... but the ship was too unsteady and at last we got her to lay flat down, and I saw at once she had so injured herself that she could not live. She struggled very hard till seven in the evening, then died very easy, and was immediately thrown overboard in the Bay of Biscay. I went to my Cabin and had a good cry over her and it will be some time before I recover from the shock.[7]

The Allies' principal objective was the Russian naval base of Sebastopol on the western side of the Black Sea's Crimean peninsula, from which the enemy threatened Constantinople. The second aim was to stem the Russian thrust from Moldavia against Silistria on the Danube. For that the Royals were landed at the unhealthy port of Varna on the Bulgarian coast, their first shipload disembarking on June 28 and the last on July 8. 'It is about the most infertile spot I ever trod on,' complained Captain Stocks in his narrative of the campaign, 'low bush woods full of toads, lizards and snakes, no grass, weeds in abundance, not a wild flower'. Both men and horses, being badly fed and underexercised, were in poor condition. Several men succumbed to cholera and other diseases while 30 horses, suffering from glanders and farcy, were shot.

Following the Russian withdrawal from Silistria the Royals awaited transports for the Crimea. Sailing on September 26 they ran into an appalling storm. 'If I live for a century,' Sergeant-Major Cruse told his wife

> I shall never forget the terrible sights ... The *Jason* [steamer] finding that she could not tow us longer with safety to herself, cut us adrift without notice at midnight, and the ship being left all at once to the mercy of the raging of the Black sea, soon became in an awful plight... The whole of the stabling broke adrift & the officers horses were dashed from one side to the other...

Captain Stocks's memory was still more ghastly: 'no sooner were the poor beasts up than down they went again.' The officers' chargers were thrown on top of the troop horses in the hold. '... Horses that had cost hundreds lying with broken backs and legs ... horses and saddles, carbines and swords, mixed up like as they had been shook up in a bag. I never saw such a wreck of as fine a troop of horses as ever in the service ... '[8] Although the other Royals transports made it to Balaclava, the Crimean port held by the Allies, Stocks's ship, the *Wilson Kennedy* was obliged to run before the storm to the Bosphorus, where it was found that only 11 horses out of 110 had survived. 'The poor Royals are annihilated without a shot being fired,' wrote Colonel Yorke. 'So great a calamity in horses probably never occurred to any regt before.' When, eventually, the party reached Balaclava, Colonel Yorke recorded that 'I take my place in the brigade as a single squadron instead of two ... On that fearful night the Regt lost more horses than at Waterloo ... Total loss, 150'. However the Colonel was able to mount his second squadron after 75 horses were sent to him by the Light Brigade.

By this time 25 men a day were dying in the Balaclava hospitals. But, on the credit side, the Battle of the Alma had been fought and won and the siege of Sebastopol was well underway. As a counter to the large Russian force threatening from the east, Raglan had a number of redoubts constructed on the Causeway heights overlooking Balaclava harbour. These were manned by the Turks. The cavalry were

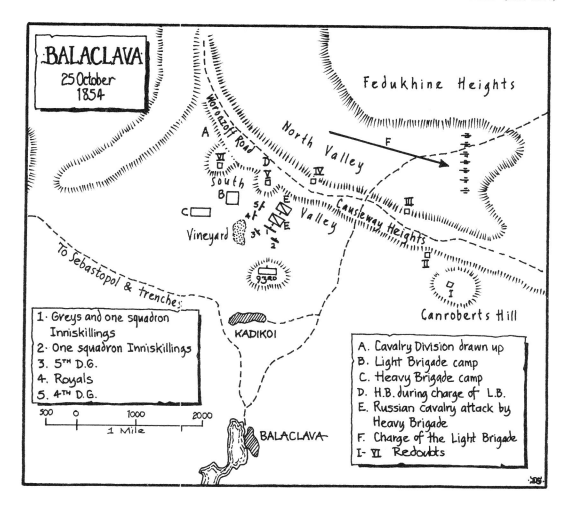

The Battle of Balaclava,
October 25, 1854

employed on patrol. 'Out all night three miles from the camp,' says Stocks's diary note for October 12, 'had an awful cold night of it, the wind has changed to the north ...' And two days later: 'the poorest fun I know of ... saw lots of Cossacks who retired when we approached and approached when we retired ... They remind you of rabbits, only not quite so harmless...' Stocks had another night out on October 18 when the Russians advanced with more serious intent, but with no serious effect. After this he writes ruefully that 'If you keep a cabman out all night he charges you double, whereas a Heavy gets nothing extra but a cold'.[9] Sergeant-Major Cruse told his wife that 'I have not undressed or had my boots off for eight or nine days and God knows how much longer it will last. This is soldiering in real earnest'.

THE BATTLE OF BALACLAVA, OCTOBER 25, 1854

During the third week of October the Russians had advanced up the Causeway Heights, and, having captured most of the redoubts, bore down on the village of Kadikoi, from which they were at first repulsed by the deadly fire of the 93rd Highlanders. Meanwhile the Royals were suffering from the Russian artillery. 'We were placed directly in the line of fire,' Colonel Yorke recorded:

All the very large shot that overcrowned the heights naturally bowled like cricket balls into our ranks ... The officers could easily escape: we had only to move our horses a few yards to let the shot pass ... but when a shot came opposite the closely packed squadrons it generally took a front & rear rank horse,and sometimes a man or a single horse. In this foolish manner we lost 7 horses and 2 men.

The cavalry divisional Commander, Lucan, who was universally disliked, suffered from poor nerves. At the least alarm he was 'excited to madness', observed Yorke, 'and abuses everybody. We are constantly fearing his want of temper and judgment should

Lieutenant Colonel Yorke. He commanded the Royals in the Crimean campaign and was severely wounded in the charge of the Heavy Brigade at Balaclava

careered into the Cossacks on the right flank, breaking their lines and dispersing them. That was the climax of the Heavy Brigade's action that day. Out on the left flank the 4th Dragoon Guards enjoyed similar success and the enemy was soon in headlong retreat – northwards up the hill.

Tennyson's poem *'The Charge of the Heavy Brigade'*, written 28 years later and not so well known as its *Light Brigade* partner, gives due credit to the regiments. Here is the last verse:

'...Lost one and all' were the words
Muttered in our dismay;
But they rode like Victors and Lords
Through the forest of lances and swords
In the heart of the Russian hordes,
They rode, or they stood at bay
Struck with the sword-hand and slew,
Down with the bridle-hand drew,
The foe from the saddle and threw
Underfoot there in the fray
Ranged like a storm or stood like a rock
In the wave of a stormy day,
Till suddenly shock upon shock
Staggered the mass from without
Drove it in wide disarray,
For our men gallopt up with a cheer and
a shout,
And the foemen surged, and wavered,
and reeled
Up the hill, up the hill, up the hill, out of
the field,
Glory to each and to all, and the charge
they made!
Glory to all the three hundred, and all the
Brigade!

The Heavies then crossed the front of the Light Brigade, but the inept Cardigan, who should have sent his regiments in pursuit, stood still. The Russian Commander, Liprandi, now sent in fighting patrols to capture the guns in the redoubts, and it was that which prompted Raglan to send his controversial order to the Light Brigade, the order misinterpreted by both Lucan and Cardigan, which led to the Light Brigade's fatal charge up the North Valley. 'About two o'clock Capt. Nolan, who was one of Lord Raglan's Aide camps [sic] came galloping down', Cruse said in his letter home, 'and as he rode past me he enquired for Lord Lucan who was close bye. "It is Lord Raglan's order that you force the enemy to retire" ... The Light Brigade went so rapid that we almost lost sight of them.'

anything serious occur. He is sure to do wrong and then throw the blame on others and in the most uncourteous manner.' But he admired his brigade commander. 'We like Genl Scarlett very much indeed, and what is better he likes us, and we are a very united Brigade of Heavies.'

Lucan now ordered the stalwart Scarlett and his Heavies to stem the renewed Russian offensive in the south valley (between the heights and Kadikoi). Yorke, seeing the Greys and Inniskillings deployed in line preparing to attack the Cossacks, moved the Royals up in extended order to support them. Scarlett placed himself at the head of the leading squadrons and bade his trumpeter sound the charge. Although greatly outnumbered, the Heavies had the best of the ensuing fight from the start. But, at the moment of impact, both the Russians' extended wings began to close in on the British flanks. Yorke, also noticing Russian squadrons extricating themselves from the mêlée and wheeling onto the flank of the Greys (very conspicuous with their grey horses and their bearskins), shouted at the top of his voice 'By God the Greys are cut off. Gallop! Gallop!'

His trumpeter sounded the *gallop*, his men gave a great cheer and his two squadrons

The Royals and Greys were sent to cover the Light Brigade's withdrawal. And '... a more terrible fire was never heard than what was opened up upon us,' Cruse told his 'own dearest Lizzie'. 'The shot and shell and bullets came down on us like hail,' said Stocks, 'and every second I expected to get one.' The casualties, which included Yorke with a shattered left leg, were heavy.[10] Nevertheless Yorke told his sister that 'I never had a better line in a Field Day,

>...The only swerving was to let through the ranks the wounded and dead men and horses of the light brigade, which were even then thickly scattered over the plain. It was a fearful sight, I assure you, and the appearance of all who retired was as if they had passed through a heavy shower of blood, positively dripping and saturated, and shattered arms blowing back like empty sleeves as the poor fellows ran to the rear... another moment and my horse was shot in the right flank.'

Yorke being evacuated to the *Arabia* in Balaclava harbour, Major Wardlaw took command of the Royals. The regiment had ridden almost the length of the North valley – they were level with the third redoubt – before Lucan ordered their retirement, by which time they had suffered a further 20 casualties. The Battle of Balaclava ended with the Russians still holding the eastern end of the Causeway heights and thereby dominating the Woronzoff road. All that death and misery had done the Allies little good.

THE CRIMEAN WINTERS OF 1854-5 AND 1855-6

After standing by day after day, in early November, through the Battle of Inkerman the British cavalry faced the Crimean winter, during which they suffered almost every sort of privation – heavy rains, snow, frostbite, their tents blown down by gales, lack of forage for the horses, very poor food for the men (salt pork was the staple diet), inadequate clothing and the threat of a variety of deadly diseases.

Sergeant-Major Cruse wrote home in January that, after the horses 'have had a good roll in the mud and after that a good fall of snow, and then the whole to be frozen on to them, it is enough to kill any animal except one cast in bronze'. Some could 'scarcely bear to be touched. The mud

having frozen on to them has taken the hair, and in many instances the flesh, off their poor bones'. In June, 1855 (while the siege of Sebastopol continued) a draft of reinforcements reached the regiment with 120 remounts. 'Such brutes ... cart horses, hearse horses, refuse ... a very different stamp of animal to what we brought out with us,' was the verdict of Captain Stocks.[11]

With more officers, men and horses reaching the cavalry during the summer, the Division was reorganised into three brigades, a Heavy, a Light and a Hussar brigade.[12] In September, while the campaign medals were distributed, the Russians evacuated Sebastopol. There was no more action for the cavalry but there was plenty of work, such as ... commissariat duties, taking supplies of biscuits to the heights for the infantry, and conveying the sick from thence to Balaclava, during all which period the health of the men, owing to continued exposure to the cold and wet, and the want of fresh meat and vegetables, was greatly affected,the prevailing diseases being diarrhoea and scorbutic affections...[13].

In November the Royals withdrew across the Black Sea to spend the winter of 1855-6 near Scutari. In March, 1855, Cruse had been promoted to cornet and sent home early. 'I expect to embark in three or four days time,' he wrote to 'my own darling Lizzie'. 'All the officers have congratulated me most heartily, and I shall partake of various dinners with them previous to my departure'.[14]

The Treaty of Paris being signed a year later, the regiment got their sailing orders in May. This time the journey was by steamship. They were sent to Aldershot, which was to serve as their station for five different postings during the 43 years that were to elapse before they went to war again. Be that as it may, the names 'Balaclava' and 'Sebastopol' were soon borne on their guidons. It was in 1856, that the Queen sanctioned the official use of the Royals motto, *Spectemur Agendo*,[15] and thence forward that slogan, too, featured on their guidons. On June 17 the Queen, 'attended by Lieutenant Colonel Wardlaw', inspected the regiment and '... walked through the temporary stables. She spoke to all the men who had been wounded and to those who wore medals,

Sergeant-Major Norris,
Royals, in 1858

and was pleased to express herself highly satisfied with the appearance of the regiment'.[16]

ROYALS EXEMPT FROM INDIA

The Royals continued to be classified as 'heavy cavalry' until 1889, the year in which the distinction between 'heavy' and 'medium' was abolished. Until then, therefore, being exempt from service in India, they divided their post-Crimean era between a variety of stations in England and Scotland – and troublesome Ireland. The Irish-American Fenian (republican) movement was strong during their first post-Crimean Irish tour (1856-61) and still rife at the start of their second (1867-73) when, once again, from their Curragh base, their troops were widely dispersed during election time when disturbance was the order of the day. In 1880, at the time their

third Irish tour began, political agitation and crime were at least as bad as ever. In January, 1882, the number of Royals on 'protection duty' had risen to over 60. It was in June that year that Corporal Wallace and the official he was escorting were shot in the back and killed. Returning to the first of these Irish stints General de Ainslie, who was then serving with them, illustrates a spartan aspect of their life:

> On the 20th of June [1859] the regiment marched to Blessington, County Wicklow, encamped there for the night and the next day proceeded to the Curragh of Kildare, where it encamped in a valley on the north-east side of the huts, and here the men built up walls of turf sods, which very much protected the horses in wet and stormy weather. The Royals remained 15 weeks under canvas and although during the last six the weather was very tempestuous both men and horses enjoyed excellent health...[17]

The regiment received congratulatory eulogies literally wherever they went. The following from the General Officer Commanding Scotland to the commanding officer in May, 1875, is typical:

> ... how much I regret the departure of the Royals from my command. During the two years the regiment has been in Edinburgh and Hamilton nothing could be better than their conduct; and their appearance, either on parade, in the field, on orderly duty, or on the streets, has always been very fine. They are a magnificent body, both of men and horses, and I am certain that, go where they may, the Royal Dragoons will never find a regiment superior to themselves.[18]

The 1860s and '70s saw many tactical changes. In 1868, for example, the breech-loading Snider carbine replaced the cavalry's muzzle-loading rifle. The drill then practised was (as it had been in the 17th century) for one man in four to hold the horses while his comrades advanced with their weapons. In 1878 the Snider gave way to the shorter Martini-Henry carbine.

In 1869 the squadron, hitherto a tactical expediency for wartime or field days, was adopted as the principal sub-unit throughout the cavalry. This restructuring had, of course, a considerable impact on Warrant Officer and NCO establishments.

1. HER MAJESTY THE COLONEL-IN-CHIEF.
From the portrait by Ricardo Macarron, commissioned by
The Blues and Royals in 1982.

2. State trumpeters with a fanfare in the Guards Chapel.

STUDIES by RICHARD SIMKIN OF UNIFORMS WORN BETWEEN 1660 AND 1914

3. 1st Life Guards

4. 2nd Life Guards

ROYAL HORSE GUARDS

5. Royal Horse Guards (The Blues)

1st Royal Dragoons

6. 1st the Royal Dragoons

7. A PRIVATE GENTLEMAN OF THE LIFE GUARDS AS SEEN AT THE CORONATION OF CHARLES II

9. (Right) DETTINGEN, JUNE 1743. George II at the battle, an impression by H. J. Ford. 'The King, dismounting and handing his horse to his Life Guards orderly, took his place at the head of the second line of Foot, exhorting them to "fight for the honour of England!"'

8. THE TANGIER HORSE (AFTERWARDS 1st THE ROYAL DRAGOONS) CAPTURING A COLOUR FROM THEIR HOSTILE ARAB NEIGHBOURS.

10. THE STANDARD OF THE BLACK MUSKETEERS OF THE MAISON DU ROI CAPTURED BY THE ROYALS AT DETTINGEN.

11. A SCENE IN THE CAMP OF THE HOUSEHOLD CAVALRY COMPOSITE REGIMENT DURING THE PENINSULAR WAR.

12. AN ARTIST'S IMPRESSION OF A MEMBER OF THE BLUES ATTACKING A FRENCH CUIRASSIER AT THE BATTLE OF WATERLOO.

13. A BLUES GUARD LEAVING HYDE PARK BARRACKS c1830. The barracks were rebuilt during the Victorian era.

14. A trumpeter of the 1st Life Guards in the late 1820s. The bearskin cap, shown here, was introduced for the Household Cavalry for State parades by George IV in 1821. It was replaced by a lighter model, by order of William IV, in 1833. For King's Life Guard and other duties the Roman helmet with a bearskin crest was worn until the 1840s when both were succeeded by the present helmet and horsehair plume.

15. A GROUP OF THE 1st LIFE GUARDS IN THE GUARD ROOM AT HORSE GUARDS IN THE 1830s. From the painting by F. R. Pickersgill. (National Army Museum)

16. LIEUTENANT FREDERICK AUGUSTUS BURNABY, ROYAL HORSE GUARDS BLUE. An explorer, balloonist and politician, he was to relinquish command of The Blues shortly before being killed at the Battle of Abu Klea on January 17, 1885.

18. A KETTLE DRUMMER OF THE 1st LIFE GUARDS. From the 1909 portrait by E. Nathan

17. SON OF THE EMPIRE. A study of the Royal Dragoons at the turn of the 19th century. From the painting by W. Frank Calderon.

19. A BLUES WATERING ORDER IN THE 1880s (From a painting belonging to The Blues and Royals). The watering order comprises the early morning excercise party for all those horses not otherwise on duty during the day.

21. THE STANDARD PRESENTED BY THE PEOPLE OF BRUSSELS TO THE SECOND HOUSEHOLD CAVALRY REGIMENT FOLLOWING THE LIBERATION OF THEIR CITY IN 1944.

20. THE BLUES SQUADRON OF THE COMPOSITE REGIMENT ON THE RETREAT FROM MONS. From the painting by Lady Butler. (By kind permission of the Royal Hospital, Chelsea.)

22. KING GEORGE VI, COLONEL-IN-CHIEF 1936-52. From the portrait by Oswald Birley (from the painting belonging to The Blues and Royals).

23. HOUSEHOLD CAVALRY OFFICERS AT THE FOUR CORNERS OF THE CATAFALQUE AT
THE LYING-IN-STATE OF GEORGE VI, 1952.

24. FALKLANDS, 1982: A BLUES AND ROYALS SCIMITAR CREW HELPING MEMBERS OF THE PARACHUTE REGIMENT TO MOVE EQUIPMENT DURING THE LAST STAGE OF THE CAMPAIGN.

25. CREW OF A LIFE GUARDS SCORPION IN BELIZE IN 1989.

26. HER MAJESTY THE COLONEL-IN-CHIEF WITH LIFE GUARDS PARATROOPERS AND A SCORPION ARMOURED CAR STOWED ON A HEAVY STRESSED PLATFORM FOR A PARACHUTE DROP.

27. Scorpions and their crews in the march past at the parade for the 1993 presentation of new Standards.

28. TROOPERS ATTENDING A NONCOMMISSIONED OFFICERS' CADRE COURSE.

29. THE BAND LEADING THE SOVEREIGN'S ESCORT IN THE MALL AFTER THE QUEEN'S BIRTHDAY PARADE.

30. CHANGING OF THE QUEEN'S LIFE GUARD ON HORSE GUARDS PARADE. Guard changing was in the Horse Guards courtyard until, in the early 1990s, the throng of spectators grew too large for either convenience or safety.

31. BOSNIA, 1995. Household Cavalrymen at Prozer waiting to form up to escort a convoy.

32. Officers conversing at the Changing of the Queen's Life Guard: the Hamilton-Russell twins. (Left) Lieutenant Edward of The Life Guards and (right) Lieutenant Mark of The Blues and Royals. They are the sons of Colonel James Hamilton-Russell MBE, a former Royal Dragoon who was Silver Stick, 1982-1986. Their grandfather, Major the Hon. John (Jack) Hamilton-Russell, was killed while commanding a squadron of the Royals in Sicily in 1943. Their paternal great-uncle was killed in the Western Desert with the Royals. Their maternal great-uncle (Lord Lewisham) also lost his life in the Second World War. (Photo: Alison Hamilton-Russell.)

33. Musicians of The Blues and Royals in State dress. (PR HQ London District.)

34. The GARTER CEREMONY showing Household Cavalrymen lining the route with the Silver Stick-in-Waiting (Colonel P. B. Rogers, The Blues and Royals) in close attendance on Her Majesty. (PR HQ London District.)

35. The Blessing of the new Standards following their Presentation by H M The Colonel-in-Chief in 1993. (Soldier Magazine.)

RADICAL REFORM

Following the Crimean War there was a growing awareness that all was not well with the army, not only in terms of logistics and the chain of command but also at regimental level. The champions of the purchase system, which had been the policy for the granting both of original commissions and for promotion since the 17th century, argued that it was the only way in which older officers (by selling their commissions) could be induced to retire and make way for the advance of younger men. The reformers replied that the system by no means guaranteed that those with the money necessary to buy a commission or promotion were suitable to hold the rank in question, or for that matter to be officers at all; and, secondly, that the question of retirement could be resolved by introducing pensions at certain ages or lengths of service.

In the 1860s a cornetcy in The Life Guards cost £1,260, in The Blues £1,200, and in the Royals about £800. There was, as we have seen, promotion from the ranks but without money (such as that held by private-to-general John Elley, of The Blues), a newly commissioned ranker would get no further than subaltern.

The reformers insisted that officers' careers should be determined only on merit; and, in condemning the purchase system, they drew attention to the case, among others, of Lieutenant Lee, of the Royals. He was promoted from Regimental Sergeant-Major to cornet in 1854, took over the regimental adjutancy in 1855, and was gazetted lieutenant in 1856. But, having become senior subaltern early in 1858, then saw some 20 juniors with ready money go over his head.

The voices of those urging a new system of officer recruitment and promotion, along with other reforms, became more confident and insistent following the testimony of the success of the highly professional Prussian army against the relatively decadent French in their campaigns of 1866 and 1870. The Prussians were effectively the first European army representative of the industrial era. That example tipped the balance in Parliament in favour of reform; which, in 1871, enabled Edward Cardwell, the inspired Secretary of State for War in Gladstone's first government, to put into practice his plans for a revision of organisation and terms of service, which included the abolition of purchase, improved pay and conditions, pensions, and, for the infantry and territorials, linked battalions. The policy of having ranker adjutants was phased out at this time.

Although a Royal Warrant of 1867 increased soldiers' pay (for the first time in 70 years) that remained dismally low. A Life Guard private's daily pay was increased from 1s 11 $\frac{1}{4}$d to 2s 0 $\frac{1}{4}$d, but after stoppages and other levies less than half the amount remained for him to spend. Incidentally, although The Blues had been on a precisely equal footing of service for 46 years, the old Life Guardsman's precedence died hard. For he was paid 3d a day more, the position being regularised in 1867.

In the course of many Army debates in the Commons in 1871, the very need for a Household Cavalry was questioned. They were an 'ornamental extravagance', declared a Liberal member, the 'revels of Knightsbridge' were a scandal; and anyhow they were no longer representative of the British army, for 'the day of heavy cavalry was over'. He spoke – as politicians so often do today on military matters – from ignorance, saying that the Prussians had shown, with the efficiency of their Uhlans that heavy cavalry was obsolescent. Captain the Hon Reginald Talbot MP, 1st Life Guards, rose to put him right. The Uhlan trooper was heavier and his horse larger than those of British dragoons. Fortunately, too, the commander-in-chief, the Duke of Cambridge, had addressed two of the Household Cavalry regiments at a review during the previous August, thus:

'In my opinion you are fit to go anywhere to do any duty you may be called upon to perform. Continue, as for many years past, your course of good military conduct, and you will be, as you always have been, the pride of the Service.'[19]

In 1882 they were to prove the truth of those words in north Africa.

COMPOSITE REGIMENT FOR EGYPT, 1882

Anglo-French influence in Egypt, which had prevailed since the Napoleonic wars, was reinforced when the Suez Canal, built by the French engineer, de Lesseps, opened in 1869; and again in the 1870s when Britain became the largest shareholder in this new, short route to India. Now four out of every

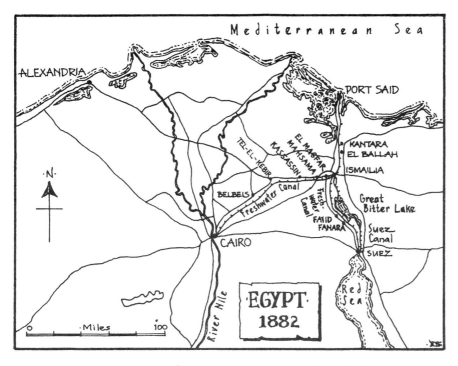

Egypt, 1882

Navy to anchor off Alexandria and an army to quell the revolt, restore the Khedive and protect the Canal, and ultimately show the French who were masters of Egypt.

General Sir Garnet Wolseley – the model for the 'Modern Major General' of *The Pirates of Penzance* – who commanded the expeditionary force, proved a master of surprise and deception. Most of his 35,000-strong army were concentrated for manoeuvres on Chobham common in the summer of 1882, (which was a bonus for secret troop movement). His Cavalry Brigade, under command of Sir Baker Russell, included the 4th and the 7th Dragoon Guards – and a composite unit comprising a service squadron of eight officers and 153 other ranks from each of the three regiments of Household Cavalry – under Colonel Henry Ewart, 2nd Life Guards, Colonel Milne Hume, the Blues squadron leader, being also Ewart's second-in-command. The 1st Life Guards squadron leader was Major the Hon Reginald Talbot, who, as Captain Talbot MP, we saw championing the Household Cavalry in the Commons in the last section of this chapter. By keeping a record of events during the campaign for his commanding officer at home, Colonel Keith Fraser, Talbot gives some vivid first-hand images of the Egyptian war.[20] We also have eye-witness accounts from an officer of the 'Seconds', Sir George Arthur.

The Prince of Wales, Colonel-in-Chief of the Household Cavalry – who had

five vessels passing through the Canal were British. Egypt was ruled, under Anglo-French protection, by a Khedive. However, by the late 1870s, the country was bankrupt and in a state of anarchy; the Khedive Tewfik was overthrown by a fanatic nationalist, Ahmed Arabi, whose battle-cry was 'Egypt for the Egyptians'. In 1882, Arabi stirred up a riot which led to a massacre of Europeans in Alexandria. While France declined to intervene, Gladstone, by then in his second Premiership, was urged, against his judgement, to dispatch a squadron of the Royal

Richard Simkin's impression of Household Cavalrymen entraining at Waterloo for Southampton for the Egyptian campaign of 1882

volunteered to be with them, but was restrained and who played a considerable part in urging the inclusion of the Household Cavalry in the force – inspected the three squadrons when they concentrated at Hyde Park Barracks on July 31-August 1, and took a very close interest in all their preparations. He also entertained the officers to dinner at the Marlborough Club. The Queen had a special request for Wolseley. Could the leading ship carrying the 'Composites', the *Holland*, pass by Cowes road so that, from Osborne, she might wave them on their way, which she did at 10.00 am on August 1. Aboard ship all ranks had their hair cut 'as short as that of a rat'. They were issued with dark-tinted goggles, against the desert glare, and cholera belts. Their first weapons, their swords (their second being Martini-Henry rifles, and their third, pistols) were sharpened, then burnt to brown them against the giveaway light of sun and moon. For the same reason all metal was allowed to rust. This was to be the last campaign (before the innovation of khaki) for which coloured tunics were worn.

By the time they reached Alexandria a fortnight later, the Royal Navy had seized the Suez Canal from Port Said to Port Suez. Wolseley promptly but stealthily moved his base from Alexandria to Ismailia by the Canal with a view to mounting his offensive against Arabi and Cairo from there.

The first action was on August 24 at El Magfar on the Sweetwater Canal (the only substantial source of (so-called) fresh water in the area). There two squadrons of the Composites put in a charge against Arabi's infantry. One shell killed a subaltern's horse, whose rider, according to the AAG, Colonel William Butler, stood up with a cry of 'three cheers for the first charger in the Life Guards killed since Waterloo!' Wolseley, in a letter to the Duke of Cambridge, the C-in-C at home, wrote:

In going round the wounded I asked a Life Guardsman, who had a nasty sabre cut over his right arm, how he came by it. He said in their first charge on the 24th instant he found himself in broken ground separated from his troop when a man on foot shot his horse and then came up at him with a sword, with which, as he was getting up, the Egyptian cut him over his guard across the arm. 'Well,' I said, 'and what became of your friend?' He replied, without

moving a muscle, 'I cut him in two, Sir'. In several instances these great giants with their heavy swords cut men from the head to the waist-belt.[21]

The following day a Blues trooper who had dismounted to take an Egyptian prisoner was attacked by him with a dagger. The trooper was wounded in the hand but, 'with a single stroke, he cut his antagonist in two, and took the dagger as a souvenir'.[22]

KASSASSIN, AUGUST 25, 1882

The soft sand handicapped both sides. It absorbed the artillery shells as readily as it sank the wheels of the supply wagons and exhausted the horses. Anyhow, by August 25, Arabi's camp at Mahsama was taken and occupied along with Kassassin (also on the Sweetwater Canal). 'We found tents which we are still using,' wrote Talbot, 'and stores of all descriptions ... we also found about twenty camels, which will be, and have been, a most welcome addition to our regimental transport.' Arabi now advanced in an attempt to recapture Kassassin, and that night the celebrated and successful 'Moonlight Charge' took place. Talbot wrote to Col Fraser:

After the sun set we had brilliant moonlight ... The 7th Dragoon Guards

The Actions at Kassassin, August 28 and September 9, 1882

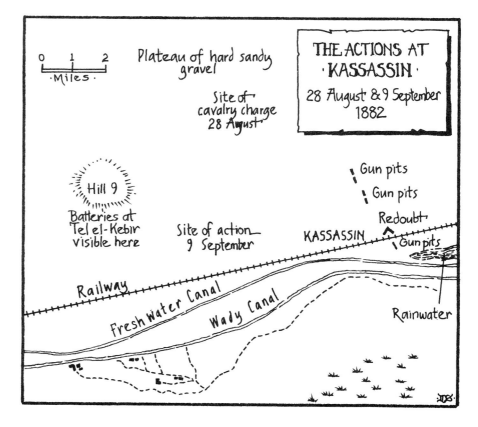

led the way followed by our RHA Battery, the Household Cavalry in rear in squadron columns … We must have marched some five or six miles when the silence was broken by the boom of a gun … and then in rapid succession were seen flashes from guns about 1,500 yards distant … on our approach, having perceived that we had got round their rear they were faced about … in a moment became visible a white line of infantry in our immediate front, which opened a tremendous fire upon us… General Lowe [Sir Drury Drury-Lowe, the expedition's cavalry commander] ordered our guns to unlimber and reply and the 7th … to clear the front of our guns, which they did by retiring, making us the first line …'Front form in two lines, draw swords, Charge!' and we were upon them … Until we got within a hundred yards they continued to fire, but in one moment the brilliant light from the firing line and the rattle of the fire and the whiz of the bullets ceased; the white line had faced about and was in flight. We rode them down in solid rank … I can imagine no more splendid sight than this moonlight charge of our fine fellows on their black horses against the guns supported by the white line of infantry, whose fire was so brilliant in the night it looked more like the lighting of some grand pyrotechnic display than anything I can describe. Then the cheer we gave, then the few seconds of silence, then the havoc and slaughter. The rout was complete, and it was only the want of being able to see that saved the guns…

Two troopers of the 1st Life Guards and one of the Blues were killed in the action. Wolseley, in his somewhat egotistical way, wrote home; 'I shall be curious to see the newspapers about the Household Cavalry. They can be laughed at no longer. I believe they will owe the continuance of their existence to my bringing them here and pushing them well to the front. They certainly are the best troops in the world. At least none could be better.'[23]

Trooper Tom Froude, of the 2nd Life Guards, echoed him in verse:

THE CHARGE OF KASSASSIN

The Body Guard of England's Queen
Have woke to life once more
The glories won at Waterloo
In stormy days of yore,
Thus answering without anger
The tongues who cast their sneers
'That we were useless save for show',
Let this assail their ears,
We were the foremost in the fight
Where'er the conflict raged.
Nor paused to count the numbers of the
foemen we engaged.
We gained the valued good esteem of
brilliant Drury Lowe,
And would have charged a thousand
guns had he commanded 'Go'.
Now glittering helmet must be worn, the
breast be clad with steel,
The prancing steed be bravely decked, the
bright spur clasp the heel,
As many scenes of pageantry will pass
before our sight,
Our flag another honour bears,
Kassassin's famous night
Will be remembered by us all, when in
the moonlight we
Charged horse and guns and infantry
and won 'The Victory'.[24]

September 1 found Sir Garnet Wolseley writing to the Duke of Cambridge again:

Believe me, Sir, the more I see of war the more convinced I am there is nothing like volunteers. These men of the Household Cavalry are teaching me a lesson, and that is that it would pay us well as a nation to obtain men of a better stamp for our Army than those we now enlist by offering double the pay we now give. This system of paying the soldiers badly give us the lowest stamp of man for our ordinary Regiments, whilst the Household Cavalry have such

Lieutenant Colonel Burnaby giving an address at a Blues NCOs dinner during the time of his command

good men that crime is unknown amongst them.[25]

TEL-EL-KEBIR, SEPTEMBER 13

During the first ten days of September the Composites were busy patrolling in preparation for the attack on Tel-el-Kebir, where Arabi, with some 25,000 Egyptian and Sudanese and 70 guns, was posted for his final stand. Wolseley's army of 13,000 or so now included a cavalry division under General Drury-Lowe's command, a reinforcement cavalry brigade having recently arrived from India. Wolseley planned a dawn attack. His forces marched with great secrecy through the night of September 12-13, the Composite Household Cavalry Regiment being on the extreme right of the line. The attack, delivered at 5.0 am, took the enemy completely by surprise and, in the words of witness Sir George Arthur:

> After half an hour's severe fighting both the fortified position and the camp of the enemy were in the hands of the British, together with forty guns, the fugitives throwing away their arms as the Indian cavalry pursued them towards Zagazig for three hours. The Household Cavalry, without stopping, made a forced march to the lock at Belbeis which was reached the same evening. Next day, September 14th, Cairo was occupied, and Arabi captured … By special order of the Duke of Cambridge the Household Cavalry were among the first to be brought home.[26]

However, the Composites enjoyed some brief comfort in camps close to Cairo, though Wolseley was not one to let discipline slip. 'The Chief of Police will post notices in Arabic,' ran one of many orders, 'that any native selling spirits to soldiers in or near any of the camps will be handed over to the Civil police and flogged on the spot and all his liquor confiscated.'[27]

On October 20 the 2nd Life Guards squadron were welcomed at Windsor by their Colonel-in-Chief and the Princess of Wales, who then proceeded to London and Regent's Park Barracks, where, with the Blues' commanding officer, Colonel Frederick Burnaby, they gave a similar welcome to his service squadron, for every man of which a public dinner was given in Holborn Town Hall. Next day the 1st Life Guards squadron marched into Hyde Park Barracks, where once again there was a 'cordial greeting from their Royal Highnesses', and, while they were duly feted, Colonel Ewart was summoned by the Queen to stay at Balmoral. She wrote to the expeditionary force commander: 'The Queen is glad to hear that Sir Garnet Wolseley entertains such a high opinion of her Household Cavalry; she would remind him that they are the only Long Service Corps in the Army.'

WITH CAMELS IN THE SOUDAN, 1884-85

The Soudan, nominally under the Khedive of Egypt's rule, was now in turmoil.

The Gordon Relief Expedition, 1884-5

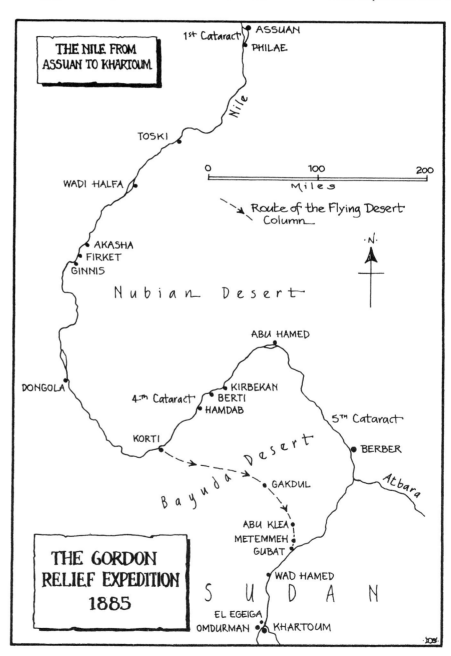

Life Guardsmen of the
Camel Corps, 1885

Mahomet Ahmed, the Mahdi – the self-proclaimed Chosen One of Allah – was intent not only on freeing his country from its Anglo-Egyptian governors, but of ruling the whole Muslim world; and many thousands of Soudanese, particularly his dervish warriors, were willing to give their lives in his cause. In October, 1883, the Mahdists were much encouraged by ambushing and more or less annihilating an Egyptian army led by Gen William Hicks ('Hicks Pasha'). The British, having decided to evacuate the province, sent the eccentric General Gordon to organise a withdrawal from the capital

Field Marshal Viscount
Wolseley. From the portrait
by Emil Fuchs. Lord Wolseley
was Colonel of The Blues
(1895-1907)

Khartoum. But, early in 1884, that riverside town was besieged on all sides. Gordon being a public hero, public opinion, led by the Queen, demanded that a relief expedition be mounted to save him and the garrison. Gladstone, still in his second Premiership, was lukewarm about such an undertaking, but relented.

Wolseley was appointed to command the expedition. He decided on a dual approach. The whole army would be conveyed by Nile steamers as far as Korti. From there one force, the 'River Column', would continue up the Nile, while the second, the 'Flying Desert Column', would proceed across the desert by camel. The Camel Corps, under command of Brigadier General Sir Herbert Stewart, included four regiments, the Heavy, the Light, the Guards, and a fourth made up of men from regiments already stationed in Egypt. The Heavy Camel Regiment, led by the veteran Colonel the Hon Reginald Talbot, 1st Life Guards, was composed of two officers and 40 other ranks from each of ten regiments of heavy cavalry, including the 1st and 2nd Life Guards, The Blues and the Royals. The officers selected from those were Major the Hon Charles Byng and Lieut Lord Rodney (1LG); Major Lord Cochrane[28] and Lieut Beech (2LG); Major Lord Arthur Somerset and Lieut Lord Binning (RHG); and Major Gough and Lieut Burn-Murdoch[29] (Royals).

The force included another notable Blue in the person of the regiment's recent Commanding Officer, Colonel Frederick Augustus Burnaby, who had been in the habit of taking long and adventurous annual leaves throughout his service.[30] In 1884-5, ever desirous of being where the action was, Burnaby chose Egypt and the Soudan for his long furlough. On joining Stewart's force he contrived to get himself a job with the baggage camels; then, being of sufficient seniority, managed to persuade Wolseley to nominate him as successor to command the Camel Corps should anything untoward befall Stewart. Lieut Sir George Arthur, of the 2nd Life Guards, the regimental historian, was also with Wolseley 'on special service'.

The expeditionary force reached Egypt on October 8. Wolseley wrote home next day: 'The great camel corps arrived at Alexandria yesterday. I am anxious to see all the fine gentlemen of HM Household Troops dressed in workmanlike fashion moving over the sands of this desert on camels!'

The (detested) beasts being distributed at Korti, the next couple of weeks was spent practising camel management and mounted parades. (Lord Cochrane was amused to see 'two or three of the camels going off with their riders, who soon succeeded in getting into laughable positions, hanging on by one leg with heads down.[31]) They set off at the end of December, their first objective being the wells at Abu Klea, 43 miles south.

THE BATTLE OF ABU KLEA, JANUARY 17, 1885

The 19th Hussars, leading the advance on desert ponies, were screened by a vanguard detachment under Major John French (the future Field Marshal Earl of Ypres) who, on January 16, reported contact with what appeared to be the Mahdi's main army. Stewart ordered the Camel Corps to deploy from column into square but to keep marching into the narrow valley leading to the wells. He called a halt in the afternoon when a zariba (defensive thorns, boxes, barrels, saddles, etc) was constructed for a bivouac. Next morning as the defensive square moved gingerly towards the wells, the enemy's sharpshooters began a fusillade, and, says Colonel Talbot, 'the Heavy Camel Regiment here lost many men, killed and wounded...

> After marching for about two miles at a very slow rate, the enemy's flags ... suddenly became animate, and a large force of Arabs, distant some 500 to 700 yards, sprang up, and advanced as if to attack the left leading corner of the square. The square was at once halted, but immediately afterwards was moved to the right on to a slightly elevated knoll – a simple movement for men, but difficult for camels, many of which remained outside the square...

Lord Binning takes up the story:

> It was at this moment that, almost at our feet, a force of Dervishes, estimated at between three and four thousand strong, sprang up as if from the bowels of the earth, and, headed by their Emirs and Baggara horsemen, charged the left face of the square. Swiftly, and with almost appalling silence, they came on, and then suddenly espying the weak spot in our defence, they wheeled like a flock of pigeons and made for the gap on our left rear ... Our men, though completely taken by surprise, fell back

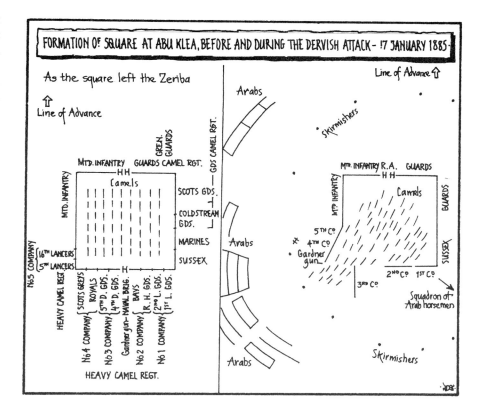

steadily in an endeavour to close the rear face ...[32]

The Gardner machine-gun 'from which', says Arthur, 'great things were expected', jammed and could not be got working again. The Heavy Camel Regiment's skirmishers, busy exchanging shots with the dervish sharpshooters, had not observed the Arab assault, which was now concentrated

The Square at Abu Klea before and during the dervishes' attack, January 17, 1885

Lieutenant Lord Binning, RHG. He gave a first-hand account of the fight at Abu Klea. We went on to command The Blues at the turn of the century

Corporal Mackintosh, Royal Horse Guards. He was obliged to relinquish his stripes in order to gain a place in the Camel Corps in 1885. He was killed attempting to save Colonel Burnaby in the square at Abu Klea

on their end of the square. Most of those skirmishers managed to regain the square, including their commander, Major Byng, who was the last but one to dash inside; the last man was overtaken and speared. Colonel Burnaby, having taken command at the point now penetrated by the enemy was killed in the hand-to-hand fighting, while Corporal Mackintosh, of The Blues, died in a very gallant attempt to save him.[35] 'It is not too much to say that, in our little force his death caused a feeling akin to consternation,' wrote Lord Binning, the Blues subaltern of the Heavy Camel Regiment. 'In my own detachment many of the men sat down and cried'. [34]

That attack was bravely repulsed, and so was the next. A squadron of Baggara tribesmen on black horses were killed to a man by volleys from the Martini-Henry rifles of the Household Cavalry, the Royals and the Bays. Major Gough and 13 of his Royals were killed in this engagement.[35]

The Mahdi's army having suffered over 1,100 casualties, from an original 16,000-strong force – in contrast to the Camel Corps' 74 killed and 94 wounded – slowly drew off, and Stewart's contingent continued their march to the wells – to find them low and the water turgid. Stewart ordered the advance to be resumed, and his Corps were within sight of the Nile on the afternoon of the 19th. But they did not gain the river without another very hot fight, in which 23 British, including Stewart himself, were

killed and 90 wounded. However, the riverside villages of Mettemeh and Gubat were occupied. Colonel Sir Charles Wilson, the new Corps commander, led an assault party of 200 men by steamer to Khartoum only to learn that the town was occupied by the Mahdi, and Gordon killed. So Wilson's detachment returned downstream to rejoin the main force.

After several more skirmishes the Camel Corps were back at Korti by March 7. Colonel Talbot's Heavy Regiment, which had started out from there with 411 all ranks, returned with only 296, a loss, from either battle or disease, of 115. Only 22 Royals survived the campaign. The Heavies and Foot Guards embarked on July 3 at Alexandria. The 14th of the month found them in Cowes Road with the Queen waiting to inspect them on the lawns of Osborne House. 'A few months later,' Arthur records, 'the detachment of the Second Life Guards, being stationed at Windsor, enjoyed the supreme distinction of having their medals affixed to their breasts by the hands of their beloved Sovereign herself'.[36]

The Royals' survivors of the Soudan Campaign rejoining their squadrons at Dundalk (County Louth) were greeted 'with honour, the whole regiment being drawn up to meet them and the officers giving them a dinner'.[37]

Fourteen years later, Kitchener's victory at Omdurman, across the river from Khartoum (1898), made Great Britain morally and practically responsible for the government of the Soudan, as an active partner in the Anglo-Egyptian condominium.

PRECEDENCE OF SILVER STICK

As mentioned in Chapter 1, Queen Victoria, pressed by the Prince of Wales, ordered the Master of the Rolls to adjudicate a propos the relevant precedence of Silver Stick and Field Officer in Brigade Waiting (an appointment granted during Queen Anne's reign to provide the monarch with an additional personal bodyguard and to endow the Foot Guards with a contact at court). In August, 1889, precedence was given to Silver Stick, not only because his office had been granted 30 years and more before that of 'Field Officer', but also because the Household Cavalry was the only military body with the prerogative of finding guards, staircase parties, etc, inside the Royal palaces.

DEPARTURE FOR SOUTH AFRICA

Serious trouble had been brewing in South Africa ever since Britain annexed the Transvaal in 1877 which the Boers had proclaimed as their republic. The resolution and strength of those Dutch settler descendants showed ever more plainly as the years passed, particularly with their victory over the British at Majuba Hill, in Natal, in 1881 (the 'first Boer War'), and again when they crushed Jameson's ill-conceived raid against Johannesburg in 1895. The situation was further fomented by the discovery of gold and diamond mines in the Transvaal, during the 1890s, and further still when President Kruger's government refused the franchise to the growing number of Uitlanders, non-Boer immigrants, whom the British, who were greedy for a share in the spoils, supported. When it became clear that the British would send an army up from Cape Colony to enforce their will on the Boers, Kruger declared war and promptly besieged Kimberley, Ladysmith and Mafeking. The Orange Free State joined him. That was in October, 1899.

Apart from Britain's 15,000 troops in South Africa, another 10,000 were sent from India, while volunteers poured in from Canada, Australia and New Zealand. The main British army of 70,000 landed in Cape Colony in November-December, with General Sir Redvers Buller commanding. The Boers, who were active long before the British could concentrate sufficient forces to outnumber them, raised more than 50,000 mounted infantry, field craftsmen and marksmen of a very high calibre, supported by a formidable force of artillery.

A British army corps plus a cavalry division were mobilised on October 7, the Royals being in the 2nd Cavalry Brigade (initially

2nd Life Guards maxim gun and 'galloping carriage'

The Queen about to
receive three cheers from the
Household Cavalry Composite
Regiment at Combermere
Barracks prior to their departure
for South Africa in 1899

The Blues contingent in
The Queen's funeral cortege
at Windsor railway station,
1901

with their old associates of the Union Brigade, the Inniskillings and Greys). The regiment, mustering 26 officers, 560 other ranks and 500 horses, under command of Colonel Burn-Murdoch, embarked at Tilbury on October 30.

It was Queen Victoria – more glorious than ever after being declared Empress of India (1876), having celebrated her Diamond Jubilee (1897) and being now the paramount symbol of Britain's greatness and Empire – who saw the Composite Regiment of Household Cavalry (commanding officer, Colonel Audley Neeld, 2nd Life Guards) off from Combermere Barracks on November 11. This was how she addressed the three squadrons, each of some 9 officers and 200 other ranks:

> I have asked you, who have always served near me, to come here that I may take leave of you before you start on your long voyage to a distant part of my Empire, in whose defence your comrades are now so nobly fighting. I know that you will always do your duty to your Sovereign and Country wherever duty may lead you, and I pray God to protect you and bring you safely home.[38]

As we shall see Queen Victoria was to welcome home the 1st Life Guards Squadron (whose station was Combermere) when the Household Cavalry came home at the end of November, 1900. But, as this (second) Boer War was to last two years and eight months, it was to be her son, King Edward VII, who occupied the throne when Major Ernest Makins led the squadron representing the Royals in the procession through London on October 24, 1902, to celebrate the end of hostilities. By then Edward VII had been King for a year and a half.

Colonel Audley Neeld,
1st Life Guards, commanding
the Composite Regiment.

1. Clifton remained Colonel until his death, aged 97, in 1869. He was succeeded by Gen de Ainslie, the regimental historian.
2. de Ainslie, 177
3. Brig-Gen Hon James Yorke Scarlett. Later Gen Sir James KCB
4. Yorke, who succeeded Martin in command, in February 1853, had served continuously in the regiment since purchasing his cornetcy in 1832. His letters to his sister are the property of Lord Anglesey, who has kindly given me permission to quote them.
5. cf Anglesey 2, 32-33, in which a 13th Hussars trooper gives a fuller description
6. From the Yorke correspondence lent to the author by Lord Anglesey. Yorke posted his first letter from Carthagenia, his second from Malta, his third from Constantinople and his fourth from Varna
7. From the Cruse correspondence lent by Lord Anglesey
8. Atkinson, 326
9. Ibid, 327-8
10. 'A grape or canister shot caught me on the left shin bone,' Colonel Yorke informed his sister, 'and smashed my leg badly.'
11. Atkinson, 334
12. The 1st (Heavy) Brigade included the 1st, 4th and 5th DG, the Royals, Greys and 6th Dragoons (Fortescue, 13, 226)
13. De Ainslie, 193
14. There appears to be no further record of Cruse's career after the Crimea.
15. *Spectemur Agendo* (Judge us by our Deeds), the motto of the Spencer family, had been used by the regiment since 1740, during the period of the 3rd Duke of Marlborough's Colonelcy
16. De Ainslie, 197
17. Ibid, 201
18. Ibid, 218
19. Arthur, II, 662
20. MS held in the Household Cavalry Museum
21. Arthur, II 674-5
22. From *Told from the Ranks* by E M Small, quoted in Anglesey, 3, 282

23. Anglesey, 3, 290
24. From the copy in the Household Cavalry museum
25. Arthur, II, 678
26. Ibid, 680
27. Quoted in Anglesey 2, 306 from the regimental magazine of the 4th/7th DG, XXII, Dec 1970, 87-8
28. Later, as Colonel the Earl of Dundonald, he commanded 2LG from 1895 to 1899
29. Burn-Murdoch, who had recently won the Grand Military Gold Cup on Major Tidswell's Larva, went on to command the Royals in 1898
30. Burnaby, also a pioneer balloonist and erstwhile MP, wrote the best selling *Ride to Khiva* following a Russian adventure in 1875-6
31. Dundonald, 23
32. Quoted from Thomas Wright, Chaper XIX, Lt-Col Lord Binning's narrative
33. The Victoria Cross was not yet awarded posthumously. Arthur remarks that, had Mackintosh lived, 'the VC would surely have been his reward'.
34. Binning went to the spot where Burnaby died and found 'a young private in the Bays ... endeavouring to support [Burnaby's] head on his knee. The lad's grief, with tears running down his cheeks, was as touching as his simple words: "Oh Sir, here is the bravest man in England dying, and no one to help him"...' (Alexander 203-6)
35. Major Tidswell, who was sent to replace Gough, died of disease in June. Burn-Murdoch succeeded him.
36. Arthur, II, 696
37. Atkinson, 343
38. Arthur, II, 700

12 EDWARD VII (1901-10)

The first fourteen months or so of the Second Boer War were the last fourteen of Queen Victoria'a reign; but, in order that the campaign should be encompassed in a single chapter, its story, as affecting the Household Cavalry and the Royals, is told here under the above reign.

THE ROYALS RIDE TO LADYSMITH

Embarking for South Africa, early in November, 1899, the Royal Dragoons endured a three-week sea voyage which was longer than expected. They arrived at the Cape (from which they were to have travelled north by rail) only to be told that, as the Boers had now directed their major offensive against Natal, the regiment was to continue round the coast to Durban, to entrain for Pietermaritzburg and there to join General Sir Redvers Buller's army, whose mission – as ordered by the new Commander-in-Chief, Field Marshal Earl Roberts of Kandahar, VC – was to go to the relief of the Natal Field Force, who were surrounded by the enemy at Ladysmith. (Over half the garrison troops of South Africa were under siege at this time – at Kimberley, Mafeking and Ladysmith.) 'These orders,' remarks 'C' Squadron Leader, Captain Ernest Makins, ruefully, 'put a stop to our serving with the Greys and Inniskillings as "The Union Brigade" which we had expected to do'.[1]

Reinforcements were so urgently needed for the Ladysmith operation that new arrivals were immediately sent up by train and placed in improvised formations as they unloaded at the station. The Royals found themselves in the brigade commanded by that good old Second Lifeguardsman, Major General the Earl of Dundonald, whom we met as Lord Cochrane in the last chapter and who had recently relinquished command of his regiment. Their brigade also included the South African Light Horse, two newly mustered regiments of mounted infantry and two batteries of Horse Gunners.

Louis Botha occupied a powerful position on the north bank of the Tugela river, and several attempts were made before he was dislodged. At the Battle of Colenso (December 15) Buller was over cautious and badly served by the commander of the brigade to Dundonald's left. As Lord Anglesey writes:

> On the left Burn-Murdoch's patrols of the Royals thrice sent warnings that the opposite bank of the river was strongly occupied. Major General Arthur Fitzroy Hart, one of the most obstinate and old fashioned of the army's generals, treated this intelligence with contempt.

Edward VII.
Queen Victoria appointed him Colonel-in-Chief of the Household Cavalry when he was Prince of Wales

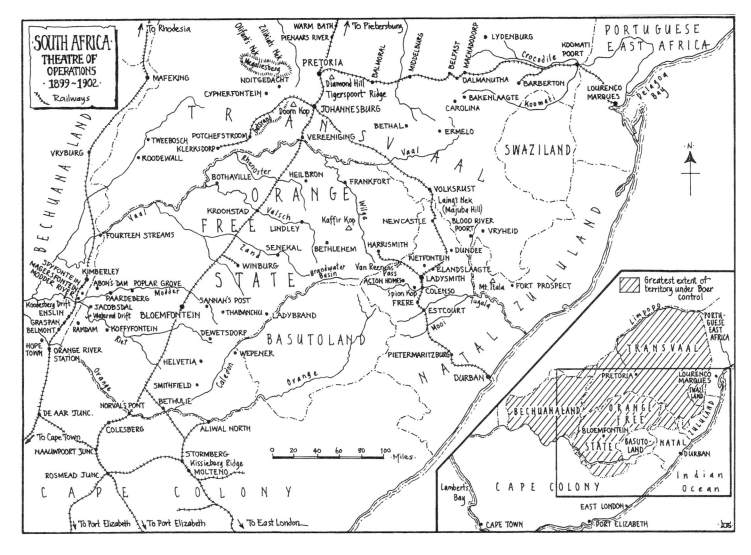

South Africa: Theatre of
Operations, 1899-1902

A Royals victim of the sea
voyage to South Africa, 1900

He proceeded to commit the closely packed regiments of his brigade to be slaughtered in a salient formed by a loop of the river which was nowhere near the drift [ford] at which he had been ordered to cross. The Royals suffered no casualties.[2]

Owing largely to the half-heartedness and incompetence of the divisional commander, General Sir Charles Warren, the next attempt to break past Botha's position foundered on Spion Kop (January 15, 1900). A fortnight later, Burn-Murdoch, who had been marching and countermarching his regiment to little effect, was complaining to Dundonald that

> I have been saddled up for the last five days. My horses have not had their backs even looked at, and I have much shoeing to be done. My men are so tired that I have cases brought before me of men asleep on their posts. My horses want hay, or, if not that, grazing.[3]

On February 1 Buller's much reinforced mounted elements were reorganised, Dundonald having the 2nd Cavalry Brigade while Colonel Burn-Murdoch was promoted to command the 1st, including the Royals (now led by Lieutenant-Colonel Hon J E Lindley[4]), the 13th Hussars, two squadrons of the 14th and 'A' Battery, Royal Horse Artillery. At last, on February 27, a bridgehead over the Tugela was established. But, even then, Buller failed to send his cavalry in pursuit. That same day, Colonel Lindley was invalided with typhoid, to be succeeded in command of the Royals by Major Lord Basing. His squadron leaders were Major R H Carr-Ellison and Captains J M Rogers and E Makins.

March 1 saw Burn-Murdoch's brigade, Royals leading, forming a protective screen on Buller's right flank. Two days later, the relieving force entered Ladysmith, the Royals

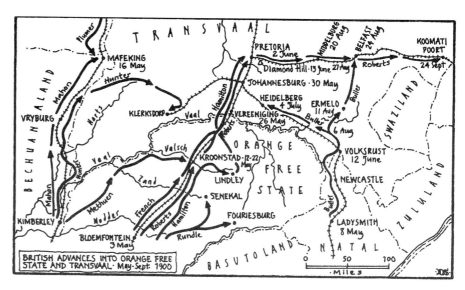

British advances into the Orange Free State and Transvaal, May-September, 1900

Men of the 2nd Life Guards on Hussar Hill, 1900

being allotted a notoriously unhealthy cantonment, which produced many cases of enteric fever in the ranks. 'Even in peacetime,' wrote Captain Makins

'Ladysmith had been well known for this scourge, and its ravages, during and after the siege, were severe ... if we had been sent further out on to the clean veldt we should no doubt have saved a good many cases of enteric ...'[5]

For the remainder of 1900 the regiment was employed largely in fighting patrol operations, or reconnaissance in force, around northern Natal; and they learned the hard way of the many advantages under which the enemy fought their campaign. As a start the Boers enjoyed

Lieutenant the Marquis of Tullibardine, DSO, Royal Horse Guards. He was attached to the Royals during the South African War

Major R H Carr-Ellison, Royals squadron leader in the South African War. He was acting Commanding Officer in 1901

internal communications; they were well acclimatised to the intense heat of the day (during the period October to March) and the contrasting cold nights; they travelled very light compared with the British; most of them had always been accustomed to riding over South Africa's vast distances; they

A Transvaal Boer

moved among friendly people; their quick little veldt ponies could endure longer periods without fodder or water than imported horses; they were organised in well disciplined commandos, supported by a formidable force of artillery (mostly officered by French and German professionals) while their columns were stiffened with well-armed units of French, Dutch and German volunteers. Their principal weaknesses were their lack of common strategic aim or, for the most part, central command and control of their widely dispersed forces, and the unwillingness of their citizen armies to go far from their homelands.

Naturally, the Boers were less prone than the British to the local diseases. In November the Royals' acting commanding officer, Lord Basing, was among those who succumbed to enteric fever. He was invalided and succeeded by Major R H Carr-Ellison. The regiment was active in northern Natal until the spring of 1901 and would not go home until the autumn of 1902. We shall return to them in due course. As for the Household Cavalry Regiment, whom we last saw taking leave of the Queen at Windsor in November, 1899, they had been to South Africa and returned to England before the close of 1900, but they had their fill of active service.

WITH FRENCH TO KIMBERLEY

Having reached Table Bay in two ships on November 29, 1899, the Household Cavalry Regiment, under command of Colonel Audley Neeld (2LG) proceeded by rail to join General Sir John French's Cavalry Division, whose immediate mission was the relief of the diamond town of Kimberley (where Cecil Rhodes was the principal figure incarcerated). Along with the 10th Hussars, 12th Lancers and two RHA batteries, HCR was placed in the 2nd brigade, commanded by Major General Robert Broadwood, a cavalryman for whom they were to have the greatest respect. Having detrained at Arundel on January 6, the Blues squadron was already in action the following day. Lieutenant the Hon Arthur Meade, RHG, kept a comprehensive diary:

> We paraded at 8.0 am, moving off in an easterly direction, parallel to the Boers' position for about three hours, the horses being very tired after their long railway journey. I was sent off with a troop to inspect ground for a new camp. At a distance of two

miles I found the squadron holding two kopjes [hills], about 150 feet high, with the enemy to their front and north. General French finding these unoccupied by the Boers, had told Fenwick [Lt Col H T Fenwick, commanding the Blues squadron] to 'hold them till seriously attacked' ... The General and his staff then returned to Rensburg, 7 miles off. The squadron had now been 3 hours under fire. ... I found the remainder of the squadron making a stand by a wire fence, and eventually they stopped the enemy. We returned to camp at 5 pm, having lost 4 men[6] and six horses, two of the latter from exhaustion. It was very lucky that any of us got away at all.

Having come off the train from Cape Town the previous evening this was not a bad first day's work, particularly considering that January and February are South Africa's hottest months. For HCR there was now a respite in which to put some condition on their horses before February 11, when, at 3 am, French's 'cavalry rush for Kimberley' as it was known, commenced. This famous ride was over flat veldt, excellent cavalry country, albeit the rain was late, the wells low and grazing short, none of which factors augured well for a division comprising, besides men, 5,000 horses, 10,000 oxen and bullocks and 12,000 mules. For the 13th Meade was recording that:

> we arrived at the Modder River at 4.12. The enemy were completely surprised; two commandos fled leaving their camp and everything standing. We came at a terrific pace and our horses were done up, many being lost – probably about 30.

On the evening of the 15th, the day on which the siege of Kimberley was raised, he was writing: 'No water all day; twenty horses died of exhaustion in the Household Cavalry alone.'

ENTRY TO BLOEMFONTEIN

Next day General French's cavalry trotted off in pursuit of the young Boer leader, Andreis Cronje, who hurried away along the Modder riverside with an army of 6,000 and a waggon train three miles long. By February 17 French had him surrounded at the drift [ford] at Paadeberg, then awaited the arrival of the infantry to capture him. The first corn ration for four days was issued on the 19th, the horses being so

Formation commander in South Africa: Major General The Earl of Dundonald, formerly commanding the 2nd Life Guards

ravenous that, when they saw it being distributed, they had to be bitted to prevent them making a dash for it. HCR was in action again on the 21st. According to Meade:

> The Boers, about 800 strong, made a sudden attack on the column when entangled in wire fences. The Household Cavalry Regiment formed up and returned the fire, while the Artillery disengaged themselves from the wire fence and opened with shrapnel when the Boers hurriedly retired ... Lieutenant Colonel Calley's horse was shot and he himself was injured by the fall.

Lt Col TCP Calley, 1LG, second-in-comand of HCR, was temporally hors de combat with several broken ribs.

After Cronje surrendered on the 27th, HCR was engaged in the Battles of Osfontein (where a 2 LG trooper was killed) on March 7 and Driefontein (March 10) before marching into the capital of the Orange Free State, Bloemfontein, on March 13.

THE ADVANCE TO PRETORIA

On March 17 French dispatched Broadwood's brigade southeast:

> ... to Thaba 'Nchu – in order to proclaim peace to the Orange Free State people and get them to lay down their arms. It was a great disappointment as we had been hoping to give our horses a rest and get them fit. 20th – At 4 pm we reached our destination. 26th – General French inspected us in the morning ...

A Boer native scout. His saddlery, captured from The Blues, was recaptured, all stamped RHG

News arrived of the death from exhaustion, at Kimberley, of Corporal-Major Blair. There was no better man in the Blues squadron' (Meade).

On March 29, Lieut Colonel Neeld, the commanding officer, went into hospital with enteric fever. Calley being still absent with his ribs injury, command now devolved upon Lt Col Henry Fenwick, of The Blues.

Meanwhile, on March 31, as Broadwood's brigade marched from Thaba 'Nchu towards Bloemfontein, that very able Boer general, Christian de Wet, ambushed his column at Sannah's post and captured seven pieces of artillery and most of the waggons. HCR – now under command of Colonel Charles Miles, 1st Life Guards – were ordered to canter their weary horses south, to sieze and guard a drift by which the 10th Hussars,

Mounted Infantry and remaining RHA might cross the Modder in safety. The 1st Life Guards suffered another 13 casualties in this operation.

Lord Roberts conducted his army's advance on Pretoria in a number of columns; to the west the Kimberley column under General Sir Archibald Hunter; then Lord Methuen's Modder column; then, proceeding by the railway line, General Sir Ian Hamilton's division, which included Broadwood's 2nd cavalry and General Bruce Hamilton's infantry; and, to the east (in a 'holding' role) Buller's Natal force. The general advance began on May 3.

HCR's next action was on May 5 near Winburg, where there was a race between two converging Boer forces and The Blues squadron (temporarily under command of Captain Viscount Sudeley) for a vital kopje on Hamilton's axis. These challengers occupied the feature at about the same time, The Blues being subjected to a galling crossfire. Two squadrons of the 12th Lancers with their maxim gun, some Mounted Infantry and RHA, galloped up in support and 'the Boers made off at top speed, pursued by shells from the 5-inch guns'. But not before Lieutenant Rose was killed and Lieutenant Hon C Wyndham wounded in the head. By the time HCR reached Pretoria the regiment had, in Meade's estimate, covered 1,592 miles in 161 days since joining the 2nd Cavalry Brigade on February 11.

Blues Troopers escorting Boer prisoners, 1900

The Boers, however, were by no means demoralised. De Wet's commandos were still at large in the Orange Free State, while Botha occupied a powerful position east of Pretoria. Roberts sallied forth to dislodge him and fought the battle of Diamond Hill (the key feature of Botha's line), where, when the Boers attempted a rush at the Horse Artillery's guns, HCR – with 1 LG on the left, RHG on the right and 2LG behind – charged and saw them off, but there was not enough left in the horses for a pursuit. Trooper Hunt was killed in this engagement. Sir Ian Hamilton occupied Diamond Hill on June 12.[7]

The regiment, still in Broadwood's brigade, led Kitchener's column, which was sent south to relieve a detachment besieged at Brakfontein on the Elands river. By August 30 they were once more at Pretoria, but, two weeks later, were on the move again; and, by September 23, back in the Bloemfontein area. It was nearly time to return to England. (All the same the regiment's official diary noted: 'Got clothing for men for first time since leaving home'.) Here are some closing notes from a 1st Life Guards journal:

> September 26th – marched; the 1st Life Guards Squadron being left to cover a convoy through the Nek near Rustenburg, repulsed the enemy who attacked the convoy ... October 1st –

Freddy (no D36) of the 2nd Life Guards, carrying a corporal major with Standard. He was the only one of the horses originally accompanying the Composite Regiment to South Africa, which returned to England. Note Freddy's campaign medal and clasps

A 2nd Life Guards 'Short Guard' on the South Carriageway returning to Hyde Park Barracks in the Edwardian Era (Hulton Picture Library)

marched out with 12th Lancers and MI and bivouacked without food or water. 2nd – were engaged about day break, drove back the enemy on Kaffir Krall, capturing 12 waggons and 10,000 rounds of ammunition. 11th – The Regiment were ordered to hand over 242 horses to the 10th Hussars and 12th Lancers. 12th – Took over the sick horses of the 10th and 12th and marched as the advanced guard of the convoy to Bloemfontein. General Broadwood said farewell to the Household Cavalry Regiment ...[8]

Broadwood wrote afterwards to Colonel Miles: 'I miss you all greatly, and can never wish to see a better regiment under my command ... I should be very much obliged if you would let the officers and men know how greatly I appreciated the keenness and dash which they always showed.' He might have added, as was generally acknowledged, that the Composite Regiment 'proved itself so excellent in horsemastership as, despite their weight and work,to exhaust fewer horses than any other cavalry unit'.[9]

On November 7 they arrived at Cape Town, and on the 29th their ship sailed into Southampton harbour. The 2nd Life Guards and Blues went into barracks in London while the 'Firsts' under Colonel Miles, entrained for Windsor. Queen Victoria drove onto the lawn in front of Victoria Tower to greet them. She said:

> It is with feelings of great pleasure and deep thankfulness that I welcome you home from your gallant and arduous services in the war in South Africa, just a year after I bade you farewell. The hopes I then expressed have been amply fulfilled. Alas! the joy of your safe return is clouded over by the memory of sad losses of many a valuable life, which I – in common with you all – have to deplore.

'So, in the failing November light, under the shadow of her mighty Castle,' concluded Sir George Arthur, 'the Queen looked for the last time on her bodyguard, whose service of loyal love had always been to her a peculiar source of pride.' She died within seven weeks of that reception.

THE RANK OF TROOPER

With the Peace of Vereeniging, which was to mark the end of the South African War in 1902, came the award of the campaign medals. King Edward, observing that the reverse side of a medal he presented to a Household Cavalryman bore the rank of 'Private', he not only objected, but ordained that, in future, all Household Cavalrymen of the lowest rank be designated 'Trooper'. The medals were duly re-engraved. This distinction remained the prerogative of The Life Guards and Blues until after the First World War.

THE ROYALS FIGHT ON, 1901-2

The chance which had taken the Royal Dragoons to Natal for the Ladysmith relief operation deprived them of a part in the dashing exploits of the Cavalry Divison, in 1900, in which HCR experienced such a gallant share. By 1901 the South African situation had changed entirely. The Boer armies were reduced to guerrilla bands; President Kruger had fled to Europe (but Botha, De La Rey, de Wet and Smuts were all still at large); Buller was recalled to England, while Kitchener had succeeded Roberts as commander-in-chief, and the Cavalry Division had been dissolved (but French commanded all the cavalry in South Africa). It was Kitchener who – frustrated by the Boer facility for slipping the British 'drives' – introduced, in April-May, 1901, a 3,700-mile system of mutually supporting tin-and-concrete blockhouses linked by barbed wire, a system which, combined with column 'drives' would eventually do as much as anything to bring about victory.[10]

Between May, 1900, and March, 1901 the Royals were in north Natal, in the vicinitiy of Newcastle, largely employed on outpost and convoy escort duty. 'The year 1901 opened quietly for us,' Makins reported. 'The only news was from home, and that was the death of the Queen, which occurred on January 22nd. Eighty-one guns were fired as a salute...'[11] On March 27 they received orders to proceed north by train via Pretoria to Belfast, to join the column commanded by Colonel Pulteney, which was one of three operating northwards from that place, a town on the Pretoria-Delagoa Bay railway. The chief guerrilla leader there was Ben Viljoen. There was plenty of action for them now, little rest and many contacts with the enemy, 'On the 21st [April] we moved off again northwards,' Makins recalled, 'into some rather hairy country... Some snipers were making themselves very annoying. 'C' Squadron … were sent on to sieze a prominent feature. They galloped on … and, dismounting, did very good time to the top. The Squadron Leader offered a sovereign to the first man up. Very good time was made, Lieut Leighton being first, Pte Bosley second and the Squadron leader third. Bosley received the prize which he now wears on his watch chain. They were sniped going up ... and, arriving at the top, there was some very pretty shooting at a few Boers ... two of which were bowled over ... June 2nd was a memorable day; we were going out on a reconnaissance, but the morning broke with a gale and a blizzard – men and horses were frozen stiff and no food could be cooked ... We saw about 150 Boers the next day, who made off south at our approach. On the 12th ... we got orders to march back to Carolina [south of the railway]. Here we had a bit of a scrap with some Boers who made clever use of the ground and it was difficult to see from where we were being fired at. Private Harris was wounded, and Private Walters was killed, being shot dead while waiting to help along a sick comrade ... On the 20th ... a member of the last draft distinguished himself by reporting that ... a large part of his mare's inside had come out. He explained that he had done his best to replace it ... We found that the mare, which was a very nice one and which we had commandered on the Elandsberg trek [February, 1901] had slipped a foal ... On the 7th [July] Lord Basing returned from sick leave, while Major Carr-Ellison went to command a Yeomanry regiment ... in the Orange River Colony. Colonel Pulteney being sick in hospital, Lord Basing took over command of the column.[12]

Casualties, and promotion outside the Royals, were such that the author of those notes, Makins himself, albeit a mere substantive captain, was to have temporary command of the regiment in February, 1902. Meanwhile, in July, 1901, the Royals were back in Pretoria. The following month found them in Basing's column, way south in the Free State. In December they were involved in the systematic clearance of the area around HCR's old battlegrounds of Sannah's Post and Thaba 'Nchu. Here is another typical entry from the Makins journal:

On January 25th [1902] 'B' Squadron started at 1.30 am to try and surround a Laager [Boer camp] that one of our native despatch riders had run into earlier in the evening. They found the Laager near Kaffir Kraal ... but while rounding it up were themselves attacked by a superior force of Boers ... [Our men] were not in a good position and had to fight their way down the hill which was the usual precipice. 'A' Squadron started at 5 am to assist them ... 'B' Squadron retired on 'A' but missed one Troop that was below and to the flank. This troop under Egerton heard the firing and scaled the hill to reinforce ... thus being exposed to the whole force of the Boers. Pte J Tynan was killed, Egerton was severely wounded together with Sergt W Glover and Pte L Mann ... One Boer was killed and two captured and they admitted to losing fire ... It rained hard all day ...[13]

At the end of March, by the Vaal river, 'Lieut Knowles, with a man named Sheehan ...

had galloped forward and caught a Boer scout and on reaching the Spruit [a deep watercourse, ususally dry] another single Boer was sighted by him. Knowles galloped on as the line halted and, when some distance in front, and nearly up to the Boer, the latter suddenly dismounted and fired straight at him and Sheehan, hitting Knowles low down in the body ... On the 28th (Good Friday) we received a telegram ... saying that he [Knowles] had died of his wound. He was a typical cavalry officer and Royal Dragoon and we were left to mourn the loss of a most promising boy whose only fault – if fault it was – was too much pluck and dash, amounting almost to recklessness.[14]

One of the strongest drives in which the Royals were involved took place in May under Sir Ian Hamilton near the railway post of Vryburg, close to the Bechuanaland border. By day squadrons were a mile or so apart with a chain of scouts in between. The line was defended by block-houses and patrolled by armoured trains. This combination presented an impassable obstacle and nearly 400 Boers, mainly belonging to two of the most formidable commandos, were captured. While peace rumours were rife, Captain Prince Francis of Teck, who had been on the staff throughout the war, reached the regiment with one of three drafts amounting to 132 men and 150 horses. Only one of the regiment's original horses now remained, the remainder being a mixture of Boer and Basuto ponies, Australians, Russians, Americans and Argentines. It is noteworthy that the Royals, with a reputation for horsemastership second to none, got through 3,275 horses between November 1899 and October 1902. As Lord Anglesey comments 'this represents the replacement six times of every horse taken out from home'.[15]

On June 1 the regiment heard that the Boers had accepted the British surrender terms, but it was not until mid-September that they entrained from Bloemfontein to Cape Town. Disembarking at Southampton on October 11 they proceeded first to Shorncliffe, then Aldershot. Their battle honour 'Relief of Ladysmith'[16] was to be shared with only two other cavalry regiments, the 13th and 14th Hussars.

INSPECTION BY THEIR COLONEL-IN-CHIEF

The German Emperor had been appointed Colonel-in-Chief of the Royals in 1894. And, although only a dozen years were to elapse before 'Kaiser Bill' became Britain's arch-enemy, the keeper of the

The Knightsbridge side of Hyde Park Barracks before the First World War (Hulton Picture Library)

8657. KNIGHTSBRIDGE BARRACKS.   L.S.& P

regiment's *Digest of Services* was recording, within a month of the return from South Africa, that:

> On Nov. 8th the Regiment was inspected by Field Marshal His Imperial Majesty the German Emperor, KG, GCVO ... After the Royal Salute ... the Regiment... marched past by Squadrons. A heavy gale, accompanied by rain, had been blowing all the morning, and it now became so bad that the trot and gallop past were dispensed with ... His Majesty then addressed the Regiment as follows: 'Royals – it has given me great pleasure to inspect you here today, the first time since your late Queen, my beloved Grandmother, whose death I lamented with you, did me the honour of conferring upon me the Honorary Colonelcy of this regiment ... I am unable to proffer my thanks to His Majesty in a more appropriate manner than by calling for three cheers for His Majesty King Edward the Seventh ...'

POMP OF THE NEW REIGN

Captain Sir George Arthur, 2nd Life Guards, marks the new reign by commenting that:

> The Court for forty years had been pervaded by a very cool colour; the Sovereign had discontinued any residence – other than for a day or two – in London, and had eschewed all social functions ... the Great Queen of imperishable memory had reigned in something like mystery as well as majesty ... now Buckingham Palace, renovated and reorganised, was to be the throbbing centre of the capital; the Sovereign would once more open Parliament in person, would convene Chapters of the Garter and lead processions of the Knights to St George's Chapel; the monarchs of Europe would, in succession be entertained in the Royal Palaces and lend their presence to Guildhall banquets ... For all such occasions the Household Cavalry must be summoned ...[17]

CLOSE OF THE EDWARDIAN ERA

King Edward VII's reign closed with his death on May 6, 1910. Apropos the King's dialogue with The Life Guards and The Blues his contemporary and fellow Household Cavalryman, Arthur, has this to say:

> No Sovereign had ever been quite so closely associated with the inner life, as well as with the outer circumstances, of the Household Cavalry. His great-grandfather, [George III] had shown a rather childish predilection for the Blues, and fretfully insisted on their being retained for an inconveniently long period at Windsor. But King Edward had at heart the real interests of the three regiments; he had rejoiced in their selection for active service in North and South Africa; he had pleaded to be allowed to serve with them in the Soudan; he had marked with close attention and eager satisfaction their every action and delighted in any distinction bestowed on them. At home he examined every point affecting their prestige or position; he recognised their special relation to the Sovereign's household. And the rightful precedence accorded to Silver Stick, under the ruling of the Master of the Rolls, was due to his firm representation to Queen Victoria.[18]

The Coronation of King George V and Queen Mary took place on June 22, 1911.

THE ROYALS IN INDIA, 1904-11

The old distinction between 'heavy' and 'medium' cavalry having been abolished and the tactical differences between cavalry regiments having been proved obsolete, the Royal Dragoons were no longer exempt from foreign service in peacetime. It was thus that they enjoyed the best part of the Edwardian era in India. They sailed, under Lieutenant-Colonel Lord Basing's command, on January 4, 1904, reaching Bombay on February 19, and proceeding thence to Lucknow, where they took over the cantonments, stables and horses of the 5th Dragoon Guards who had been posted to South Africa. First at Lucknow and then at Agra (1907-10) and Muttra (1910-11) the Royals achieved an unreservedly successful first Indian tour, which ended in November 1911, when they themselves left for

South Africa. There was to be considerable trouble in store for them there.

1. Makins, 9
2. Anglesey, 4, 77
3. Dundonald, 135
4. Col Lindley went on to be Commandant of the Imperial Yeomanry School of Instruction, 1901-3; he commanded the 3rd Cavalry Brigade, 1907-10; and was founder of the Cavalry School at Nether-avon. He was appointed Colonel of the Royals in 1910.
5. Makins, 5
6. Captain Ricardo and four men were taken prisoner
7. The entry in the Regiment's official diary for June 13 says: 'The First Life Guards squadron lost 70 horses during the past month'.
8. Arthur, II, 763-4. A Life Guards horse, 'Freddy' was the only one of the original HCR horses proceeding to South Africa, which returned to England.
9. Ibid, 764
10. Anglesey, 4, 219; Pakenham, 499
11. Makins, 67
12. Ibid, 77-90
13. Ibid, 136
14. Ibid, 166-8
15. Anglesey, 4, 323
16. The Royals also secured, of course, the battle honour 'South Africa' which was common to The Life Guards, Blues and all other campaign units.
17. Arthur III, 2-3
18. Ibid, 13

13 GEORGE V (1910-35)

THE ROYALS LEAVE INDIA

Nineteen-eleven was the last year of the Royals' pre-war Indian tour. January was a red-letter month for them. Although the initial menace of the Hun was only three-and-a-half years away, the German Crown Prince, the son of their Colonel-in-Chief, spent a sporting and social week with them at their new station, Muttra, that month. (And – the wheels of State turn slowly – it was not until January, 1911, that the battle honours 'Tangier, 1662-1680' and 'Fuentes d'Onoro' were accorded to the Royals.)

November was a time for a change of command. Lieutenant Colonel Henry de Beauvoir De Lisle – who had first made a name for himself as captain of India's champion regimental polo quartet (the Durham Light Infantry team) and had subsequently served in the 5th Dragoon Guards, before transferring to the Royals and taking over command of them from Lord Basing in 1906 – now himself handed over the regiment, the new lieutenant colonel being their South African War diarist and future honorary Colonel, Ernest Makins.

November, 1911, too, saw them back in South Africa. They sailed from Bombay to Durban via Mauritius and took over the camp ('bleak, bare and comfortless, tin huts everywhere') at Roberts' Heights, near Pretoria, from the 3rd Hussars. The Regiment's first major event there was their week's celebrations – staged late on account of their posting – for the 250th anniversary of the raising of the Tangier Troop (1661).

A POLICE ROLE IN JOHANNESBURG

Otherwise the great drama of the Royals' South African tour was the part they played with the 10th Hussars in quelling the riots, following the strike by workers in Johannesburg in July-August,

King George V dressed as Colonel-in-Chief of The Blues

Brigadier-General Ernest Makins, commanding the 4th Cavalry Brigade, 1914. A former commanding officer of the Royals (1910-14) he went on to be Colonel of the Regiment (1931-46)

1913. Lieutenant the Hon Julian Grenfell described some of the Regiment's unpleasant duties of that year in letters home:

> Johannesburg. Sunday, July 13, 1913. We got to Jo'burg at about 2 o'clock [am] on Friday [July 4] and got a feed – the men had nothing since 7 the night before ... There were tremendous crowds and a good deal of shouting ... The people who looked like trouble were the real Jo'burg roughs who are rougher and dirtier than any other roughs in the world ... When we left [Park] station we got into the thick of the hooligans; everyone yelling and bottles and stones flying and roughs upsetting the horses with whips – led by a woman who was trying to pull the men off their horses ... We stood-to till 2 am [July 12] and then we were summoned into the town again ... There had been a good deal of street fighting, people shooting and throwing sticks of dynamite from the tops of houses ... and three of our horses had been killed ... We went to the main Police Station and as we got there the police brought in 60 of the hooligans whom they had rounded up in a pub. You never saw such brutes .. While we were at the place [the Rand Club] they didn't dare touch us, because I had men lying down across the street above and below with rifles at the ready ... they did not fire till 5 or 6 of the men had been hit with bullets and slugs and several of the horses. Sunday, July 20. We're still here, loaded to the muzzle and ready to sally forth at any minute ... It's such a poor game – broken bottles if you don't shoot, execrations if you do – heads they win, tails we lose ... Potchefstroom Sunday, August 3. We are just this moment (7 pm) back from Jo'burg by train. The strike is finally burst up – for the present ... If they had decided it we should have had a pretty thin time, as they had all got dynamite, made up into bombs in bicycle pumps, which they were going to throw from the house-tops on to our devoted heads ...

The officer commanding Potchefstroom District expressed his

> ... admiration of the conduct of the Royal Dragoons ... under the most unpleasant circumstances under which cavalry can be called to act i.e. to support the police in preventing loss of life and damage to property against a hostile crowd, which heaped insults on the troops, threw missiles ... and was intent on firing indiscriminately. The greatest possible credit is due to Colonel Makins, his squadron leaders, officers, NCOs and men for their steadiness and discipline in face of fire ...[1]

On August 3, 1914, the Regiment rode out of camp for manoeuvres (with the 10th Hussars and the infantry from Pretoria), but next day news arrived of the declaration of war with Germany, so the exercises were cancelled. Mobilisation was the order of the day while, in Germany, the Kaiser repudiated his rank as a British field marshal along with his Colonelcy of the Royals. The Regiment, bringing with them their little South African ponies, disembarked at Southampton under their new commanding officer, Lieutenant Colonel George Steele,[2] on September 19 and proceeded to Ludgershall.

ROAD TO THE GREAT WAR

The First World War grew out of a Europe whose industrial expansion, causing great gulfs between rich and poor in the early 1900s, led to widespread unrest. No nation was rendered more prosperous by the industrial revolution than the Germans who wanted further outlets for their trade and thus became increasingly imperialistic. Germany, hating and fearing Russia (though her greatest hatred of all was reserved for England) was determined to form a hegemony with Austria, and, with that in view, was intent upon dominating the foreign policy of the Austro-Hungarian Empire, and then upon crippling Russia.

When the Emperor's nephew and heir, the Archduke Francis, and his wife, were murdered at Sarajevo on June 28, 1914, Austria sent a draconian ultimatum to the Serbs, who failed to concede to all the demands. Whereupon Austria, backed by Germany, invaded Serbia. Russia immediately went to Serbia's defence. The Germans asked the French if they would remain neutral in the event of a Russo-German war. The French declined. The Germans assumed they could deal with the French by one quick blow. The British Foreign Secretary, Sir Edward Grey, asked both parties for assurances a propos Belgian neutrality. The Germans replied, on August 2, by invading Luxembourg, whose neutrality was also guaranteed. On August 2 the British Prime Minister, Asquith, issued orders for mobilisation. On the 4th Sir Edward Grey advised Belgium to resist invasion and promised to join France –with whom we had signed the Entente Cordiale in 1904 – and Russia in support of her. Germany then invaded Belgium.

READY FOR THE GREAT WAR

Britain was not unprepared for war. Under the imaginative reforming zeal of a dour Scottish barrister-turned-statesman, Richard Haldane (1st Viscount Haldane, Secretary of State for War, 1905-12) the Edwardian era and the early years of George V's reign saw many improvements in the military hierarchy and organisation. The post of commander-in-chief had been abolished and replaced by that of Chief of the Imperial General Staff, a general staff being formed from top to bottom of the army at the same time. Haldane did away with the Militia and Volunteers and replaced them with the Territorial Army. And he ordered a reorganisation of the United Kingdom army into the formations in which it would go to war. In 1914, therefore, there was a British Expeditionary Force of seven divisions more or less ready for action. And there was a strong body of men in reserve. On August 5 Lord Kitchener was appointed Secretary for War in the Cabinet, while General Sir John French was poised to take command of a British Expeditionary Force.

The account of the Great War which follows is confined to the principal actions in which Life Guards, Blues and Royals were engaged.

The Royals found themselves in the 6th Brigade – led by their old commanding officer, Brigadier General Ernest Makins – of the 3rd Cavalry Division (under Major General Sir Julian Byng, later 1st Viscount Byng of Vimy). The 7th Cavalry Brigade of the same division was, by special authority of King George V, composed of the three regiments of Household Cavalry (less their initial service squadrons).

THE HOUSEHOLD CAVALRY COMPOSITE REGIMENT, 1914

Meanwhile, the three service squadrons of The Life Guards and Blues had been prominently in action from the very beginning. Therefore we now turn to the Western Front and the Household Cavalry Composite Regiment, which, under command of Lieutenant Colonel E B Cook, First Life Guards, took their place in the deployment of the 4th Cavalry Brigade – completed by the Third Hussars and the Carabiniers and commanded by a former Life Guardsman, the Hon C E Bingham[3] – between the River Sambre and the Condé-Mons canal on the 19th of August. This was the day before the Germans entered Brussels with the intention of advancing on Paris. They met and fought the Allied forces (under overall command of Marshal Joffre) in the Battle of Mons on August 23-24.

General Sir John French, the British commander, was holding the line of the canal with, on his right, three French regular armies and, holding positions to his left, a corps of French Territorials. An onslaught of 10 German divisions, preceded by a massive artillery bombardment, however, forced the Allies into retreat, General Allenby's cavalry providing the rearguard. And our cavaliers, scorched by the August sun, rained upon at night and deprived of sleep, slumped and dozed across their horses' withers as they trudged south in those foul conditions to a point less than 10 miles from the French capital.

But the enemy commander, Von Kluck, underestimated the tenacity of the Anglo-French forces, who, by September 5, stood their ground. Within three days of that it was the Germans who were on the run; and, by the middle of the month, the Allies were back over both the Marne and the Aisne. Frustrated in their attempt to occupy Paris,

The 1st Life Guards Squadron of the Household Cavalry Composite Regiment on mobilisation at Hyde Park Barracks, August, 1914

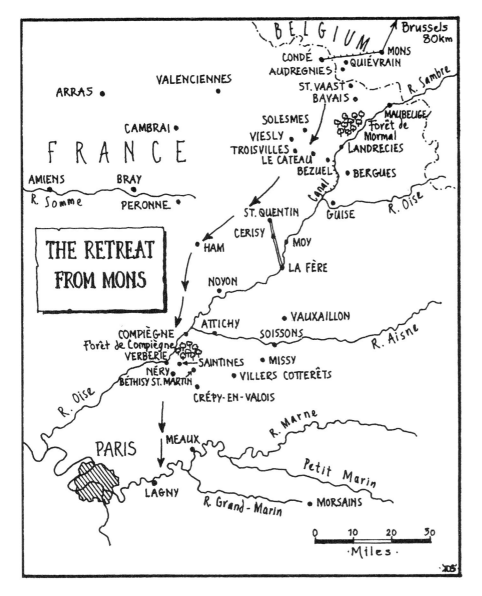

The Retreat from Mons,
August, 1914

the Kaiser and the German High Command turned their attention to the Channel ports, duly switching their offensive north-westward. If the Germans were to achieve those objectives, Britain and her Empire would lose the war. So General French, with the authority of the Generalissimo, Marshal Joffre, moved his army from the River Aisne to Flanders, to be deployed east of Ypres – that vital centre of communications which held the key to Calais and Boulogne – and south through Armentières. The concentration area would be around Lille.

Allenby, now a corps commander with two cavalry divisions, was to hold the southern sector, behind the River Lys, the Household Cavalry Composite Regiment occupying trenches east of Warneton (with the minimum number of horseholders in

relative safety behind). The line extending 10 miles north of that was allotted to French units, while the British Corps to their left, in the Ypres salient, contained General Byng's 3rd Cavalry Division.[4] The Royals (still under Lt-Colonel Steele) in Brigadier-General Makins' 6th Brigade, and the 7th (Household) Brigade, the two regiments of Life Guards and The Blues (less, of course, the service squadrons in the Composites, but brought up to strength with reservists), were sent to the Western Front by special sanction of King George V early in October. The Household Brigade was commanded by a line cavalryman, Brigadier-General Charles McMorrough Kavanagh, while the three regiments were initially led by Lt Colonel the Duke of Teck (1LG), Lt Colonel AFH Ferguson (2LG) and Lt Colonel G C Wilson (RHG). On October 18 the Household Brigade was entrenched west of Zandvoorde with the 6th Brigade to their left.

FIRST YPRES, OCTOBER-NOVEMBER 1914

From October 18 onwards the Allied positions were subjected to sniper fire all day and every day and constant artillery bombardment night and day. On October 19 the Germans, with a three-to-one superiority in numbers, blasted their way across the Lys against Allenby's positions – more weapon scrapes than trenches (because the cavalry had no entrenching tools) – and the Composites were severely punished. That afternoon Major Lord John Cavendish, the First Life Guards squadron leader, was killed, Lieutenant Anthony Murray Smith, the regimental machine gun officer, mortally wounded, and 50 others either killed or otherwise rendered non-combatant. Next day, Cook, the commanding officer, was hit by shrapnel and evacuated, Major Viscount Crichton, of The Blues, succeeding him, while command of the Blues squadron devolved upon Captain Bowlby (who, before the battle was finished, would be the regiment's senior surviving officer). Writing to Colonel Fitzgerald – commanding The Blues reservists at home – Crichton said:

> ... We got into rather a hot place last week ... We are holding a very extended front, in fact bluffing, and the Germans came on pretty strong and forced us out of our trenches with shrapnel and rifle fire; it was when retreating that we lost our men; the very next day Royden,

John Astor and three men were hit with a shell and I found myself in command, but my exalted state will be short lived ... as I fear we are to be broken up and sent back to the Seventh Brigade to stiffen them up a bit ...[5]

Twelve miles farther north, beyond the French lines, the 7th (Household) Brigade and the 6th were also fighting against great odds. Every available man being issued with a rifle, horse-holders found what cover they might in the rear, holding up to eight mounts each. The Germans were much inferior in weapon handling and marksmanship. Atkinson records a Royals officer remarking that 'they shot abominably. A man in my troop kept raising his cap to the Germans and saying "third-class shots, third class!"'[6] Field Marshal Lord Wavell, himself an infantryman, wrote in his biography of Allenby that 'the fate of the war [at the first Battle of Ypres] depended on the fact this cavalry had been trained to use the rifle with an effect that no horsemen or infantry in other European armies could match'.[7] But that was not preventing dreadful British casualties in men and horses.

The Hon Julian Grenfell wrote of life in the trenches at Zandvoorde, during the last week of October, thus:

I have half my troop, 12 men, in a trench in a root field with the rest of the squadron about 100 yards on each side of us and a farm half knocked down by shells just behind us. We get our rations sent up once a day in the dark, and two men creep out to cook us tea in the quiet intervals. Tea is the great mainstay on service ... The men are splendid, and happy as schoolboys ... Nobody grumbles at one for being dirty. I have only had my boots off once in the last ten days and have only washed twice. We are up and standing to our rifles by 5 am when doing this infantry work, and saddled up by 4.30 when with our horses. Our poor horses do not get their saddles off when we are in the trenches.[8]

The German High Command selected October 30-31 for their great breakthrough to Ypres and the ports. The Kaiser went to Prince Rupprecht's headquarters and exhorted his troops: 'We will finish with the British, Indians, Moroccans and other trash, feeble adversaries who surrender in great numbers if they are attacked with vigour'. It

The Royals entering Ypres, October 13, 1914

was indeed a most devastating attack all along the line, the worst of it coming against the Household Brigade's trenches as related by Trooper Ernest Hook, a Lifeguardsman:

We had no protection from the shelling as our trenches were on the forward slope ... and, although our gunners put up a great show they were no match for

Major The Viscount Crichton, Royal Horse Guards. He succeeded to the command of the Composite Regiment on the death of Colonel E B Cook, 1st Life Guards, in October, 1914, and was himself killed in action shortly afterwards

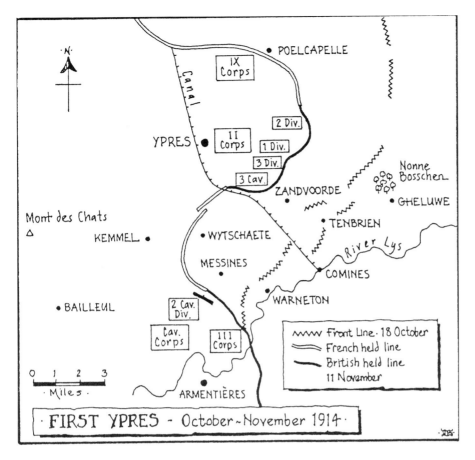

FIRST YPRES - October~November 1914

Front Line · 18 October
French held line
British held line
11 November

The First Battle of Ypres,
October-November, 1914

the Jerries heavy stuff. We could see
their infantry in great masses about 1000
yards away. Just about then I was hit by
a shell that nearly took my left arm off
and my officer sent me to the rear. It was
the end of the war for me. I believe that
later on one of our squadrons was
surrounded and completely wiped out.
[It was].[9]

Sir George Arthur, who had the advantage
of interviewing the survivors, returns to the
southern sector on October 31 and Lord
Crichton's command like this:

> Under the rays of the moon, the
> Germans, open-mouthed and heavy-
> handed, came, as it seemed, straight for
> the Composite Regiment ... At 200 yards
> the Regiment opened fire and poured in
> round after round and .... saw live men
> climbing over their dead comrades
> simply to fall themselves. The Germans
> swung left-handed, short of the Blues'
> trenches, and made for the Life Guards,
> surging into their trenches to engage
> in hand-to-hand fighting ... In all this
> din and turmoil Crichton seemed
> to be everywhere and with a word
> of encouragement at everyone's elbow

... When the squadrons were
pushed irresistibly a little way back
intercommunication became almost
impossible, but Corporal Eason was able
to report their retirement to Bowlby ...
ten minutes later the same messenger
returned, now bleeding from a wound,
to repeat the information, adding that
the enemy had worked round and was
nearly behind 'C' Squadron (RHG). At
that moment two machine guns opened
fire from the rear, and the Blues were
thus under attack from three sides ...[10]

Crichton leaving Bowlby in charge of what
little was left of the Composites, rode off to
make contact with the neighbouring 20th
Hussars, and was never seen again. By this
time his successor's (Bowlby's) command
was reduced to 30 men of the First Life
Guards, three of the Seconds and about 30
Blues. (Two First Life Guards brother-officers
who were also brothers-in-law, Captain Lord
Hugh Grosvenor and Lieutenant the Hon
Gerald Ward were among those who died
side by side.)

The 7th (Household) Brigade were in
reserve – 'doing Fire Brigade duty', as it was
called – in a wood in the Ypres salient when
four columns of Prussian Guards found a gap
by Klein Zillebeke between Lord Cavan's 4th
Guards Brigade and the French on their right,
who had been forced to withdraw. And, says
Arthur:

> It would seem as if a path had really
> been laid for an insolent German
> entrance in Ypres. That path was to be
> barred and closed by the British
> Sovereign's Bodyguard ... Kavanagh
> hurried his troops at top speed along
> the Zillebeke road to the point where
> their presence and prowess were
> imperatively needed ... The line – The
> Second Life Guards on the right, the
> First Life Guards on the left and the
> Blues in their immediate rear – moved
> at the double up to the wood
> at Zwarteele, and met the Germans
> emerging from it, and drove them back
> through it at the point of the bayonet.
> The spirit of the Household Cavalry was
> infectious; the French quickly took
> heart and [came up on]... Kavanagh's
> right ... Gerard, Northampton and
> Edwin Brassey were wounded almost at
> once ... and, before the threshold of the
> wood could be reached, the Blues had
> lost their Colonel. A borrowed rifle in

his hand, a cheery laugh bubbling up, Gordon Wilson[11] was a few feet ahead of his men when a bullet pierced his brain ...[12]

Major the Hon Hugh Dawnay, by then commanding the Second Life Guards, was another who died in that encounter.

So the fighting continued with the utmost ferocity until November 20, by when the remnants of the Household Cavalry Composite Regiment were absorbed into the 7th (Household Cavalry) Brigade – and by when the Allies can be said to have saved Ypres and the Channel ports. Among many other instances of gallantry and self-sacrifice Atkinson cites that of the Royals' previously mentioned Julian Grenfell on November 17:

About 11 am ... the Germans suddenly developed a tremendous bombardment ... They seemed to be searching for our guns, so the troops in the line escaped more lightly than might have been expected. Lt Grenfell meanwhile went out in front to investigate. He crawled out to the German front trench to find it empty. Barely had he reached it before a single German approached whom he shot. He then waited some 20 minutes and then heard noises as of many men approaching through the woods. He waited till they came into sight, shot down their leader and made off at 'a sort of galloping crawl' which got his important news back to our lines. His timely warning that an infantry attack was coming was passed on to the 10th Hussars and to the guns behind ...[13]

[Grenfell, whose daring exploits were already a legend, received a DSO in February, 1915.]

Here is Lord Wavell's verdict on the performance of the Cavalry corps in October-November, 1914 '... In holding at bay so greatly superior a mass of enemy infantry they performed a feat of defence unrivalled in history by any other cavalry'.[14] Atkinson succinctly concludes:

'The German failure to take Ypres and break through to the Channel Ports had completed the process of establishing one long front from Switzerland to the North Sea. It left both opponents entrenched behind a flankless barrier the other had failed to penetrate, too exhausted to do more than accept the deadlock for the moment and hope for better

fortune when they could renew the attempt to break through. With opportunities for the employment of cavalry thus relegated to a problematical future, the British Cavalry were naturally drawn back well behind the trench line ...'[15]

As for the enemy, they were to keep up the challenge for another four bitter years. There was very little cavalry work, as such, to be done by the cavaliers, but any amount of foot soldiering from the dug-outs. The war of movement was over. It was said that the loose-limbed confident-looking Household Cavalryman – on average appreciably taller than his comrades of the Line – could be much more readily distinguished from a distance as a foot soldier than he had been in his khaki mounted guise.

With a number of yeomanry regiments arriving from England, the decision was taken to regroup in order that those should be mixed with regulars. Thus in the 3rd Cavalry Division, The Blues joined the 10th Hussars and the Essex Yeomanry in the 8th Brigade, their place alongside The Life Guards being taken by the Leicestershire Yeomanry. The Royals and the 3rd Dragoon Guards had the North Somerset Yeomanry as their new comrades-in-arms in the 6th Brigade. The average strength a cavalry regiment could muster for the trenches at this time was about 275 rifles.

SECOND YPRES, 1915

The enemy, still recognising Ypres as the key communications centre before the ports, launched a new offensive in April, 1915, this time supported by poisoned gas. They broke through the French line, outflanked the Canadians and threatened the British Cavalry Corps, who had taken over from the French in the salient in February. The cavalry were now subjected to a continuous artillery barrage, from which they were somewhat better protected – with deep communication trenches and dug-out shelters – than they had been with the 'scrapes' of 1914. And there were new weapons for the foot soldiers, such as more effective defilading mortars and rifle grenades.

Initially, the Second Dragoon Guards (Bays) were on the left of the line, then Seven Brigade, then Eight, and, on the right, Six. Our map shows the theoretical deployment for the various stages of the second Battle of Ypres; but, as the fight developed, regiments' positions became confused. The bombardment reached a crescendo on May 13 when, says Arthur:

As dawn broke damp and cold – to give way to biting wind and drenching rain – it seemed as if Hell itself had suddenly been let loose. Every enemy gun crashed out in a chorus of hate and destruction. The trenches were swamped, blown sky high and, by 4 o'clock, the bombardment had become so intense as to exceed all its heavy predecessors; and so for three solid hours.[16]

The German infantry began advancing at 7 am, mainly against 6 Brigade, so the cavalry were forced to withdraw to a reserve position. But the assault petered out. And, when a counter-attack was ordered for the early afternoon, Blues and Royals found themselves cheek by jowl, with The Blues' new Colonel, Lord Tweedmouth, the senior officer among those squadrons present:

Zero hour (2.30) approached and the Blues and Royals stood waiting to make what must have seemed an almost hopeless attempt. 'Fix bayonets and dry your butts!' (a very necessary precaution when cold steel meets the

The Second Battle of Ypres, May 13, 1915

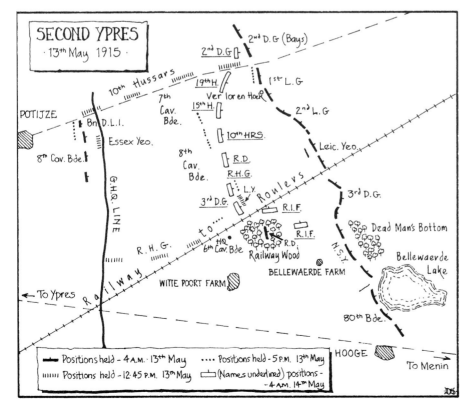

human body). Old Blues will always look back to that moment and conjure up the picture of their Colonel, Lord Tweedmouth, thinking with gratitude of the example he set them. He stood, calm as ever, watch in hand, ready to launch his attack. He dropped his watch back into his pocket. 'Advance!'... Six hundred yards had to be covered, the chief support coming from the [8th] Brigade's own machine gunners ... The attack succeeded, nay more ... Alastair Leveson-Gower... reached the objective with only two of his troop unwounded. He himself was hit in the thigh and will be long remembered surveying calmly the situation, a small unwounded German beneath him, and an immense cigar in his mouth. Afterwards, as he delighted to narrate, he was carried back by two good friends, both Corporals, by name Coffin and Churchyard.[17]

But casualties were very heavy. The Third Cavalry Division lost a total of 91 officers and 1,052 other ranks at the second Battle of Ypres. The Life Guards alone suffered 4 officers and 47 men killed. Bowlby, of The Blues, who had been the senior survivor of the Composites, was among the dead. Colonel Steele, the Royals distinguished commanding officer, died of his wounds after this action, as did the heroic Captain Grenfell DSO, a very gifted young officer. (Apart from his leadership qualities, he is remembered as one of the 'war poets', examples of his work being honoured in many anthologies. A couple of verses from his Into Battle may be found at the end of this chapter.[18]) Five other Royals officers and 21 other ranks were killed, eight men 'missing believed killed' and six officers and 94 men wounded.

Thousands more young men had been called up. In August the first service squadrons of the three Household Cavalry Reserve Regiments combined to raise six troops to form an independent cavalry squadron for the Guards Division, to be employed either with horses or bicycles. Their first action was to be at Loos, four miles south-south-west of Bethune, to which we shall shortly turn.

HOOGE, MAY-JUNE, 1915

At the end of May the Germans tried their luck at the south end of the Ypres salient, near Hooge, where the Third Cavalry

Division relieved the First on the 29th, the Royals (now under command of Lieutenant-Colonel Henry McNeile) and The Blues proceeding to adjacent trenches in Sanctuary Wood, with the Third Dragoon Guards on their left and the Tenth Hussars and the Second Life Guards on their right. Enemy artillery fire seems to have been the main feature of this action. But, owing to brave and skilful reconnaissance patrolling, the German attacks were frustrated. Lance Corporals Bishop and Chick, of the Royals, were among those mentioned in despatches for such work.

LOOS, SEPTEMBER 25-26, 1915

In August the Division (as part of General Haig's First Army) was moved farther south in the Allied line, to a point some five miles south-south-west of Bethune. And there, on September 25 and 26, the Sixth and Eighth Cavalry Brigades (still containing, respectively, the Royals and The Blues) but not the Seventh (with The Life Guards), advanced from the Hohenzollern Redoubt to be involved in the Battle of Loos. Although they stormed and took the village, the reserves, upon which Haig had counted, did not materialise, so there could be no exploitation. Suffice to record a little memoir of Corporal-of-Horse Lowson, Royal Horse Guards:

At 8 o'clock in the evening of the 25th we were told we had to go up and hold

the trenches somewhere in the vicinity of the famous Hohenzollern Redoubt; so off we trekked. On the way we got heavily shelled and our Machine Gun Squadron stopped the worst of it, Troopers Terry and Small being killed and five others badly wounded ... The scene going up was indescribable, the road and the fields were one mass of dead horses, men and smashed transport ... The next afternoon on our left we saw a battalion of the Foot Guards making an attack on the Hohenzollern Redoubt. They were going down like ninepins. I enquired of Lord Tweedmouth who it was attacking, and he told me it was the First Grenadiers. I had a brother in that battalion and I very much wanted to go over and see if he was alright ... We were just under a ridge, and, on top of it, I saw a wounded man waving his hand, and I got Lord Tweedmouth's permission to go out and try and get him in ... When I reached him there were two or three Germans lying not far away ... they let fly at me, but luckily they weren't marksmen. I shook my fist at them and started dragging the wounded man in. He ... had been badly hit in the back with an explosive bullet. I ... took him down to the dressing station where Capt. Bodington (RMO) was busy with the wounded. Shortly after that Captain

Reservists of the 2nd Life Guards and Royal Horse Guards who were part of the Household Cavalry's Divisional Cyclist Contingent, parading on the lawn at Combermere Barracks in 1915

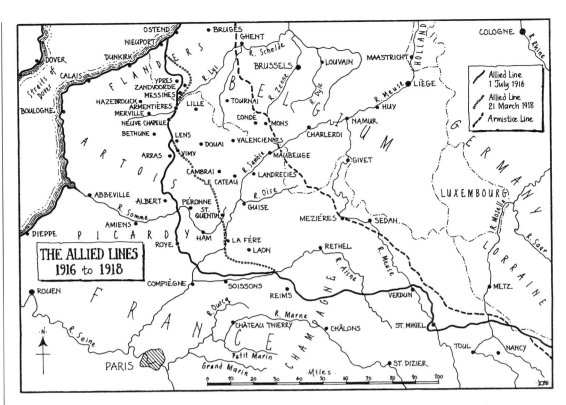

The Allied Lines, 1916-18

Bodington and his assistant, Cpl Maj Scarborough, were both hit ....[19]

The BEF, now under command of Sir Douglas Haig, resigned itself to another winter of stalemate and trench warfare. On December 20 the Royals' commanding officer, Lieutenant Colonel McNeile, was killed with a broken neck, falling from his horse, to be succeeded by Major Frederick Wormald from the Eighth Hussars. They and the Household Cavalry still had their horses, but saw less of them as time passed. In December the Cavalry Corps formed a dismounted division, each Division of the Corps providing a brigade of three battalions while in the New Year all the cavalry machine gun sections were brigaded.

1916: THE YEAR OF THE SOMME

During 1916 the Cavalry were often moved about, withdrawn into reserve, sent up into the trenches, suffered a good deal more shelling, were involved in much patrol work, retired once more, then posted to the front line again. But they took no major part in the Allies' push on the Somme, which began on July 1 and finished in a quagmire in late September. Although the result of that offensive looked, at first sight, to be a poor return for the long casualty lists, it did reduce, as never before, the German army,

which was retired to the Hindenburg Line in March, 1917.

THE BATTLE OF ARRAS, APRIL 9-11, 1917

April, 1917, found the Cavalry Corps concentrated west of Arras, for what was to be the battle of that name. The 6th and 8th Brigades led their advance on April 9, with the 7th in reserve. It was another month of ghastly weather; and, although Arras was cleared of Germans and Vimy ridge and Monchy were taken, further advance was more or less halted in the mud. Here is the Royals historian:

Shell-holes afforded what scanty shelter there was against the intense cold. Snow and blizzards made the night miserable alike for horses and men. No hot food could be obtained; the only consolation was that as yet the [6th] Brigade had escaped being seriously shelled, though Major Tomkinson, acting as liaison officer between the Division and the Thirty-Seventh Division, had been wounded in the face and leg, and three of his orderlies had also been hit ... The effect on the roads and tracks was to ... delay the process of bringing forward the artillery whose support was needed for the attack on the rearward German line ... about 9.0 pm the Twelfth Division came forward to take over Monchy ... whereupon the brigade toiled back over the snow to Arras and bivouacked miserably on the racecourse, cold and wet and hungry. Several men collapsed completely and frost-bitten feet or hands were numerous, while the state of the horses, over the hocks in icy slush and snow, was pitiable.[20]

Bulkeley Johnson commanding the 8th Brigade was killed by machine gun fire at this juncture. Lord Tweedmouth led the Brigade for a few days, Lord Londonderry assuming command of The Blues, who now occupied the celebrated Orange Hill by Moncy. Captain Buckmaster's[21] diary entry gives a further impression of the conditions:

> ... dug a hole and got into it to sleep, but before we got to sleep the snow came down. I never closed my eyes, my feet were too cold, and I had only a biscuit or two since breakfast ... Reveille at 2 and back we rode to Arras race course ... It was still snowing hard ... Talked to 2nd Life Guards who heard 8th Cavalry Brigade had broken through ... We saddled up at 11 am and rode straight back to last night's ground. Cavalry track ... with snow up to horses' hocks. Many falling ... No sleep again in a shell hole. It was snowing like hell and bitterly cold. Perhaps it was a godsend as the horses were getting no water and, had it been hot, could not have stayed the course. We were shelled all night and lost many horses ... We were saddled up by daybreak. I was so stiff with the cold that Smith, my groom, had to lift me into the saddle...[22]

SECOND-LIEUTENANT JOHN DUNVILLE, VC, ROYALS

The Royals, who got through Arras with six killed and 27 wounded, went into a rest area after the battle – until May 12 when the Cavalry Corps, now concentrated around Peronne, were ordered to take over a stretch of trenches opposite the Hindenburg Line. On June 25 four of their officers and 96 other ranks were detailed to carry out a raid on some German trenches. Lieutenant Ronald Henderson was in command of the party with Lieutenant Richard Helme and Second-Lieutenant John Dunville commanding the

2nd Lieutenant John Spencer Dunville, VC, 1st the Royal Dragoons. Dunville, who won his Victoria Cross in France in June, 1917, died in hospital from his wounds

two fighting patrols into which it was divided, while Lieutenant John Bickersteth led a covering party armed with Hotchkiss rifles.[23] The force was supported by a dozen scouts from the Third Dragoon Guards and the North Somerset Yeomanry, and Sappers with Bangalore torpedoes.[24] Atkinson takes up the story:

> At the appointed point, 450 yards out, the assaulting and covering parties lay down to await the barrage. At 1.10 am it began and the scouts and torpedo parties went forward. In 2nd Lt Dunville's party something went wrong with the first torpedo, which failed to explode. The RE then started cutting the wire by hand, covered by 2nd Lt Dunville who, as the enemy had taken the alarm and started shooting, deliberately placed himself between the sappers and the fire, which seemed to come from rifle pits in advance of the main trench.[25]

Second Lieutenant Dunville, dying in hospital next day, was awarded a posthumous Victoria Cross. '... Although severely wounded [he] continued to direct his men in the wire cutting and general operations until the raid was successfully completed', ran his citation, 'thereby setting a magnificent example of courage, determination and devotion to duty ...'

By July the Royals found themselves in the same billets they had occupied after the First Battle of Ypres. By October they were in reserve with 6 Brigade, in the Somme valley east of Abbeville. (It was at this time that a Royals officer serving on the staff was asked by a French officer why his cap badge was adorned with an eagle. 'And you have worn this for a hundred years because you defeated us?' the Frenchman exclaimed on being informed. 'I take that as the greatest compliment!')

THE HOUSEHOLD BATTALION

Meanwhile there had been plenty of volunteers offering their services to The Life Guards and Blues in London and Windsor, but insufficient horses to mount them. The proposal for a Household Battalion was therefore submitted to the King who by then had made several visits to Household Cavalry units at the Front. And, on August 30, 1916, the GOC London District was writing to the senior Household Cavalry officer at home: 'His Majesty approves, and it is his distinct wish that it be formed as quickly as possible from the three regiments ... HM was extremely strong about it.' Captain Wyndham Portal (1LG) being promoted to command this new unit they proceeded to France in November, joining the Tenth Brigade in the Fourth Division. 'Here and now it was to show its Household Cavalry traditions and training,' says Arthur, 'for be it remembered that, under a thin crust of foot drill, every man remained a cavalryman at heart.' They entered the trenches on December 8 and were to have their full share of the fighting. One particular hero emerging from the Battalion was Corporal-of-Horse Hamill who, having won a Military Medal in April, 1917, on the Third Army front, secured a bar to it in July when

> ...night after night [he] would patrol the north bank of the Scarpe river east of Roeux Bridge, with the special object of discovering possible crossings for future operations and with the incidental result of locating several enemy posts. On the night of July 15th-16th this intrepid NCO and four men swam the river ... to be greeted by an angry but innocuous burst of rifle fire, and to be very awkwardly hung up by the entanglements with which the bank was heavily protected. Despite wire and fire, however, the party secured – and swam back with – the information required ...[26]

During the Passchendaele 'push', in the autumn of 1917, the Household Battalion advanced over a distance of 600 yards towards their objective, Requette Farm, then attacked and took it in the face of desperate odds, and lost 400 of their number in the endeavour. Yet when they were disbanded in February, 1918, they could still muster 18 officers and 424 other ranks. 'As your Colonel-in-Chief,' wrote the King, 'I have followed with pride and admiration your doings at the front ... you have added yet another chapter to the grand traditions of my Household Cavalry.'

MACHINE GUNS, 1918

In the spring of 1918 the King was asked to give his blessing to another departure for his Household Cavalry. Not only was it increasingly clear that there was little prospect of further scope for horsed cavalry in the conflict, but the difficulty of finding adequate remounts had become acute, particularly for the six-feet-tall men of The Life Guards and Royal Horse Guards. Moreover the need for more reliable machine gun units had increased. What were required for that arm were men of superior intelligence and discipline who would convert easily to the role. It was both fair and logical that the Household Cavalry should fill it. This, says Arthur, went to the roots of the constitution of the Household Cavalry,

> who are essentially liable to be employed wherever and however the Sovereign may please and may direct, with the implicit understanding that, when the specific duty is accomplished, they must be returned to their immediate service, mounted or dismounted, about the Sovereign's Person.[27]

Early in April they went to the Vickers machine gun school, on the coast near Etaples, north of Abbeville (where, most tragically, on the night of May 19, they lost 43 killed and 82 wounded in an air raid). Each machine gun battalion comprised nearly 50 officers and 800 men with 64 Vickers. By the third week in May they were allotted to formations, the First Life Guards and Blues (the First and Third Battalions) going to the First Army front, east of Bethune, and the Second Life Guards (Second Battalion) to Four Corps, east of Albert. And they scored a universally fine reputation for their efficient

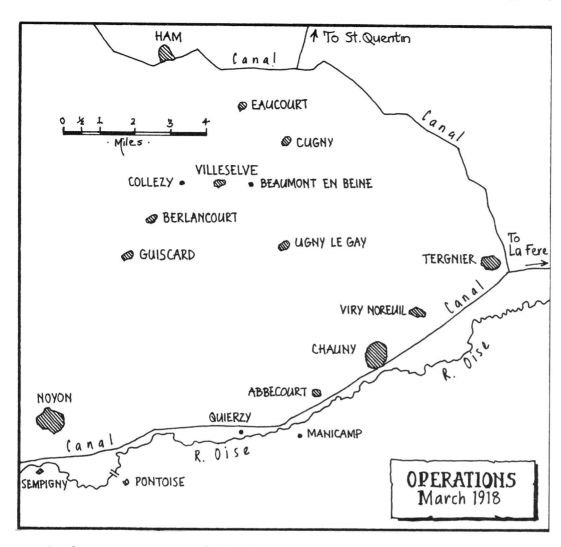

Operations, March, 1918

creeping barrages in support of advancing infantry.

The First Life Guards and Blues, along with a battalion of the Army Cyclist Corps formed Lindsay's Force (later Brassey's) which, in cooperation with the Canadian Corps dashed up, in September, to seize the crossings of the Canal de L'Escat, while The Second Life Guards (under Lt Col Hon A F Stanley), covering the Forty-Sixth and Forty-Seventh Divisions, helped those formations to cross the Hindenburg Line and capture the Hindenburg Canal. The Blues Battalion was still in action early in November when they provided a barrage for the First and Thirty-Second Divisions as they stepped over the Canal de Sambre, days before Marshal Foch received the surrender of the newly formed German Government. Between 1914 and 1918, therefore, the Household Cavalry filled, for the Franco-Flanders front, a composite regiment, a cavalry brigade, a divisional

squadron, two cyclist companies, a rifle battalion, three machine gun battalions and a siege battery.[28]

THE ROYALS, 1918

When the German offensive of March, 1918, opened the Royals were at Devise, seven miles south-east of Peronne, about to march to Beaumont-en-Beine, between Ham and Chauny, where they received orders to find a dismounted company. This was composed of seven officers and 217 men under Captain W P Browne. On March 23 news came through that the Germans had broken through our line at Ham. Whereupon each regiment of Six Brigade was detailed to raise a mounted squadron (to be commanded by Major Williams, 10th Hussars), the Royals officers being Lieutenants Cubitt, Cooper and Harris, leading about 50 men. Capt Browne's party, well dug in, stood their ground all through March 23, while next day the

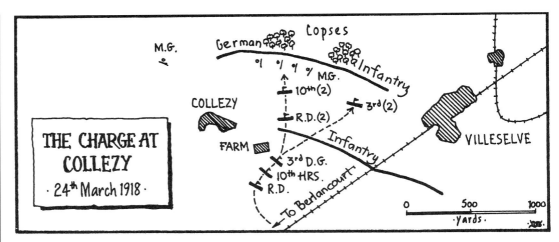

The Royals' charge at Collezy,
March 24, 1918

little detachment of horsed cavalry carried out a most successful charge by the village of Collezy, four miles south of Ham. The position was described as 'rather shaky' when Williams's squadron rode up a branch of the Guiscard-Villeselve road:

> Trotting up this side-road, which was sunken, the squadron reached the southeast edge of the village of Collezy, undetected. Here it sheltered behind a big farm while the officers did a hasty reconnaissance. About 600 yards ahead German infantry with several machine guns were established in front of two substantial copses. To the squadron's right our infantry were still hanging on, but another advance by the Germans must have outflanked them. Though the last 200 yards to be covered was ploughland Major Williams did not hesitate. Sending the 3rd DG's troop on ahead against the most easterly of the two copses with the object of drawing the enemy's attention and distracting him from the main attack, he launched the other two straight at the infantry and machine guns. The charge ... caught the Germans quite unprepared ... They had been marching and fighting for several days and the sight of cavalry, swooping down on them, sword in hand, was too much for them ... Opening out a little as they dashed forward, the 10th and the Royals covered the ground at a gallop. Many fell, including Lt Cubitt,[29] but the German fire was wild and did not stop the horsemen ... cutting them down right and left.[30]

By the end of March the Royals were together once more, ready with the Third Cavalry Division to help stem the German attack around Hamel and Villers-Bretonneux. On April 9 they were moved north under the First Army; and, in May, back again, when the Germans made a bid for victory south of the Aisne. General Haig's August offensive found the regiment with the Fourth Army astride the Somme. In September and October, the Sixth Brigade, Royals out in front, supported the Fourth Army in the Le Cateau district. On October 9, says their historian:

> As the Royals' leading squadron [Captain Browne's 'C' Squadron] came dashing through the firing-line northeast of Maretz the infantry burst into loud cheers, and, tired as they were, sprang to their feet and hurried forward. The advance drew some rifle and machine gun fire ... but the speed of the advance prevented either infantry or machine guns doing much damage and the Royals swept on, unchecked ... Seeing the Royals threatening their retreat the German infantry cleared out of Renmont as they had quitted Honnechy ...[31]

On November 6 the Third Cavalry Division marched north to bolster the Second Army's offensive in Belgium. At Leuze, on November 11, their advance was stopped by the glorious news of the Armistice.

THE GUARDS MARCH AND HOUSEHOLD CAVALRY REQUIEM

On March 22, 1919, the King directed that the Household Cavalry and the Foot Guards battalions should march past him at Buckingham Palace, after which each man received his Majesty's '...

acknowledgement of the selfless services rendered to himself and his Empire through four years of toil and agony'. A fortnight later the King and Queen led the congregation at the Household Cavalry requiem in Westminster Abbey. Sir George Arthur witnessed the finale:

> From high up in the Triforium over the east end the gold-laced trumpeters, who had passed through the south transept into the ambulatory, sounded the Last Post and the three ringing regimental calls; from the west end of the Abbey Church came the reply of the Reveille; and, before its echoes had faded, a gathering thunder of drums led up to the crashing of bands and the outburst of choir and people in the National Anthem. The whole occasion lasted but a short half hour; for many years to come there would be many to dwell on every moment of it.

THE MEMORIAL AT ZANDVOORDE

The Household Cavalry War memorial which stands at Zandvoorde, was unveiled by Field Marshal Earl Haig, Colonel of The Blues, representing the King, on May 4, 1924 – a most fitting site, considering the number of Royal Dragoons, as well as members of the Composites and the 7th (Household) Brigade who died for their country nearby. 'We have here in these scenes amid which we now stand and in the memories they evoke,' said Lord Haig,

> 'a high incentive to our endeavour. Many splendid stories of desperate chances bravely and surely taken, of unselfish and enduring heroism, go to make up the history of our regiments in war. But glorious as that history may be, the names of these Flanders villages ... conjure up deeds as glorious and as fateful, and devotion as complete and unrestrained, as any that can be found in the stories of the past ...'

THE LIFE GUARDS BECOME ONE REGIMENT, 1922.

The 31 regiments of cavalry, which the Nation had supported during World War One, were bound to be affected at least as much as any other arm of the Service in the post-war Army run-down. Under Lloyd George's Government and the Geddes Axe of 1922 numerous amalgamations were effected, among them the merging of the two regiments of Life Guards – a terrible blow to both the 'Firsts' and 'Seconds'. But, clearly, the Household Cavalry could very easily perform their duties with only two Regiments. The Blues were, at one point, also quite closely threatened by Geddes with amalgamation. (It is worth noting here that when amalgamations of cavalry regiments were mooted in the 1960s the call went up from the Line Cavalry – 'why not merge The Life Guards and Blues?' When it was pointed out that the Household Cavalry had already suffered an amalgamation, in 1922, lancers, hussars and dragoons cried with one voice 'the two regiments of Life Guards were as good as wedded anyway!' But it was not so. There was as much jealousy and rivalry between them as any existing in the army.)

The new Regiment was given the name 'The Life Guards (1st and 2nd)'; then, in June, 1928, simply 'The Life Guards'. (Note the capital 'T'!) They began life at Regent's Park Barracks.[32]

THE ROYALS, 1918-35

The Royals remained as part of the Army of Occupation, on the Rhine, until August, 1919, when Colonel Wormald led them home to Hounslow, where, in December, 1920, he handed over to Lieutenant Colonel Henry Tomkinson.[33] In December the regiment, with three full strength sabre squadrons to deploy, left for Ireland, for Co Galway. There, in face of the greatly increased IRA threat, they were out, night and day, on patrol duty or providing search parties, in cooperation with the Black-and-Tans and the Royal Irish Constabulary. When the situation became calmer they moved to the Curragh. That was in 1922, the year in which the King became their Colonel-in-Chief (he being the first to fill the Colonelcy since the Kaiser's resignation in 1914).

In the spring of 1923 the Royals were posted to Aldershot, where the King and Queen spent a day with them in the summer. Two years later his Majesty presented them with a new guidon, the left face of which bore the old battle

Changeover of the regiments, October, 1935: A scene on The Great West Road. The Life Guards (*right*), on their way from Hyde Park Barracks to Combermere Barracks, pass The Blues (*left*) proceeding from Windsor to London

honours and the right face ten of their new honours – YPRES 1914-15, LOOS, SOMME 1918, HINDENBURG LINE, PURSUIT TO MONS, FRENZENBURG, ARRAS 1917, AMIENS, CAMBRAI 1918 and FRANCE AND FLANDERS 1914-19. In December, 1926, they returned to Hounslow, and, a little less than a year later, set sail for Egypt under command of Lieutenant Colonel Edward Miles, who had just succeeded Lieutenant-Colonel Walter Hodgson.[34]

After a couple of years spent in and around Cairo the Royals transferred to that most rewarding of all British military stations in the inter-war years, India. They were at Secunderabad (where Lieutenant Colonel Francis Wilson Fitzgerald took over from Colonel Miles in 1931) until October, 1932, when they moved to Meerut. ('The Regiment ... handed over in Secunderabad to the 17th/21st Lancers,' recalls Brigadier Roddy Heathcoat-Amory, 'with whom for some reason we had to share the barracks for a week. This might have been a strain to good relations, but ... both Regiments had always been good

friends and the week went off well with parties and friendly rivalry between us.') They remained at Meerut until November, 1935, when they sailed for a brief sojourn in Egypt before returning to England (Shorncliffe). Here is a farewell cameo of military life in India by Brigadier Heathcoat Amory:

During our final training season at Meerut the Regiment took part in what must have been the last mounted Brigade charge in the history of the British or Indian armies. The manoeuvre took place on a maidan, or open space ... The Royals, commanded by Frank Fitzgerald, was the centre Regiment with an Indian cavalry regiment on either side. The poor Black Watch were the 'enemy' and the recipients of our charge. The Brigade was in two ranks stretching for about a mile-and-a-half. Presumably the Brigade Commander was in front, but I didn't see him. The order was given to draw swords. Then, successively to walk, trot and canter. I don't think the order to charge was ever given, because by then horses with hard mouths could scarcely be restrained, and Squadron and Regimental Commanders were riding hard in order to stay in front. By a miracle there were no casualties among the Black Watch who were lying in the open. My horse collided with a signalling mirror on a tripod which did the apparatus no good, but luckily I avoided its operator and didn't run him through with my sword ...[35]

Here is another, provided by Colonel James Hamilton-Russell regarding his father, Capt the Hon John (Jack) Hamilton-Russell, Royal Dragoons:

In 1935 my father won the All-India pigsticking contest for which the prize was the Kadir Cup. This was not only an achievement in itself, but also because it was won on one of his troop horses. On account of that my father was debarred from the regimental team. He thus won it as an individual![36]

LAST YEARS OF GEORGE V

The Household Cavalry kept Regent's Park Barracks until 1932, when The Life Guards, the last cavalry to be stationed there, transferred to Hyde Park, that barracks and Combermere having been, respectively, the town and country homes of the Corps ever since. In 1925 the King presented The Life Guards (First and Second) and The Blues with new Standards on Horse Guards Parade. The Life Guards (First and Second) – to emphasise the still distinct identities – receiving two regimental and four squadron Standards.

Although ominous shadows now drew over Continental Europe and elsewhere, they were not much observed in Britain and the Empire. There was thus an air of considerable stability during the last years of King George V. The marriages of his younger sons, the Dukes of York (1923), Gloucester (1935) and Kent (1934) gave great public satisfaction (and much additional activity for the Household Cavalry) while the response to the Silver Jubilee celebrations, in the summer of 1935, proved the Monarchy to be as popular as scarcely ever before since Tudor times. Then, in January, 1936, to the nation's great dismay, the King died.[36]

The Prince of Wales was now Edward VIII.

1. Atkinson, 389
2. George Frederick Steele joined the Royals in 1892. He was Adjutant during the Boer War.
3. Bingham had been adjutant of the Second Life Guards and Commanding Officer of the First
4. The 3rd Cavalry Division, along with the 7th Infantry Division, was grouped in General Rawlinson's IV Corps
5. Arthur III, 73
6. Atkinson, 401
7. Wavell, *Allenby, A Study in Greatness*. p 145
8. Atkinson, 406
9. Ascoli, 225
10. Arthur, III, 75
11. Colonel Wilson had begun to display gallantry at an early age. He had been one of the two Eton boys who, with their umbrellas, subdued Queen Victoria's would-be assassin in Windsor in the 1880s, and handed him over to the police
12. Arthur, III, 108-9
13. Atkinson, 413
14. Wavell, 148
15. Atkinson, 416
16. Arthur III, 125
17. Ibid, 127-8
18. Into Battle (2nd and last verses):
... And life is colour and warmth and light,
And a striving evermore for these,
And he is dead who will not fight;
And who dies fighting has increase.

The thundering line of battle stands,
And in the air death moans and sings;
But Day shall clasp him with strong hands,
And night shall fold him in soft wings.
19. Arthur, III, 140-1
20. Atkinson, 442-3
21. Buckmaster, who fought as a trooper with the Colonial Cavalry in the Boer War, was commissioned in The Blues in 1914. After the Great War he founded Buck's Club, with his old commanding officer, Lord Tweedmouth, as President and Chairman.
22. Arthur, III, 168
23. The newly invented Hotchkiss was an air-cooled light machine gun, issued principally to the cavalry and pack artillery.
24. Bangalore torpedoes, first fashioned at Bangalore, the capital of Mysore, India, were designed to be exploded across barbed wire entanglements and minefields, to create free paths
25. Atkinson, 447. See also J B Bickersteth, pp 64-5
26. Arthur, III, 176-7
27. Arthur, III, 193
28. The 520th (Household) Siege Battery, commanded by Major Hon J J Astor, 1st Life Guards, was armed with 6-inch tractor-drawn guns. It was formed in April, 1918.
29. Lt. Hon W H Cubitt, who had joined the Royals in November, 1914, died of his wounds on March 24, 1918.
30. Atkinson, 453-4
31. Ibid, 465
32. Regent's Park Barracks, built to John Nash's design in 1820-1, stand between Albany Street and the branch of the Regent's Canal running just to the east of that. The barracks is now (1996) occupied by 20 Transport Squadron of the Royal Logistic Corps. The route from Regent's Park to Whitehall (for the King's Life Guard) was already inclined to be heavily congested.

33. Col Tomkinson, who joined the Royals in 1901, held temporary command of the 10th Hussars in 1918. An international polo player, he was a member of the last all-England Westchester Cup team before the war (1914) and was in it again for the first post-war series of that challenge (1921)

34. Hodgson transferred, as a subaltern, from the Middlesex Regiment in 1902; he commanded the Royals from December, 1923 to December, 1927

35. R Heathcoat-Amory, *Reminiscences*, 1989. p55

36. In a letter to the author.

37. It was at the funeral of George V that the Household Cavalry marched for the last time in mounted review order.

14 EDWARD VIII (1936)

Although the reign of King Edward VIII was to last only from January to December, 1936, it seems appropriate to employ his chapter for a sketch of the Household Cavalry between the wars. The Life Guards and The Blues exchanged stations (London and Windsor) annually, passing one another on the Great West Road as they proceeded with their horses between the two barracks. Perhaps there has been no better description of a soldier's existence in the Corps at this time than that provided by Tim Bishop, a trooper, and subsequently a lance corporal, in The Life Guards.[1] He begins with his arrival at Combermere:

> The room ... was spacious with a high ceiling and situated directly above the stables. A hideous black stove, out in the centre, was guarded all round by a bleak little curb of whitewashed concrete. A dreadful black pipe rose from the stove to disappear through a hole in the ceiling. There was a trestle table and forms. Against the walls, closely aligned, stood diminutive iron bedsteads, without mattresses or blankets, folded to chair size. Three pegs and an empty tin locker served each bed. The floor was of bare boards. As the room was not in use all was quite remarkably forlorn, the true abomination of desolation. Worse, there was an adjoining 'ablution room', with stone floor, urinal, and cold-water taps – cold water only. Even had one joined out of desperation, as perhaps some boys had, it was a poorish welcome ...

> We had just decided that we had been forgotten when a young NCO burst in and took us to 'draw biscuits'. By this time we were feeling in need of something more substantial.

But the 'biscuits' turned out to be small mattresses (three laid end to end made one soldier's bed). We also drew blankets and a pillow-canvas, the shape of a suet roll, stuffed tight with horse-hair and bone hard. Lest we dislocate our necks we folded our pullovers, coats or towels for pillows that night. We were then shown the troopers' mess and told to go in and get 'tea'. Somewhat timidly we entered this crowded and noisy room and found ourselves placed on benches at trestle tables with a plate of fried egg and chips. Still clad conspicuously in our civilian suits we were surrounded by cheerfully curious and rowdy soldiers in canvas dung-arees that reeked of stables. Their every other word, it seemed to me, was the same four-letter one, even inserted quite often into the middle of ordinary two-syllable words. It was used as a verb, noun or adjective and without inhibition.

The cavalry reveille lasts just over a minute ... On our first morning I felt proud to listen to it for it now concerned me personally. But then we recruits were not embroiled in the general hubbub preceding a morning's mounted drill in the Great Park. From the top balcony outside the room I was to have a bird's eye view of the squadron to which I had been posted ... I looked down on a gleaming array of shining cleanliness. Even in khaki the Life Guards were dazzling. The summer coats of the horses shone. Bits, buckles, stirrup-irons, spurs ... blinked and twinkled. Not only was the steel burnished, buttons, cap-badges and titles winked and flashed. The blue sky was reflected in the polished

seats of the saddles (polished seats and surcingles, soaped flaps) ...

We were but the newest of recruits, who had not as yet even drawn canvas dungarees in which to work in the stables ... to my disappointment it was not a gleaming sword but a much-used broom which I was handed (or had hurled at my back) in the half light of the following dawn...

Several things took a bit of understanding. First, perhaps, the shouting of the NCOs at Reveille: 'Rise and shine, bed in line! ... The sun is burnin' your bleedin' eye-ball'; and this on a pitch dark and freezing morning in January. Then there was the unofficial but total and dreadful ban on the wearing of pyjamas ... that and having to share ablution facilities ... The shirt and underwear worn during the day were the recognised form of night attire ... One was usually so tired that it did not matter much anyway. Secondly, the mucking out of stables which followed at 6.30 am using only the bare hands. No stable implements were permitted young soldiers ... Bedding, that would have been thrown out of a civilian stable, was carried in warm, sticky, ammonia-scented and ton-weight armfuls, to be dumped in the yard ... to be spread to dry by 'old' soldiers with forks ... when wisps were made for use at evening stables you made them from this used bedding, never from hay or clean straw ...

Filthy, the food. A slab of yellow, soap-like cheese and one large white and pungent slice of raw onion was quite frequently the last meal of the day ... And a breakfast of bacon smothered in fried onions could surely stymie the hungriest ...

To start with ... our ride was taken by a hard-as-nails Scottish corporal. Compared with the kindness designed to encourage the learners of today, our instructor just stared at us in horrified disbelief. Then: 'So you,' and we jumped at the suddenness of his shout, 'you think you are going to be Life Guards?' He turned his horse and circled us at a collected trot, very nicely done. Then he faced us once more. I liked him when I became a corporal myself, but now his eyes were not friendly. 'It is my view,' he said, 'that, given luck, none of you will survive.' He rode another circle, fist on thigh, before addressing us in a more quietly reasonable tone. 'For a mon like me who loves his hairses,' he explained, 'it hurts to see people like you having the damned impairt'nance to try and set on their backs'...

When the regiment galloped past King Edward VIII in Windsor Great Park in 1936 His Majesty is reported to have remarked that the lines of the galloping half-squadrons were 'as inflexibly straight as blocks of wood'. Watching the newsreels that same evening they looked to be just that. The pace was a gallop, the soldiers in full review order (the officers wearing frock coats and forage caps by order of the King, because he himself was thus attired)... At the parade's conclusion, we were played back to barracks down the sun-flooded Long Walk to the strains of 'Colonel Bogey' ... With the King riding at our head it soon began, with its second part, to sound grander than all the symphonies. An aura of splendour surrounded one, from the glossy black quarters of the horses in front to the gilt and silver of royal ciphers emblazoned here, there and everywhere around...

It was during my second term at Windsor I was given promotion more important to me than any [since]... it meant much more than having a couple of stripes and a crown ... and wearing aigulettes on my left shoulder in full kit. Never again would I do sentry-go, getting out of bed at a quarter to one on a frosty morning in order to patrol on foot the deserted Horse Guards ... never again would I pray for the chimes of Big Ben to come crashing musically down Whitehall signalling for me a return to bed at 3 am till I must leave it again at 6 ...

That year the Blues came to Windsor. The Life Guards rode to London ... Twenty trumpeters sounding 'Stables' under the clock at Knightsbridge at 11 am ... every night 'Last Post' floating up from the darkness below had the power to stop me in my tracks. At such

Opposite page:
Edward VIII riding back to Combermere Barracks after inspecting The Life Guards in Windsor Great Park. He is flanked (*left*) by Major General The Earl of Athlone, Colonel of the Regiment, and (*right*) by Lieutenant Colonel the Hon E H Wyndham, commanding. It was the express wish of the King (who did not relish the prospect of cuirasses and helmet) that the officers should wear frock coats

times I would think 'Who would be a civilian?' Now that I am one I still do but the saying 'Once a Life Guard, always a Life Guard' is quite a comfort ...[2]

During the 1930s regiments of horsed cavalry saw the first glimmers of mechanisation. Thus, in 1930, the echelon transport of The Life Guards, Blues and Royals was mechanised. During the reign of Edward the Eighth Austin 7 motor cars with wireless sets were issued. But, notwithstanding the lessons of the Great War – even while Mussolini's bombers and fighter aircraft were cutting up the Abyssinian army (as the clouds of the Abdication crisis drew over Britain) – the generals still saw a battlefield role for the *arme blanche*. In particular they still foresaw a useful role for horsed cavalry in hilly country. There was a policing task for which horsed cavalry were particularly suited.

Nearly two years into the new reign, that of George VI, the Royals (one of the only two line regiments of cavalry left with horses – the other being the Greys) sailed to Palestine, where they were still to be found at the outbreak of the Second World War.

1. Bishop gained a place at Sandhurst shortly before the Second World War, in which he served as an officer in the 12th Lancers
2. Bishop, pp 3-20

15 GEORGE VI (1936-52)

George VI, Colonel-in-Chief both of the Household Cavalry and of the Royals, succeeded to the throne on December 10, 1936, his Coronation being on May 12, 1937. Within 27 months of that Britain declared war on a Germany whose National Socialist government had embarked on a blatantly criminal campaign of expansionism in Europe. September 1, 1939, was the day that drew Britain and France into the war, the day that Hitler invaded Poland, a nation with which both Allies had signed pacts of mutual assistance. They declared war two days later.

THE ROYALS IN PALESTINE

Meanwhile the British government had been facing a growing crisis in Palestine, which had been occupied by General Allenby's army in 1918 and which became a British Protectorate under the Balfour Agreement of 1920. Owing, in great measure, to Nazi Germany's persecution of the Jews, many of them had fled to Palestine, causing a heightening of tension between the native Arabs and a growing Jewish population, who, demanding a permanent national home there, were increasingly in support of the militant Zionist movement and its terrorist branch. During the 1930s a campaign of Arab nationalism was launched against Jew and Briton alike; and, when the British government put a strict limit on Jewish immigration, the Jews turned anti-British as well as anti-Arab.

That was the situation when the Royals were posted to Palestine, under command of Lieutenant-Colonel Cyril Swire, in 1938. Naturally, in such circumstances, horsed cavalry proved a most effective form of mounted police, and the Regiment, assisted by their attached motorised squadron, of the Fifth Royal Inniskilling Dragoon Guards, spent the next two years carrying out patrols, bandit hunts and cordon-and-search

operations in the hills and villages surrounding their Judaean camp, and intercepting Jews who entered the country illegally. The Royals, between them, won a Military Cross, two Military Medals, six Mentions in Despatches and five C-in-C's certificates for their good work in these operations. In November 1938 the Divisional commander in Palestine asked the commanding officer whether he thought his horses were any use. At which Colonel Swire wrote a fulminating letter home to the Colonel of the Regiment (Ernest Makins): 'He [the general] said that if we could not do it [guard a stretch of railway line] mounted, we

The Royal Family. The King, Colonel-in-Chief of the Royal Horse Guards, is wearing The Blues' tartan, (tailored from a roll of tweed presented to him by the late (10th) Duke of Beaufort

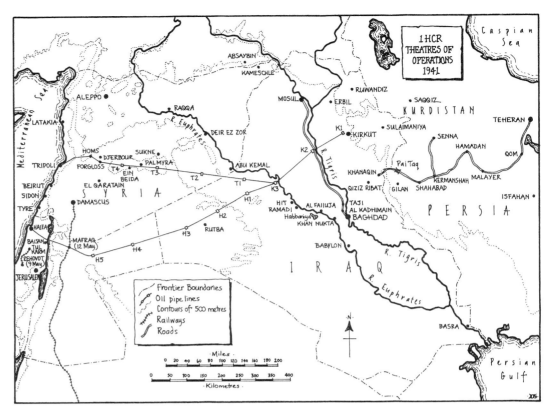

Theatre of Operations,
1HCR, 1941

could "rough up" our horses!! or he might have to send them home ... Montgomery is the gentleman's name, and I am told he is one of the brains of the Army'.[1]

THE ROYALS SAY FAREWELL TO THEIR HORSES

It was now widely acknowledged that there could be no role for horses on the battlefields of the day. And, with the dramatic unfolding of events of 1940 – Dunkirk, the air battles over England, Russia still allied to Germany, the heavy fighting in north Africa – the Royal Dragoons felt as though they had

been committed to a backwater. On the foundation of the Royal Armoured Corps (April, 1939) both they and the Royal Scots Greys (along, of course, with the Household Cavalry) were specifically excluded from it. However, Lieutenant Colonel Reginald Heyworth (who had taken over from Colonel Swire in March 1939), after due consultation with his senior officers, applied to the War Office for the Royals to be mechanised. He was fairly promptly given the choice of tanks or armoured cars. He chose the latter; and the Regiment, having handed over their horses in December, 1940, were busy in the process of conversion, with the help of experts from the Royal Tank Corps, the 11th Hussars and the armoured car wing of the mechanical, gunnery and wireless school in Egypt.

THE MARMON-HARRINGTON MARK III

The vehicle upon which the Regiment was now based was the South African Marmon-Harrington Mark III, a somewhat thin-skinned armoured car mounted with a .303 Vickers machine gun, a Bren gun and a .5 inch anti-tank rifle. The Royals were organised with three sabre squadrons and a headquarters squadron, each sabre squadron deploying five troops, each of

The Royals' horse lines in Palestine. The coastal plain of Esdraelon is in the background

three Marmon-Harringtons. Within the troop, only the troop leader's vehicle carried a wireless (a number 9 set). Colonel Heyworth decided that his Regiment should wear distinctive workmanlike berets, and the colour he chose was grey.[2] Adorned with the Napoleonic Eagle the berets looked most impressive.

EGYPT TO SYRIA

Following the British withdrawal of an infantry division and an armoured brigade from the desert to counter the German invasion of Greece, the Axis forces retook Cyrenaica, which General Wavell's army had so recently captured. While 'C' and HQ squadrons of the Royals continued to train, in May, 1941, 'A' (Major Pepys) was posted to Egypt, under the 11th Hussars, and 'B' (Major Hermon) to help take on the Vichy French forces in Syria where the Household Cavalry were also now in action. And to whose first phase of the war we now turn, starting at September 1, 1939 (at the order for general mobilisation when The Life Guards were at Hyde Park and The Blues at Windsor).

THE HOUSEHOLD CAVALRY REGIMENT, 1939-41

Under the mobilisaton scheme for the Household Cavalry, there was a Composite Regiment at Windsor, ready to take the field (but – owing to a shortage of ammunition – with flags and policeman's rattles to represent automatic fire!); a Reserve Regiment at Knightsbridge, to continue with London duties; and a Training Regiment, also at Windsor, to produce reinforcements. The Composite Regiment (initially under command of Lieutenant Colonel Jack Speed, of The Life Guards) contained two Life

Guards and two Blues squadrons and a mixed headquarters squadron, with a signals troop, a machine gun troop and an anti-tank troop. Some of their mounts were experienced troop horses, but the bulk of them were hunters, bought by the Remount Depot (Army Veterinary Corps). Early in October, 1939, the Regiment moved to the vicinity of Nottingham to join the Warwickshire and the Royal Wiltshire Yeomanries and the 1st Bn Essex Regiment in the 4th Cavalry Brigade, which, with the 5th and 6th Brigades, composed the 1st Cavalry Division.[3]

In February, 1940, the Household Cavalry Regiment – the word 'Composite' was dropped from the title in January – crossed the Channel for the first leg of their journey to Palestine. At Dunkirk the horses were unboxed and transferred to French boxes for their road journey to Marseilles,[4] their next destination being Tulkarm, near Haifa, where they spent some months on internal security duties before proceeding, in September, to patrol the Syrian border. Meanwhile Lords Athlone and Birdwood, the two Gold Sticks, approached General Sir Edmund Ironside, the Chief of the Imperial General Staff, to apply for a role for the Household Cavalry, other than with horses, while Lieutenant Colonel Andrew Ferguson, now commanding HCR, made a similar plea to General Wavell. Thus, early in 1941, the decision was taken to convert them to a motorised cavalry regiment. Accordingly, thirty-five 15-hundredweight trucks were delivered, the horses having been handed over to the Remount Squadron at Ramle.

THE ROAD TO BAGHDAD

Iraqi oil was the agent by which HCR saw their first action. British fuel interests were protected under the Anglo-Iraqi treaty of 1930, while RAF stations were established at Basra and Habbaniya. In March, 1941, however, when the pro-German Raschid Ali became Prime Minister, he abrogated the treaty and sent his army, assisted by Germans, to besiege Habbaniya.

On May 8 Habforce, found from the Cavalry Divison, was organised to relieve the garrison. The advance guard, Kingcol (named after Brigadier Kingstone, 4 Brigade commander), was led by HCR in their 15 cwt trucks, three to a troop. Our men travelled and fought the Iraqi campaign over a distance of 500 miles in temperatures of 120 degrees in the shade with a daily water ration

General Wavell flanked by (*left*) Lieutenant Colonel Andrew Ferguson commanding 1 HCR and (*right*) the veterinary officer, Veterinary-Major B R Body

(always dirty water) of half a gallon per man. Their weapons were the rifle and bayonet, the unreliable Hotchkiss gun and one Bren gun and one two-inch mortar per troop. There were no radios at troop level. After some heavy fighting and much menace from the air the force relieved Habbaniya on May 18, then advanced on Baghdad in two columns, Kingstone in the south and Colonel Ferguson (with 16 sections of the Arab Legion under Glubb Pasha) in the north. The Iraqis surrendered on the 31st.

On June 5, Major Eion Merry (RHG) put together Mercol to round up the Iraqi firebrand, El Fawzi el Raschid, who was still holding out with 500 men, and they chased them over the Syrian border (across which, at that time, no pursuit was permitted). Then Major Eric Gooch (LG), taking command of Gocol, went in search of Doctor Grobba, the fugitive German envoy to Baghdad, and Grobba, too, was sent scurrying into Syria.

During the Iraq campaign Major Henry Abel Smith (RHG) returned to England to relieve Lieutenant-Colonel Lord Forester (RHG) in command of the armoured car regiment formed from the Household Cavalry Training Regiment, to be part of the Guards Armoured Division. This had been the 2nd Household Cavalry Motor Battalion. By the time Major Abel Smith reached Windsor, the battalion had become an armoured car regiment – 2HCR. So the Regiment in active service in the Middle East will be known henceforward as 1HCR

SYRIA AND THE VICHY FRENCH

On the collapse of France, in June, 1940, the French forces in Syria adhered to the pro-German Vichy government. Syria was bristling with German agents, while, in May, 1941, 120 Axis warplanes were landed there. When Britain decided to occupy the country, Habforce was detailed for the task, with the old Roman town of Palmyra as their first objective. 1HCR, less A squadron, duly began their march, at the head of the column, along the Euphrates valley from Habbaniya on June 15, 1941; and, a week later, were deployed in front of the Roman ruins, which, with the surrounding palm groves, afforded excellent cover for the enemy. The French, at first possessing total air supremacy, held out for nine days. 'The Vichy forces now saw their opportunity to smash the Brigade,' says Somerset de Chair (the Blues officer who was Kingcol's

Intelligence Officer),[5] in his book *The Golden Carpet*[6]. 'And every available aircraft was switched to the attack ... All morning [of the second day]

the air was filled with the throb of engines and the roar of bombs ... They swarmed over in relays and cruised round in circles, pitching out bombs on the heads of the helpless troops below. The occasional retort from Bren guns or Hotchkisses perched on their slender tripods, did not even sting them up except one de Woitine, which was sent with a whine and a crash into the sand by the Regimental Corporal-Major's batman in the Household Cavalry lines. He was given an immediate award of the Military Medal – standing there on the bare desert, without the cover even of a slit trench, firing back at an aircraft pouring lead and iron past him'.[7]

At last, however, the Brigadier received some air support, and Palmyra fell on July 3, the official Franco-Syrian surrender being at Homs on the 7th, although large pockets of resistance remained. Meanwhile a patrol led by Lieutenant Gerard Leigh made contact, at El Quaratain, with 'B' Squadron of the Royal Dragoons who had fought their way north from Palestine with the Indians, Australians and Free French. The campaign closed with a victory parade at Aleppo. Winston Churchill thought that the confidentiality imposed on these operations was quite unnecessary. 'Action this day,' he wrote to the Secretary of State for War on July 6,

Why have we not been told that the Blues, Life Guards and Essex Yeomanry [sic – he meant Essex Regiment] took part in the capture of Palmyra? These units have long ago been identified by contact and there cannot be any military reasons for not disclosing this interesting piece of information ...[8]

PERSIA

It had been decided that the German influence in Teheran must be quashed. So the 4th Cavalry Brigade, now renamed 9th Armoured, led by the Household Cavalry, set out for the Persian capital early in August and occupied it, without a shot being fired, on September 17 – at the same time as the Russians came in from the north. Ten days later the Brigade began their 900-mile march back to Palestine.

HCR, whose primitive vehicles bore the

Marmon-Harrington armoured cars of 'B' Squadron of the Royals at the Victory parade at Aleppo after the Syrian Campaign

identification number 55, were now referred to in the Middle East as 'the Flying 55'.

Perhaps the first personal accolade for their success in all these operations should have gone to Captain Lord Roderic Pratt (LG), the technical adjutant, who, on arrival in Palestine, had worked as the foreman's assistant and pupil at the Haifa Ordnance Depot, and was responsible for the roadworthiness of the trucks – across such monumental distances, in appalling conditions – and for the training of the drivers.

THE ROYALS IN THE EIGHTH ARMY

Greece and Crete were occupied by the German army; Rommel had the upper hand in the Western Desert; and, while, on the oceans, the U-boats triumphed, in June, 1941, an exultant Führer made the fatal move of invading Russia. Six months later the United States entered the war on the Allied side. (It was at this time, too, that the commando leader, Colonel Robert Laycock,[9] of The Blues, stormed Rommel's headquarters, inflicting many casualties, but failing to find the German Panzer general at home.)

In July, 1941, the Royals led the advance of Habforce to Homs, while their 'C' Squadron (Major Scott) remained in north Africa until the autumn when they rejoined the Regiment at Aleppo. In mid-November the

8th Army's offensive to relieve Tobruk began, and the Royals were wanted in Egypt. By December 10 their Marmon-Harringtons had relieved those of the King's Dragoon Guards.

For the next eighteen months – while suffering the exhausting heat of the day and the piercing cold winds of the night, mirage, flies and sandstorms, all the problems of communication, navigation, re-supply and medical access over vast distances and (in the early phases) the ever-present fear of air attack – the Royals would be armoured reconnaissance soldiers of the desert. The three sabre squadrons would each have the capacity to deploy five troops, or 'officer patrols', each of three armoured cars, of which only the troop leader's vehicle carried a wireless set. Their principal task was to see without being seen, to stalk without being stalked, to report enemy movement. Armoured cars being much in demand they found themselves switched frequently from one formation front to another, and often in a variety of independent groupings. For example, in mid-December, 'A' Squadron leader, Major Tony Pepys, composed Pepcol, having under his command a troop of the Northumberland Hussars, a company of the Rifle Brigade and a section of Sappers. On Christmas Eve that little unit was the first into the Cyrenaican capital, Benghazi.

On December 27, the day that 'A' Squadron rejoined the Regiment, the universally popular Colonel Reggie Heyworth died from

Household Cavalrymen cleaning saddlery, Palestine, 1941

a bomb splinter following a Stuka attack. Major Pepys assumed command until the regimental second-in-command, Major Ronnie Joy, who had been wounded in the same air strike, returned from the field hospital to wear the mantle. At this time the Germans went on to the offensive again and the Anglo-Commonwealth forces were thrown back to Gazala, the Royals holding a patrol line between Bir el Hamarin and Bir Tengeder, until the end of April, 1942, when they were withdrawn to recuperate and to refit their worn-out cars. In May they helped to fight the rearguard action from the Battle of Knightsbridge; and, in June, when the Germans retook Tobruk, the Royals held a

OC 'Smithforce':
Captain G A Murray Smith,
Royal Horse Guards

Theatre of Operations,
Mediterranean Area, 1941-3

new patrol line by Sidi Rezegh. But Tomahawks began to appear in the sky, and there was now almost a state of air parity. On July 13 General Montgomery took command of the Eighth Army, which was soon poised for the Battle of El Alamein. Meanwhile 1HCR had made contact with the Royals again, albeit tenuously.

SMITHFORCE

It was while I HCR was back in Palestine that they learned that they were to become an armoured car regiment; and, in February, 1942, instructors from the Royals and the 11th Hussars, were sent to convert them. Since the new establishment meant a reduction from four sabre squadrons to three, there were men to spare. So the regiment was required to produce a force of five officers and 115 other ranks to man '101 Royal Tank Regiment', a deception unit of wheeled vehicles disguised as Crusader tanks. Being commanded by Captain Tony Murray Smith, of The Blues, this strange little band was familiarly known as 'Smithforce'.

During 'Smithforce's first commitment in the Western desert, between April 13 and 15, they were given a wrong map reference by Headquarters 1st Armoured Division, which put them way out in front of the patrol line, between Bir el Hamarin and Bir Tengeder, which was held by the Royals, who were duly astonished to see them there. 'Smithforce' was attacked by a squadron of Italian tanks. Fortunately, however, the Stukas which were sent in support attacked their own tanks instead of the 'ghosts' of

Murray Smith's command. (He called this 'Smithforce's finest hour'!) Back at Cairo, on May 2, he handed over his dummies to the Yorkshire Dragoons and drew out new vehicles made to look like General Grant tanks, with which he returned to the front in time for the Battle of Knightsbridge.

Meanwhile, in March, 1 HCR had been sent from Palestine to boost the defence of Cyprus, where they took over a motley collection of vehicles. It was not until the end of August that they were called to Egypt. There they drew not only their quota of antiquated Marmon-Harringtons, but also a number of the better armed, thicker armoured Daimlers, so that each troop could have two Marmon-Harringtons and one Daimler, the latter being mounted with an armour-piercing and high-explosive capacity 2-pounder and a 7.92 Besa machine gun whose rate of fire was 700 rounds a minute.

EL ALAMEIN, OCTOBER-NOVEMBER, 1942

July, 1942 found the 8th Army on the Alamein line. Being flanked to the south by the yielding sands of the Qattara depression, this was the last cohesive line of defence before the Nile delta. And – while the front was fortified with mines and barbed wire and considerable reinforcements, South Africans, Australians, New Zealanders and Indians, as well as British, with improved equipment, came forward to bolster the Army – General Montgomery's exhortations made clear there was to be no more retreat, only advance.

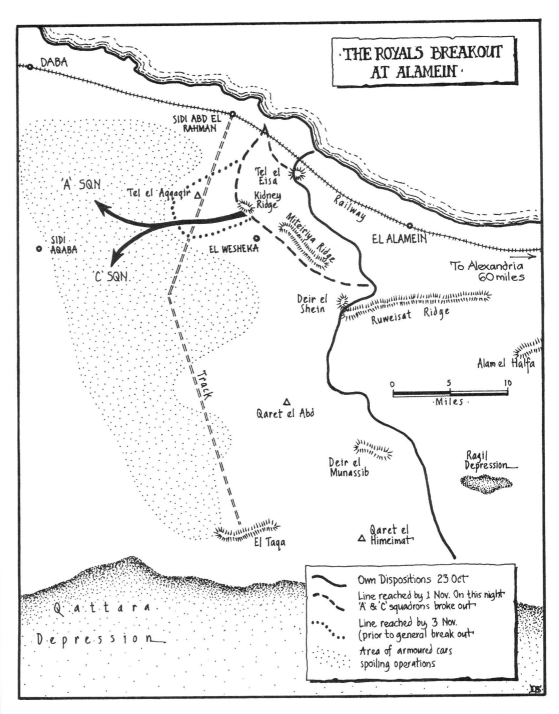

The Royals breakout at El Alamein, October–November, 1942

The Royals were ahead of the Household Cavalry in modernisation. Having dispensed with their old Marmon-Harringtons and being supplied with two Humbers (carrying 15mm guns) and a Daimler per troop, they were sent, during the fourth week of September, to a line in advance of X Corps (Lt Gen Lumsden) at the northernmost end of the front. Colonel Joy being posted to the 4th Light Armoured Brigade, Colonel Tony Pepys was now commanding officer. And while, a month later, the Germans were

subjected to a barrage from a thousand artillery pieces the 8th Army moved into new assembly areas, the Royals squadrons were busy conducting traffic through paths in the minefields. On October 31 the 51st Highland Division captured the vital feature of Kidney Ridge, and, after dark, Colonel Pepys sent two of his squadrons 'A' (Major the Hon Jack Hamilton-Russell)[10] and 'C' (Major Roddy Heathcoat Amory) to exploit the success. 'In our overriding responsibilities of providing information on enemy movement

and positions,' says Heathcoat Amory, 'we seldom had the opportunity to inflict much damage to him. Now all this was to change, anyhow for the next few days ...'[11] Pitt-Rivers takes up their adventure:

> The night ahead was full of flashes and the sounds of battle; but, to the south, where their course lay, all seemed quiet. A late moon was rising. The column threaded its way through tanks and anti-tank guns, which waited with engines throbbing, to go forward ... The armoured cars sped blindly ... into the territory of the enemy. Soon they were aware of troops on either side of the track. Sleepy guards sat rubbing the backs of their hands, or ran over to consult with one another about the strangers passing through their position. They could not be enemy, these Germans thought, so far from the battle and arriving in column of march ... The column passed quietly forward. They [saw] gun crews sleeping by their guns. The guards watched them through bleary eyes and stamped their feet. Already the east was green behind them ... but, by the time it was light, they were fleeting through the open desert ...[12]

Having created a good deal of havoc in the Italian bivouac areas, the squadron leaders decided (so as to cover more ground) to separate. 'A' moved north-west, 'C' south-west. They repaired their punctures (inflicted by enemy air) from British three-tonners captured by the Germans at Tobruk; they found fuel replenishment in enemy echelon areas; they leaguered at night in sandy depressions, or hidden by scrub; they cut the Axis telephone lines; and, during their three days (November 2-5) of piratical raids they destroyed 181 wheeled vehicles, three tanks, an armoured troop carrier, a medium gun, three field guns, 17 anti-tank guns, 20 Breda guns and one aircraft. They were also responsible for the capture of hundreds of prisoners.

1 HCR:
SEPTEMBER, 1942 – APRIL, 1944

Parading for the first time as an armoured car regiment in Egypt on September 25, 1942, 1 HCR received their orders for El Alamein on October 23. They were to take over the observation posts of the 11th Hussars and Yorkshire Dragoons at the southern end of the 8th Army's line, in front of the 7th Armoured Division. Many of their patrols cut their teeth in the new role with exchanges of fire with the enemy during the great battle, and they helped to round up more than a thousand surrendering Italians. But, still having Marmon-Harringtons while most of the other armoured car regiments were mounted exclusively in Humbers and Daimlers, the Regiment was denied the glamour of joining General Montgomery's offensive into Libya.

A quite different task awaited 1 HCR, which was now under command of Lieutenant Colonel Eric Gooch, The Life Guards. It was decided at the Casablanca conference (January, 1943) that the attempt should be made to entice Turkey into the war by economic help (from the Americans) and military backing, based on the 10th Armoured Division, to which 1 HCR was now assigned. The Regiment duly found themselves deployed on the Turco-Syrian border for nearly a year. However, during the summer of 1943, being entirely re-equipped with Humbers and Daimlers, they prepared to take their place in the Italian campaign.

END IN AFRICA, START IN EUROPE, 1943

Although the triumph of El Alamein – coupled with the defeat of the German forces, amid the snow and ice at the gates of Stalingrad – marked the turning-point of the war in the Allies' favour, there was still plenty of bite left in the depleted Afrika Corps. And, after the great desert battle of October-November, 1942, the Royal Dragoons experienced a further six months of continuous north African campaigning, through Cyrenaica (where Lieutenant

Colonel Pepys lost a foot from a German mine, being relieved by Lieutenant Colonel Barne), through Tripolitania where the Regiment took a major part in overwhelming the formidable Mareth Line (and where Lieutenant-Colonel Lloyd succeeded Lieutenant-Colonel Barne); to Tunisia, where the country became increasingly broken and hilly (and where, on April 19, the Regimental intelligence officer, Captain the Hon Desmond Hamilton-Russell was killed while on a visit to his brother the 'A' Squadron Leader) until, at last, on May 8, 1943, 7 Armoured Division entered Tunis, and 250,000 enemy troops laid down their arms. Meanwhile 'A' Squadron had left for Egypt to prepare for the invasion of Sicily (Operation 'Husky') which was to be the springboard for Italy. For the landing 'A' Squadron came under command of 4th Armoured Brigade, subsequently the Highland Division, then the Canadians; and its troops were operating semi-independently. 'The troop leaders were learning the technique of fighting in close country,' says the regimental historian.

And, instead of waiting for the hidden enemy to open fire, they began to use their machine-guns upon any cover which might serve the enemy purpose. ... Upon one occasion a troop discovered some enemy concealed beneath haystacks on the far side of a canal and quickly had them burning. Frequently the shell-fire set the fields

The Royal Family's Household Cavalry Guard at Balmoral in 1943. Front row (*left to right*) Cpl F Taylor (LG), HRH Princess Elizabeth, Lieut Lord Rupert Nevill (LG), HM The Queen, Cpl of Horse HS Friend (LG), HRH Princess Margaret, Cpl J Lockhead (RHG)

alight ... The heat was very great and the enemy shelling, accurately directed from the high ground to the north, kept the crews in their cars all day and filled the plain with the stench of rotting animals ...[14]

After three weeks of heavy fighting the Sicilian campaign was over; and, soon after that, the Italians negotiated a separate peace. The greatest tragedy for the Royals was the loss of 'A' Squadron Leader, Major Hamilton-Russell, who was killed when his jeep turned over in a shell crater. Major Bowlby was flown up from north Africa to replace him. Now began the contest for Italy where the Germans deployed 15 divisions. The 8th Army landed in Calabria on September 3, and the Anglo-American bridgehead at Salerno was secured on the 9th. A fortnight later the armoured cars of 'A' Squadron of the Royals were on the Calabrian roads. The remainder of the Regiment (who, in June, had been inspected by the King at Tripoli) sailed to Taranto in September, and, in November, drove north to Lucera to join the hitherto independent squadron. Before the month was out, however, they were under orders to return to Britain, for the Second Front was in the planning stages. It did not seem that mountainous Italy afforded much scope for armoured cars. But 1 HCR soon found that there was a job to be done there.

ASTRIDE THE APPENINES, 1944

We left 1 HCR enjoying a relatively quiet life on the Turco-Syrian border where, in July, 1943, they saw the end of their old Marmon-Harringtons, those being replaced by Daimlers and Humbers. In February, 1944, the Regiment, by now in Egypt, handed over their vehicles to the 27th Lancers. They sailed, under Colonel Gooch's command, to Naples to join the 8th Army early in April, by which time the Italian campaign had been fought for nine months, the struggle for the mastery of Monte Cassino and Kesselring's Gustav Line raged, and the breakout from the Anglo-American bridgehead at Anzio was still a month away.

The leg of Italy being bisected by the broad and craggy Appenine range with, in the south, constricted coastal plains on either side, there was very little room for armoured car manoeuvre during the advance to Rome. So, for phase one of 1 HCR's five and a half months in Italy they were largely

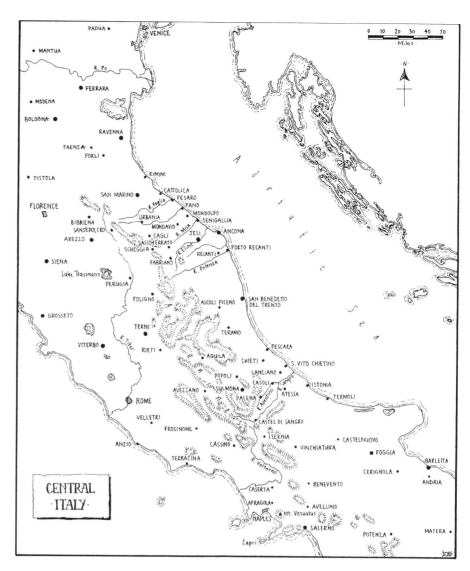

employed on foot reconnaissance, fighting patrols and the manning of observation and listening posts. They were to be up against some of Hitler's bravest and most tenacious veterans, well trained and well equipped, in thickly wooded mountains, liberally sown with mines and booby traps, and in dreadful weather conditions which frequently rendered the roads, as well as the tracks, impassable.

Operating on the front of the 4th Indian Division they began in the vicinity of Palena and Casoli on the river Aventino, a tributary of the Sangro. Among the many encounters recorded in the regiment's official history is this account of how a Military Cross was won by Lieutenant Lawrence Rook, who captured a German sergeant in an observation post, complete with marked maps, showing positions and reference codes:

He [Rook] had moved out through the

Central Italy, theatre of operations, 1 HCR, 1944

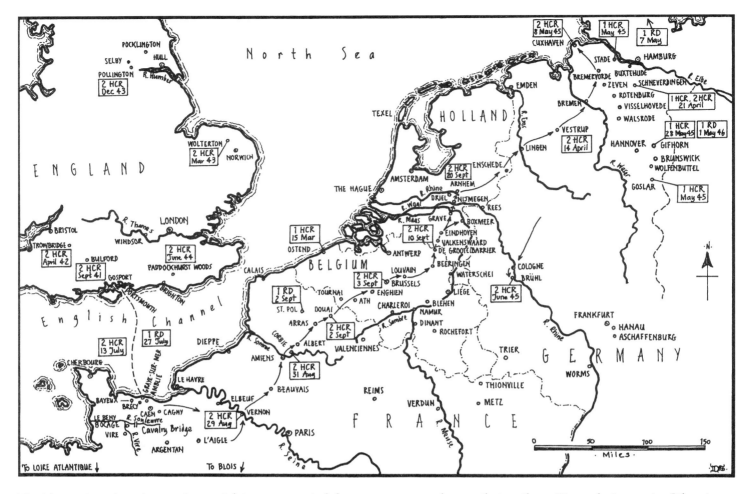

The Advance through north-west Europe, 1944-5

night accompanied by one man, and established his OP at first light. He observed a German OP, got into it, took the German NCO completely by surprise from behind and thrust his pistol into his ribs, marching him off with all his maps and papers without a sound. The rest of the German post was not more than 100 yards away and he could hear them talking. He also had to pass through a minefield on his way.[14]

The Allies overran Cassino during the second half of May and entered Rome on June 4 while the Germans withdrew to the Gothic line. Thus, by mid-June, the mountain warfare phase was over for 1 HCR. On July 9 the Regiment, having skirted Rome, advanced on the 10 Corps front a few miles south-west of Perugia. Now mounted, with their reconnaissance troops, or 'officer patrols', each based on two Daimler armoured cars and two scout cars, they deployed four squadrons, at first with two forward and two in reserve; and later, when their front extended to 20 miles, with three squadrons up. It was during this time, too,

that, the King being at 8th Army headquarters, Colonel Gooch went to give him a report on his Household Cavalry.

On August 2, the day on which six extra Humber scout cars arrived to boost the Regiment's mobility, they were transferred to the 6th Armoured Division, whose commander was Major General Gerald Templer (one day to be Colonel of The Blues and the first Colonel of The Blues and Royals). In a typical, if relatively mundane, troop contact quoted in the official history, the author describes how, on August 6, Lieutenant Coats, of 'B' Squadron, supported by two of the squadron's rifle sections, mounted in White armoured personnel carriers, was ordered to report whether a certain route was suitable for tanks:

At first light he [Coats] moved onto Trappola, having a good deal of difficulty as the road was steep and a bridge had been blown. On arrival at the outskirts of the village two Italians reported that some Germans were in the last house at the other end. Coats ... made the usual street-fighting plan of sending one section up the front of the row of houses and the other up the back ... With the two Italians acting as guides one section under Corporal Sherwin moved through the orchards on the right; the other, under Lance-Corporal Conway, moving up the main street ... when they were about fifty yards from the [enemy-held] house a German came out and was shot ... A considerable number of bullets now started whistling overhead, so Coats sent a runner to see how Conway's section was getting on. He went via the [his armoured] cars and came back with all kinds of questions as to how many Germans there were, and did Coats need any help from the Squadron Leader? So Coats went back to his wireless to answer all these questions ... he went on and addressed himself to the problem as to whether the track was fit for tanks. It was not; indeed it finally petered out altogether ... As a result of the report made by this patrol an operation planned for 6th Armoured Division on the following day was cancelled.[15]

In mid-August they were switched to the Polish Corps, whose commander was General Anders. He was to reward them, for their sterling service, with the emblem of the Mermaid of Warsaw, the red-and-white badge of which, with King George's permission, would adorn a sleeve of all ranks.

On September 7 the Regiment moved from the Adriatic coast to 10 Corps front again, this time coming under command of the 9th Armoured Brigade and operating forward, frequently amid torrential rain, from Perugia to Monte Carpegna which overlooked a splendid panorama, including most of the Republic of San Marino and the plain of Lombardy. The whole area which they traversed was very heavily mined and all the roads and tracks cratered. Towards the end of the month, with the 4th Indian Division closing up on their right and the KDGs on their left, 1 HCR was squeezed out and withdrawn from the line. On October 10 they sailed home to England.

Meanwhile, the appointment of Lieutenant Colonel Commanding Household Cavalry[17] had been created, Colonel Andrew Ferguson being the first to fill it (along with the office of Silver Stick, when in attendance on

the Sovereign) which would, henceforward, be invested in the post. In that context it should be mentioned that all ranks who had served continuously abroad since the war began were already entitled to the month's Python leave.

During the summer Ferguson, knowing it was undesirable for 1 HCR's career in Italy to be interrupted by a large exodus of its members on leave, paid a visit both to the Regiment and to General Alexander, the Supreme British commander in the zone, and asked him, inter alia, for 1 HCR's Python to be deferred until their tasks in the campaign were completed.

As soon as the Regiment was installed at Aldershot at the end of October those entitled to Python got their month's leave. Early in December the King paid the Regiment another visit.

EXPANSION OF THE CORPS

The Life Guards and Blues operated more or less independently of one another before the Second World War, the exigencies of which were to change that situation radically. Colonel Ferguson, the first 'Officer Commanding the Household Cavalry', was responsible for supervising the domestic needs of both Regiments, for keeping the Regimental records, and for maintaining a regular flow of the highest quality of officers

General Montgomery expaining the campaign situation in Normandy to personnel of 2 HCR and the Royal Northumberland Hussars in August, 1944. Lieutenant Colonel Henry Abel Smith, Royal Horse Guards commanding 2 HCR, is in the centre of the group with his adjutant, Capt Arthur Collins (with his head turned away), next to him. (Imperial War Museum)

and men for the whole Corps. Nearly all the remaining horses had been sent to Melton Mowbray. There were now two composite armoured car regiments to be manned, each of which had more than doubled its strength in both officers and men since the pre-war Household Cavalry Regimental establishment.[17] Finding sufficient suitable young officers – in competition with the Foot Guards, Greenjackets and some Line Cavalry regiments with strong officer recruiting traditions – was an ever-present problem. Then there was the Training Regiment and the Sovereign's armoured car escort (codenamed 'Morris Mission', under command of Major the Hon Arthur Baillie, LG) not to mention numerous extra-regimental appointments, such as the Household Cavalry Commando Platoon.[18]

NORTH-WEST EUROPE, 1944-5

Both 2 HCR and the Royals were more or less in the vanguard of the campaign in north-west Europe from July, 1944, to the end of it, which is to say May, 1945, whereas 1 HCR, having enjoyed four and a half months, after their Italian adventure, in Britain, did not arrive at the front until March, 1945. This section of the chapter is therefore largely concerned with the first two regiments named. Of the histories. *The Second Household Cavalry Regiment* by Roden Orde (who served with the Regiment from start to finish) is a classic, perhaps the finest account of armoured car warfare ever written. All the 2 HCR quotes in this chapter, unless otherwise stated, are from Orde.

Orde's book deals not only in depth with the organisation and the fighting, but, including liberal quotes from participants of all ranks, it gives very vivid descriptions of all the dramas and horrors encountered, such as the elan and bloodthirstiness of the revengeful Maquis, the devastation caused by the Allied air forces and artillery, the misery of refugees, the courage and the spiteful acts of the retreating Germans. It also has time for many refreshing moments of humour and gaiety. This brief history – brief in time, long in text (600 pages) – presents a magnificent portrait of the camaraderie and esprit de corps of a good armoured cavalry regiment.

From the moment Major Henry Abel Smith reached Windsor from the Middle East to take over 2HCR (already converted from motorised infantry to armoured cars) from Lieutenant Colonel Lord Forester in July, 1941, he set about galvanising his command for war, sending officers, NCOs and men on driving and maintenance, wireless and gunnery courses, conducting squadron and troop tactical drills and generally working the regiment in the field and in the classroom for all they were worth.

Meanwhile it had been decided that an additional armoured division would be necessary for the Second Front, the role being assigned to the Foot Guards – with, first Major General Sir Oliver Leese Bt.[19] as commander, and, subsequently, Major General Allan Adair – and with 2HCR providing the armoured reconnaissance element. The Guards Armoured Division was initially in Lieutenant General O'Connor's 8 Corps of General Dempsey's 2nd Army.

The four sabre squadrons of a British armoured car regiment would now each go to war with five Daimler troops, each of those having two armoured cars and two scout cars ('dingos'); a 'heavy' troop, which contained two 75 mm-armed 'Matadors'; and a support (or 'blitz') troop which deployed three dismounted sections, who travelled in White armoured personnel carriers. The command cars were the capacious American Chevrolets ('Staghounds') which were mounted with a 37mm gun and two Browning machine guns. Colonel Abel Smith's adjutant was Captain Arthur Collins, and his Regimental Corporal Major, Mr Jobson (the only member of the Regiment who had served in the First World War).

'C' Squadron of the Royals passing through Falaise

General Sir Bernard Montgomery, commanding 21st Army Group, addressed the Regiment in his breezily optimistic manner in February, 1944; and, in the following month, the King and Queen spent a day with them, being escorted by a troop under command of Captain Thomas Clyde. The Anglo-American invasion having been launched on June 6, 2 HCR sailed for Normandy on July 12-13, their first action being, a few days after landing, in advance of 8 Corps' Operation 'Goodwood Meeting', the objective of which was to break out south of Caen to a line overlooking Falaise. There, a combination of the closely wooded and hedged nature of the Bocage country, the mines and the powerful defiance of the German 88mms and Bazooka anti-tank guns, compounded by wet weather, brought the squadrons to a halt with seven of their strength killed.

To their left the Royal Dragoons, who had landed on July 27, were in the relatively quiet van of 12 Corps.

The Anglo-American armies, enjoying total air superiority, were not to be denied in their mighty swing south and east. On July 29 2HCR were diverted south to lead 11th Armoured Division. Lieutenant Powle's troop of 'C' Squadron having found an undefended track in the Fôret l'Eveque, forming the boundary between two German divisions, reached the river Souleuvre (then six miles behind the enemy lines); and, in due course, joined by a troop of tanks from the Northamptonshire Yeomanry, captured a vital crossing, to be nicknamed 'Cavalry Bridge'. ('The capture of this bridge and the advance southward which it made possible,' says 11th Armoured's historian, 'was unquestionably a turning-point in the campaign in France'.)[20] Roden Orde remembers the scene in 'D' Squadron harbour area:

In harbour stoves hummed merrily ... soon it grew dark, and drivers made a final check-up to assure themselves that tanks were full of petrol, that oil levels showed no unaccountable drop and that stowage of kit permitted unrestricted traverse of the turret. I watched Corporal Harrison, 'Rev' up Harry, indefatigably touring the squadron area with his water-cart of chlorinated ditch water ... A torch flashed on, groping for a mislaid article. A scout car lid closed with a metallic crash ...

The German 7th Army having been trapped and more or less crushed in the 'Falaise Pocket', 2 HCR next led the Sherman and Cromwell tanks of Guards Armoured up to the Somme. If the highlight of the Royals' war was El Alamein, one of 2HCR's was their capture of the three Somme bridges, known as Faith, Hope and Charity at Sailly-Laurette, Corbie and Vecquemont on August 31. Let General Horrocks give the accolade:

We had definite information that the Germans were striving to establish defences on the line of the river and it was imperative to take every possible risk in the hope of being able to seize the Somme bridges before the Germans had time to organise their defensive arrangements in detail. The orders to advance were only received by the [2HCR] squadrons at 0100 hours when they were settling down to a well-earned night's rest. The ensuing advance must have been a nightmare; the men were already tired before they started, it was pouring with rain and the roads were blocked with every form of traffic, including German tanks. Nevertheless, the leading troops, commanded by Groenix van Zoelen, Buchanan-Jardine and Hanbury on the right and Peake on the left, pushed on relentlessly and the seemingly impossible was achieved – the bridges were all captured intact. But what was even more important, having enlisted and armed members of the French resistance movement ... the Regiment succeeded in holding these bridges until the Grenadiers arrived – a most memorable night's work which could only have been achieved by well-trained deter-mined men whose morale was high'.[21]

The Royals, too – operating on the flank of General Horrocks Corps and patrolling ahead of 7th Armoured Division – had been heading for the Somme, and found a way over in the suburbs of Amiens before extending the bridgehead west and north. 'Lieutenant Bradstock moved his troop swiftly into the village of La Chausée Tirancourt,' says their historian,

and found himself at once in the centre of an enemy stronghold. Entirely surrounded, he gathered his cars into the central square where he fought off all attacks, shooting with his sten gun from the top of his turret at Germans

General Montgomery presenting the Military Cross to Lieutenant D F Bradstock, 1st The Royal Dragoons (Imperial War Museum)

2 HCR: Lieutenant Colonel Henry Abel Smith and (*left*) Captain Arthur Collins entering Brussels in their Daimler command car. (Imperial War Museum)

who assailed the troop with anti-tank grenades. When the troop finally forced its passage out of [the village] they left 20 SS men dead upon the ground ... by last light the Royal Dragoons had penetrated beyond the river to a depth of five miles.[22]

Corporal Boon of 'C' Squadron, 2HCR, was the first Allied soldier into Belgium and, according to a *Times* war correspondent, in an article entitled 'Cavalry Spirit' 'A' Squadron Leader, Major Bowes Daly (a Master of Foxhounds) raced Major Peter Herbert (an amateur steeplechase rider) in their respective 'Motor Chargers' to be first into

Brussels. During the advance, on September 3, Trooper Conry-Candler of 'C' Squadron was very badly wounded after his vehicle was knocked out by a Bazooka. 'He must have fainted,' Orde recalls,

for the next thing that he remembers was finding himself in hospital in Brussels with two good-looking German nurses holding his hands imploringly and asking him in perfect English "what will happen to us now?"

They did not have to wait long. That very evening 2HCR, with Corporal-of-Horse Dewar and Trooper Ayles in the leading 'A' Squadron 'dingo', were first into the city. Guards Armoured pushed on; and, the following day, Lieutenant Hanbury, of 'D' Squadron reached Louvain on the Dyle. On questioning some civilians Hanbury was told 'the bridge is prepared for demolition, it would be suicide to go on'. Which, opined the troop leader, 'seemed a trifle pessimistic'.

It was as a result of the action at that bridge that he won the Military Cross and his intrepid Corporal-of-Horse – W L Thompson[23] – earned a DCM. After which, Orde recalls, 'at a little cafe at the corner of the Brussels road

... came the strains of a song, punctuated by prolonged cheering. I walked across. Seated at the entrance to his bivouac, each arm round the waist of a Belgian girl, his own men forming a grinning and admiring semi-circle, was Lieutenant Hanbury. He was singing, as if without a care in the world, 'The Big Rock Candy Mountains'.[24]

2HCR went on to play an important part in the Irish Guards' capture of a vital bridge over the Meuse-Escaut canal on September 10. 'If anyone wanted to know "whether Jerry was up the road",' wrote the Micks' war historian,

'the answer was always "ask the Household Cavalry to go and see". Above all they could always be relied on somehow and somewhere to find a way round any obstacle, natural or unnatural. This evening the Household Cavalry found something splendid – a fine new unmapped German-built military road running due north from Exel to Overpelt and then turning due left at de Groote barrier.'

Having observed the German presence at de Groote barrier from a high factory window overlooking the place, Lieutenant

Creswell and Corporal-of-Horse Cutler sent back a detailed report of the situation. Next day Lieutenant Buchanan-Jardine, of Major Jackie Ward's 'D' Squadron, made his famous dash with two scout cars into Holland – he was the first to cross the border – several miles behind the enemy lines, and rendered his report on the bridge athwart the Dommel at Valkenswaard. ('Doubts that it might be too fragile to hold the Shermans were soon put at rest by the sight of a German Mark IV tank which moved slowly forward out of Valkenswaard and settled like a giant toad in the middle of the bridge'.)

The Anglo-American airborne attempt to turn the Siegfried Line by outflanking from the north, failed in the face of hardening German resistance. Nevertheless 2HCR reached Nijmegen and Arnhem by the evening of September 20, of the operations of which date, a Divisional staff officer wrote that 'patrols of the Household Cavalry,

> dispersed to the four winds, as much as thirty miles apart, were reporting fantastic engagements. In one place, cut off entirely from us, they had discovered a ferry in perfect working order ...[25]

Late October found 2HCR with OPs overlooking the Maas. On November 2 the Royal Dragoons drove up to take over from the Inns of Court, who, at that

Daimler scout car driver. One of the many drawings by Corporal Eric Meade-King adorning Roden Orde's history of 2 HCR

juncture, were under Colonel Henry's command. On November 9, General O'Connor, commanding 8 Corps, was writing 'Dear Abel Smith, Again I feel I am greatly indebted to you and your Regiment. I can honestly say I have never yet met a unit which so wholeheartedly carries out the spirit of the instructions that are given to them ...'[26] After ten days 2HCR was withdrawn and Colonel Pepys and the Royals took control of the sector.

In mid-December, Hitler having reinstated von Runstedt in command of his Western Front, the Ardennes counter-offensive was launched against the Americans who eventually halted and turned it. On March 30, 1945, 2HCR crossed the Rhine with Guards Armoured. Orde described the emotion:

> The strange gripping feeling as the car dips to the water's edge. The Military Police signalling frantically to close up ...

The Royals in the outskirts of Kiel en route for Denmark, May 1945

The Mayor of Brussels handing over the ' The Brussels Standard' to personnel of 2 HCR. Corporal-of-Horse J Neill, who went on to be RCM of The Blues, is nearest the camera. (Imperial War Museum)

The musical, almost mesmeric, sound of the rumbling sleepers as they take the weight of the wheels and the pontoon boats bob and dance as the current strains against the anchoring ropes ...

By this time 1 HCR, brought to the Continent by Col Gooch – but subsequently commanded by Lieutenant Colonel Walter Sale – were up with Guards Armoured, rendering the two Household Cavalry regiments side by side. Although there was not to be much left of the campaign 1HCR had their share of action. At 0800 hours in the last week of the war, for example, a troop of 'B' Squadron

> advancing up the coast road from Stade had a sharp little action with some Hitler Youth holding out in some cottages. Corporal Allen, an extremely popular NCO, was killed in this engagement. The party of Hitler Youth ... came in for some very rough handling ... by the time the squadron leader had succeeded in calming the enraged reconnaissance troop.[27]

The Royal Dragoons crossed the Elbe on May 1; and, on the following day, they received the surrender of no fewer than 10,000 Germans. On May 6 the Regiment was delegated to represent 2nd Army in the liberation of Denmark. Colonel Pepys was flown to Lüneburg Heath, Headquarters 21st Army Group, where General Montgomery ordered him to take the Royals to

Copenhagen. After six months in Denmark, the commanding officer, on November 3, was received in audience by King Christian before the Regiment proceeded to Germany where they remained for the next five years.

LIFE GUARDS AND BLUES RE-FORMED

In May, 1945, 1HCR occupied barracks in Goslar, 2HCR in Bruhl. Colonel Gooch, who had succeeded Colonel Ferguson as Regimental Lieutenant Colonel, master-minded the reconstitution of the Household Cavalry into Life Guards and Royal Horse Guards. In July, 1945, all Blues personnel in 1HCR were sent to the new Royal Horse Guards at Bruhl, while all Life Guardsmen in 2HCR went to the new Life Guards at Goslar[28]. Meanwhile, in order to resume the Household Cavalry's State duties without delay, a body of pre-war men, who had been posted home on Python, formed a composite mounted squadron at Hyde Park Barracks. And that would soon expand – when sufficient trained dutymen were available – into a squadron from each Regiment.

When, on July 28, 1945, the inhabitants of Brussels turned out in their thousands to pay tribute to the Guards Armoured Division, the formation which had liberated their city eleven months previously, men of the old 2HCR, along with representatives from the Grenadier, Coldstream, Irish and Welsh Guards, were presented with Colours by the Mayor. Major E J S Ward commanded the Household Cavalry detachment, while RCM Poupart, Corporal-Major Berrisford and Corporal-of-Horse Neill formed the Colour party. 'In the Royal Park the GOC [Major General Adair] took the salute,' Captain Orde concludes; 'and, after the Colours had been shown to the men, the Division received the order "Dismiss" with ears still ringing with the cheers of the Brussels multitude.'

THE TURBULENT PEACE

It was a very troubled world that still faced Britain following the final defeat of Nazi Germany in the early summer of 1945. Not only was the hot war to continue in the Pacific until Japan's capitulation early in September, but the Russians, who promptly occupied Eastern Germany and the best part of the rest of eastern and central Europe – with a militantly jealous eye on Western Germany, too – and, in alliance with Communist China, were clearly intent upon setting up communist regimes in every part of the world. Berlin, divided between the four Allied powers, the United States, Britain,France and Russia, stood like an island in the Soviet zone of the new divided Germany, while the British Army of the Rhine (formerly the British Army of Occupation) had rather more than its share of the zonal border to survey and defend. It was the Allied resistance to these threats, coupled with the new blackmailing menace of the atomic bomb, which prompted a massive Allied presence in Western Germany until the early 1990s.

The Life Guards, The Blues and the Royal Dragoons, counting, as three of the Army's nine armoured car regiments,[29] displayed a quite different image from their horsed days of the 1930s, not only because they stood at twice the strength, but also because National Service outlasted the war by some 15 years, which meant the training of intake after intake of young conscripts, a great tax on the patience and enthusiasm of regular officer and NCO instructors and a heavy burden on squadrons, particularly when on active service. However, that commitment was considerably alleviated, in 1951, with the establishment, at Carlisle, of the 67th Training Regiment, which was to cater for the armoured car trade training and testing of both regulars and National Servicemen.

The careers of the three Regiments with which we are concerned at this time have been quite recently recorded, and in some depth, in *Challengers and Chargers: A History of The Life Guards, 1945-1992* (published 1992) *and The Story of the Blues and Royals: Royal Horse Guards and 1st Dragoons* (1993). This account (and in the following chapter) of their postings and activities, during the period 1945-96, will therefore be confined to bare outlines.

THE LIFE GUARDS

When Lieutenant Colonel Walter Sale (RHG) relinquished command of 1HCR in April, 1945, to take a staff appointment, he was succeeded by a Life Guardsman, Lieutenant Colonel 'Boy' Wignall, who was thus to be The Life Guards' first commanding officer when the Regiment was reconstituted at Goslar in July. In March, 1946, Colonel Wignall led The Life Guards from Western Germany through the Russian zone to the British sector of Berlin where, apart from busy guard and escort duties, they enjoyed a pleasant recreational interlude for a couple of months before returning to BAOR en route for Egypt.

In fact that posting was for Palestine, but the delicate situation in Egypt was such that they remained there until May, 1947. Under the Anglo-Egyptian Treaty of 1936 British forces were to garrison the country for twenty years. But Arab nationalism was

Back to mounted duties. An inspection at Hyde Park Barracks in September, 1945. (*Soldier* Magazine)

already waxing strongly, and the Egyptians were determined to sack all foreigners at the earliest opportunity. The Life Guards were the last troops to be evacuated from Cairo into the comparative seclusion of the Canal Zone.

The situation in Palestine, as outlined close to the start of this chapter when first the Royals, then 1HCR, were there, had deteriorated considerably. Arabs and Jews had been literally at each others' throats day and night, while large numbers of the universally hated British Army and Colonial Police were frequently attacked, many being killed. Anyhow, the sovereignty of that unhappy land remained British until the Government renounced the Mandate in May, 1948, by which time The Life Guards had endured a full year there, and were involved in some bitter fighting, while their soldiers displayed many acts of great initiative and courage. Even as they drove away they were attacked by the Egyptian air force, who had joined the fray on behalf of the Palestinian Arabs. The Regiment sailed home on June 6; they remained at Windsor, as the Training Regiment, with one sabre squadron retained for demonstration purposes. Subsequently they reverted to the full service regiment role. In March, 1952 The Life Guards handed over Combermere Barracks to The Blues, having, during the previous month, played their part in the funeral of their Colonel-in-

The demonstration troop of The Blues close to the East German border in August, 1949 (*Soldier* Magazine)

Chief, the King. At the time of the Korean War, The Life Guards were put on an operational footing, training becoming the task of a new unit, the Household Cavalry Training Cadre.

ROYAL HORSE GUARDS

The Blues soldiered in Germany for the best part of the last years of George VI's reign. In April, 1946, they moved from Bruhl farther north-east in the Ruhr, to Menden; and again, in the winter of 1948-9 – by which time Lieutenant Colonel Sir Peter Grant-Lawson had taken over command from Colonel Sale – still farther north-east to Wesendorf – close to the Soviet zone frontier. Their tasks varied from helping to control the Black Market and the large numbers of 'displaced persons', and internal security in general, to keeping a watch on the zonal border which the Russians and Communist East Germans had now wired and interspersed with watch towers. Before and after the outrageous Soviet blockade of Berlin, which lasted from June 1948 to May 1949 (during which time the Allied garrisons were re-supplied by air), squadrons were detached for duty in that city, and The Blues provided the escort for the first post-blockade convoy. The Regiment scored some outstanding sporting successes during this tour, on the athletic grounds and playing fields as well as in a number of equestrian events.

In November, 1950, the Regiment transferred to Wolfenbüttel, near Brunswick, taking over Northampton Barracks from the Royals, and staying there until March, 1952 when – under command of one of the great wartime leaders of clandestine operations, Lieutenant Colonel David Smiley – they returned home to Windsor, having lost their Colonel-in-Chief on February 6.

THE ROYAL DRAGOONS

The Royals, too, spent the late 1940s with the Rhine Army, and like their close comrades in The Blues, patrolled the Soviet border when they were not trade training or on squadron and regimental exercises. Reluctantly, as we have seen, they gave up the delights of Denmark in November, 1945, for Eutin in Schleswig-Holstein. But that was also shortlived; for, in September, 1946, they were moved on to Dedelsdorf, just north of Wesendorf, close to the East German frontier; and, a year or so later, south

Members of The Blues Mounted Squadron awaiting an inspection in 1949

again to Wolfenbüttel where their best friends, The Blues,[30] relieved them late in 1950. The Royals, too, achieved some very significant sporting successes during this time.

Under their new commanding officer, Lieutenant Colonel Roddy Heathcoat Amory, the Regiment was sent (en route for Egypt) to Chester where, at Dale Barracks, their Colonel-in-Chief inspected and spent a day with them on December 5. They had a relatively quiet ten months' training at Fayid in the Canal Zone, until, in October, 1951, the Egyptian Government declared their Treaty with Britain null and void, and put its army on a war footing. So thereafter, until their departure from Egypt in 1954, the Royals were closely involved in Internal Security duties. It was during this time (1951-3) that their future Colonel, Lieutenant Colonel Desmond Fitzpatrick, commanded them. It was during their Egyptian sojourn, too, that their Colonel-in-Chief died.

THE MOUNTED SQUADRONS

The Household Cavalry Training Regiment, which had supplied reinforcements to the two service Regiments during the war, now dispatched recruits to The Life Guards and Blues for armoured car trade training (driving and vehicle maintenance, wireless, gunnery and assault, or support, troop) – or, from 1951, for the same purpose, to 67th Training Regiment RAC. They also dispatched volunteers for mounted duty, after completing their basic military training, to the Composite Mounted Squadron at Hyde Park Barracks, to undergo twenty weeks' riding school and sword drill. And, during the summer of 1947, sufficient recruits had passed through riding school to enable the new Regimental Lieutenant Colonel, Colonel Abel Smith, to expand the Knightsbridge element into a squadron from each Regiment. From that time forward, therefore, instead of the King's Life Guard being a mixture of Life Guards and Blues, the two squadrons alternated in finding the King's Life Guard. During that summer the King gave permission for full dress to be worn for the wedding of Princess Elizabeth to Lieutenant Philip Mountbatten RN, and it was worn, thenceforward, for all State occasions.

In 1950, when the King heard it proposed that the Household Cavalry should come under command of the Director, Royal Armoured Corps, he sent for the new commander of the Brigade of Guards and London District, Major General Julian Gascoigne and told him, 'I cannot possibly have that. The first thing you have to do as Major-General is to arrange to bring the Household Cavalry under your command in the same way as the Brigade of Guards is'.[31] Hence the Household Cavalry and Brigade of Guards became one in the Household Brigade, and subsequently the Household Division. *Septem Juncta in Uno.*

In 1952 it was decided that the Lieutenant Colonel Commanding Household Cavalry, the Silver Stick, should have his own headquarters and staff at Horse Guards, and that the Mounted Squadrons should make up an independent command with the title Household Cavalry Mounted Regiment.

From February 6, 1952 until March 29, 1969, the Colonel-in-Chief of the Household Cavalry and the Royal Dragoons was Queen Elizabeth II, as she has continued to be, since that day, of The Life Guards and The Blues and Royals. It is the stories of the two Regiments during her long and illustrious reign, so far, that will now be reviewed.

1. Pitt-Rivers, 4
2. Notwithstanding the support of Montgomery the grey beret failed to secure War Office approval.
3. The only reason a horsed cavalry division was kept on the wartime establishment was the lack of sufficient mechanised equipment to convert all the regiments.
4. A most graphic account of the rigours of this journey is given by Col Smiley in his autobiographical *Irregular Regular*
5. RHG supplementary reserve, 1938; MP, 1935-51
6. Household Cavalry students of the campaign would do well to read de Chair's book in conjunction with Colonel Wyndham's history of 1HCR
7. De Chair, 195-6
8. Second World War, Vol III (*The Grand Alliance*), appx G page 622 (Reprint Society)
9. Major General R E Laycock CB DSO (1907-68) Chief of Combined Operations (1943-7), Governor of Malta (1954-9)
10. In order to get their letters past the censors, without interference, Hamilton-Russell and his wife wrote to one another in hunting code. Hamilton-Russell's, written the day before El Alamein, starts 'Darling, I am just off to Kirby Gate, my coat is smart, my top boots polished, my horses's mane plaited and lovely ... the scent is good, the country the cream... the whole pack of bitches and dogs ... and riding our best horses'.
11. Reminiscences, 97
12. Pitt-Rivers, 60
13. Ibid 84
14. Wyndham, 104
15. Ibid, 116
16. The 'Lieutenant Colonel Commanding the Household Cavalry' although a full Colonel, is technically 'Lieutenant Colonel to the two Regimental Colonels'
17. From approximately 15 officers and 350 other ranks to 40 and 700 respectively
18. This had been formed under command of Capt Lord Sudeley, RHG, in 1940
19. Gen Leese left to take over a corps in the Western Desert in September, 1942
20. Quoted by Orde, 102-3
21. Foreword to Orde, viii
22. Pitt-Rivers, 108
23. An accomplished horseman and equitation instructor, Thompson was to be appointed Lieutenant and Riding Master to the Household Cavalry in the 1950s
24. Orde, 287
25. Ibid, 325-6
26. Ibid, 386
27. Wyndham, 145
28. But 1HCR and 2HCR did not assume their new titles until August.
29. The others were the King's Dragoon Guards, 11th Hussars, 12th Lancers, 13th/18th Hussars, 15th/19th Hussars and 16th/5th Lancers
30. See page 67 of *The Story of The Blues and Royals*
31. Quoted from *A Modern Major-General: The Memoirs of Julian Gascoigne (1903-1990),* Edited by Merida Drysdale and Bamber Gascoigne (privately published, 1992)

16 ELIZABETH II

(1) FOUR REGIMENTS 1952-69

This section of the Queen's reign surveys, briefly, the stories of four regiments from the accession to the spring of 1969. Those four – as at the end of the last chapter – are The Life Guards, the Royal Horse Guards, the Household Cavalry Mounted Regiment and the Royal Dragoons.[1]

THE MOUNTED REGIMENT

Before the Second World War the King's Life Guard, mounted since the 17th century at the Horse Guards, Whitehall, was found – day in, day out every year – by either The Life Guards or The Blues, according to which Regiment was stationed in London. Now the composite Mounted Regiment, firmly established at the end of the last reign, was, as it remains today, based on two sabre squadrons,[2] which alternate in finding what became, on February 7, 1952, The Queen's Life Guard – a 'long' guard, composed of an officer, a corporal-major (carrying a Squadron Standard) and 15 other ranks, when the Monarch is in London; or a 'short' guard of 13 men, under a corporal-of-horse, when she is away. There are three regular State occasions when the Household Cavalry turn out en masse. Those are for the Sovereign's escorts furnished for the Queen's Birthday Parade, in June, and the State Opening of Parliament (when there is also a staircase party at the House of Lords) in November. The third is to line the route, dismounted, and to find a staircase party for the annual Garter ceremony. There are generally at least two other events during the year requiring escorts (such as visits by foreign Heads of State).

The Mounted Regiment has, since 1952, been an independent, self-contained Lieutenant Colonel's command, with its own medical, veterinary, catering, rough riding (equitation) and farrier staffs, along with its own procedures, in cooperation with the Royal Army Veterinary Corps, for the purchase and training of remounts – black horses for the troops, greys for the trumpeters, skewbalds, piebalds or greys for the mounted drums. During the period under review the mounted squadrons followed one another to the summer camp (at Stoney Castle, Pirbright, Surrey) so that one squadron remained in London to mount the Queen's Life Guard. But that arrangement was soon to change.

It was in the early 1960s that the Government decision was taken to rebuild Hyde Park Barracks. During demolition and the building of the present barracks (1965-9) alternative accommodation was found for the Mounted Regiment at Wellington Barracks, Birdcage Walk, temporary stables and a riding school being erected on the sides of the barrack square. The announcement that the Royal Horse Guards were to merge with the Royal Dragoons came three years before the Mounted Regiment rode from Wellington to the new Hyde Park.

It has often been claimed that the Household Cavalry's mounted dutymen have a busier routine than any other soldiers in the Army. By no means all mounted dutymen were sent for tours of duty with their respective service Regiment; and there was always quite a high proportion of regular officers, noncommissioned officers and troopers with the armoured cars who were never posted to Hyde Park Barracks. During the period of National Service the Mounted Regiment was composed entirely of regulars.

HOME AND ABROAD IN THE '50S AND '60S

Until the late 1940s the Regiments of Household Cavalry had never served abroad except in wartime. That policy was not to be repeated after 1945.

For the first decade of the Queen's reign the two service Regiments, along with the

Inspection of The Life Guards by their Colonel in Windsor Great Park, 1958. The inspecting party is composed of (*left to right*) Major A J Dickinson, Royal Horse Guards, Regimental Adjutant Household Cavalry; Major I B Baillie, Squadron Leader; Lieutenant Colonel A Meredith Hardy, Commanding Officer; Captain R I Ferguson, Adjutant; Field Marshal Lord Harding of Petherton, Colonel of the Regiment; Colonel W H Gerard Leigh, Officer Commanding the Household Cavalry; and W O I Henderson, the Regimental Corporal Major

Royal Dragoons, continued to form three of the Army's nine wheeled armoured car regiments – until the early 1960s when it was decided that all the Cavalry of the Line and the Royal Tank Regiment, too, should alternate between tanks and armoured cars.

Between 1945 and 1992 the Household Cavalry was normally represented by one service Regiment at Windsor, the other being abroad. The main role of the home service Regiment was, as it remains, within the order of battle of the Strategic Reserve. Apart from training to fulfil that function, employment was also found for them, when expedient, in such unsoldierly tasks as substituting for workers on strike, or filling sandbags and helping to reinforce our North Sea wall during a time of flooding. They were also called upon to protect vulnerable places against the possibility of airborne landings by Warsaw Pact forces. The second function of the home-based regiment, during the 1950s and '60s, was to provide basic training for the recruits of both Regiments. The Household Cavalry avoided conversion to tanks (until 1969) because it was the Sovereign's express wish that one of the Regiments should be at Windsor, where it is not expedient to station tanks.

Until the collapse of the Soviet threat, the dissolution of the Warsaw Pact and the end of the Cold War I (British) Corps stood in Western Germany in the forefront of the NATO shield with three armoured car regiments ready to deploy as the ground 'eyes and ears' of the British Army of the Rhine, in the event of an attack across the 'Iron Curtain'. (The object of that barrier of wire, guard dogs and watch towers, incidentally, was less to deter the Allies than to prevent unhappy East Germans – Communist Germany's essential labour force – from escaping to the West.)

Those three Corps armoured car regiments invariably included either The Life Guards, The Blues or the Royal Dragoons. They remained based on the Daimler armoured car and the Daimler Scout car (Dingo) until the mid-to-late 1950s, a period which marked the advent of a new fleet of vehicles, six-wheeled Saladins (mounting 76 mm guns), Ferret scout cars (with .30 Browning machine guns) and the troop-carrying Saracens, which also served as command vehicles. Armoured car regiments spent a high proportion of their time on the BAOR commitment (although not nearly so high as tank regiments did on their commitment).

This being the heyday of National Service, the Regimental year in the Rhine Army began with trade training and testing. It continued in the spring, for the most part, with troop training, which progressed in the summer, to squadron and regimental training and culminated, in the autumn, with formation manoeuvres. Regiments had also to be ready, at very short notice if necessary, to 'bomb up' and deploy to battle stations. But a large proportion of a Rhine Army soldier's time was spent at sport and other recreational activities, and great trouble was taken within the squadrons to keep men entertained on free afternoons and evenings.

The Household Cavalry in BAOR stabled a number of black horses, primarily with which to train volunteers for the Mounted Regiment, but also for recreational and competition purposes; and, eventually, with which to ride with the Weser Vale bloodhounds, the hunt founded by The Blues and Royals³ at Detmold in 1969.

At the start of the Queen's reign The Life Guards were with the Rhine Army and The Blues were at Windsor. The Royal Dragoons were in Egypt's Canal Zone – until 1954, when The Life Guards relieved them. In 1955 a squadron of The Life Guards was sent, briefly, to underpin the British forces in Aden; and, at the end of the year, the same squadron was dispatched (again, briefly) to Cyprus where the security situation had become tense owing to the Greek Cypriot demand for '*Enosis*', or 'Union with Greece', while that movement's terrorist organisation, EOKA, had 'declared war' on the British administration.

Meanwhile, the Royal Horse Guards (who were themselves soon destined for that troubled island) and the Household Cavalry Training Cadre (which was under their command) had been living a very full life at Windsor between 1952 and 1955, during which time the demolition of the Victorian Combermere buildings began in preparation for the erection of the present barracks.

The Blues had, among a host of other experiences, played their part at the Coronation; mourned the death of their friend, Queen Mary; received (with The Life Guards) new Standards from the Queen; won the 1954 Cavalry Cup (Association Football); produced pentathlon, swimming, fencing and equestrian champions; helped, with the cooperation of the Duke of Edinburgh, to found the Guards Polo Club; gained the Household Cavalry's first toehold in the Guards Independent Parachute Company⁴; and converted to the new two-man Ferret Scout car which was to stand them in such good stead during their three and a half years

of anti-terrorist operations in Cyprus, where they were to be in a state of frequent triumph and occasional tragedy (1956-9).

The Royals, having left Egypt and received a new guidon at Tidworth, returned to Rhine Army, first to The Blues' old station, Combermere Barracks, Wesendorf, then to Harewood Barracks, Herford, which was to be another Household Cavalry home-from-home. The Life Guards were on stand-by for the Suez campaign of the autumn of 1956. A contingent sailed to the eastern Mediterranean. But, in the event of the

Members of the Royal Horse Guards performing an act in the Regimental revue *Watch your Backs!* performed in Cyprus in the Spring of 1959. (*left to right*) Corporals-of-Horse R Taylor, P Roper and R Hoggarth

A Saladin armoured car and Ferret scout car of The Life Guards on convoy duty on the hazardous Dhala Road in Aden

The Blues marching through Windsor on May 19, 1959, having returned from their triumphant tour of Internal Security duties in Cyprus. They are led by their commanding officer, Lieutenant Colonel the Hon Julian Berry, OBE

Aden which had been long claimed by the Imams of Yemen. From there they detached a squadron to Oman (where Colonel David Smiley, of The Blues, commanded the Sultan's Forces – resisting rebellion by the tribal leaders – with Major Kenneth Timbrell, of the Royals, as his DAA and QMG). Another squadron was later detached to Sharjah on the Gulf.

Sweltering in temperatures of over 130° Fahrenheit, The Life Guards' 'D' Squadron lost eighty per cent of their scout cars through enemy action in the space of three months. For one offensive against the rebels in their mountain stronghold a dismounted troop – with 56-lb packs and Browning machine guns carried on donkeys – was found from the Squadron. A surprise attack by that troop, with the SAS, forced the rebels out, and they narrowly avoided capture by an armoured car troop as they fled to Saudi Arabia.

In November, 1959, The Life Guards handed over their Aden commitments – including the hazardous Dhala road convoy, and the squadron detachment at Sharjah – to the Royals. But the Royals spent only one year in the Middle East before being dispatched to Malaya, with one squadron in Singapore, Britain being pledged to underpin

quickly curtailed Operation Musketeer (November 5-7) only one of their vehicles was disembarked at Port Said. At Windsor they pioneered the Household Cavalry's airportable role and, in August, 1958, they proceeded to the British Protectorate of

In 1960 the Royals proceeded from Aden to Malaysia. Here a Ferret Scout car crew cover a foot patrol across a ford in Malaysia

Soon after converting to Centurion tanks during the winter of 1962-3, at Tidworth, two squadrons of the Royals found themselves with Ferret scout cars again, 'keeping the peace' in Cyprus. The troop shown in this picture was fresh from intervening in a feud between Turkish and Greek villagers. (Public Relations Strategic Reserve)

the new Federation of Malaysia. By October, 1962, the Royal Dragoons were at Tidworth converting to Centurion tanks. In 1963 they celebrated their Centenary (which occurred in 1961) by exercising their privilege of marching through the City of London with 'Guidon flying, drums beating and bayonets fixed'.

The Blues, following their anti-terrorist campaign in Cyprus, found themselves at Windsor, in an exciting airportable role (with the 1st Guards Brigade group) before returning to Cyprus for four months in 1960. Independence had by no means brought peace to that island, where hostility between the Greek and Turkish Cypriots was on the boil. In 1961 The Blues celebrated their Tercentenary; and, in 1962, flew back to Germany, and to Herford, to those good barracks previously occupied by the Royals, and, since 1960, by The Life Guards, whom they relieved. On May 26, 1965, The Blues took part in the Rhine Army parade for the Queen, at Sennelager, the largest ever of its kind, as did the Royals. The Blues returned to Combermere in 1966.

1960 had been a particularly intensive year for the Mounted Regiment. Apart from their regular commitments there were heavy programmes for the State visits of President de Gaulle, the King and Queen of Thailand and the King and Queen of Nepal, not to mention Princess Margaret's wedding. But then no year was other than action-packed for the Mounted Regiment. Five years later the Household Cavalry were honoured with the Freedom of Windsor.

The Life Guards, back at Windsor, were now (1963) on the two-squadron airportable basis, each squadron deploying five troops, each of four Ferret scout cars. In January, 1964, they found a squadron for the United Nations force in Cyprus (UNFICYP). Soon that squadron was joined by another and subsequently by regimental headquarters. They were home at the end of 1964, but not for long, being warned for duty in Malaysia the following Spring. For this they were reinforced with a squadron of The Blues. They flew to the Far East and occupied camps at Seremban (Western Malaysia), Sarawak and at Singapore. With the Chinese fomenting unrest in Hong Kong, in 1968, a Life Guards squadron was sent to give a hand in quelling the consequent riots in the Colony, their hosts being 48 Gurkha Brigade. The Regiment returned to Windsor in 1969 to adopt a new role as the reconnaissance element of the Allied Command Europe (ACE) Mobile Force – more elaborately known as Allied Command Europe Mobile Force Land Component (AMF(L)), a roving mission which took them to the NATO flanks, anywhere between Norway and Turkey, so that the Household Cavalry were to divide much of their time during the 1970s

Early in 1963 the Royals received the Freedom of the City of London. Here are their trumpeters at Armoury House on the day, with (*behind*) Major J A Dimond, MC (second-in-command) and (*right*) Lieutenant Colonel R E (later General Sir Richard) Worsley, Commanding Officer. (Photo: Kenneth Balfour)

between the snow-clad north and the gruelling temperatures of the eastern Mediterranean.

In 1969, The Life Guards were, in addition to their many other responsibilities, the first to represent the Household Cavalry with a squadron in strife-torn Northern Ireland. It was the year, too, in which the Royal Horse Guards merged with the Royal Dragoons to form a new Regiment of Household Cavalry, The Blues and Royals.

(2) THREE REGIMENTS 1969-92

When, in the mid-1960s, the Government announced that there was to be a further

Field Marshal Sir Gerald Templer, KG GCB GCMG KBE DSO. He was Colonel of the Royal Horse Guards from 1962 to 1969 and of The Blues and Royals from 1969 until his death in 1979. He was the principal mastermind behind the working of the amalgamation

series of Defence cuts, it was made clear that the number of armoured and armoured car regiments would be much reduced. The Life Guards felt relatively safe. For their 'Firsts' and 'Seconds' – two Regiments as different in character and outlook as any two in the Cavalry of the Line – were fused into one after the First World War, as we saw in Chapter 13. Only three cavalry regiments, the Royal Horse Guards (Household Cavalry) and the Royal Dragoons and the Royal Scots Greys (Royal Armoured Corps) had so far escaped any form of amalgamation. All three were promptly made aware that they could not remain untouched. And very soon General Sir Desmond Fitzpatrick, Colonel of the Royals, was telling the commanding officer that it was now a question of 'with whom'?

The Royals' first instinct was to unite with their old comrades in the Union Brigade, the Greys (2nd Dragoons). But, since the Greys was essentially a Scottish regiment, recruiting from Scotland, the Royals feared they would lose their own identity in such a move. They shared quite a substantial common heritage with The Blues, who were old friends and who looked upon them as the next best Regiment in the Army. Thus General Fitzpatrick (who was then vice Chief of the General Staff) approached Field Marshal Sir Gerald Templer, The Blues Colonel, who told him 'we have been expecting you!' The Regiments could not have asked for two finer soldiers than those to negotiate the details of the merger.

To take up the thread of the Royals' story, from the early '60s, they had scarcely completed their full conversion to tanks at the end of 1962 and early in 1963 than two of their squadrons found themselves in Cyprus with Ferret scout cars. Eighteen months later they left Tidworth to join 20th Armoured Brigade at Detmold. They were still there at the end of 1967 when the announcement of the forthcoming amalgamation with The Blues reached them; and still there in 1968-9.

The Blues were at Windsor when they received the news that they would next be doing a stint with tanks. Shortly after that they heard that they were to merge with the Royals.

Lieutenant Colonel Richard Vickers, a former Royal Tank Regiment officer, who had transferred to the Royals to command them in July, 1968, was selected to lead the new

In October, 1970, the Household Cavalry Mounted Regiment rode from their temporary accommodation at Wellington Barracks into the new Hyde Park Barracks. Here the two Colonels, Admiral of the Fleet Earl Mountbatten of Burma (Life Guards) and Field Marshal Sir Gerald Templer (Blues and Royals) return the salute of the Blues and Royals squadron as they enter the new entrance for the first time. (*Soldier* Magazine)

Regiment which was formally united at the Royals station, Hobart Barracks, Detmold, on March 29, 1969. Field Marshal Templer, their Colonel, took the vesting parade, two days later, at which he read out the loyal address to the Queen. On April 2 Her Majesty inspected the Queens's Life Guard, that being the first occasion on which a Sovereign had done so. Most of the initial Royals volunteers for mounted duty found the Knightsbridge challenge more difficult than they had imagined it would be, and failed to pass out of riding school. However, by the Spring of 1969, the situation had improved, and former Royals were well represented in the Queen's Life Guard of April 2.

1969 was another especially onerous year for the Mounted Regiment. After the vesting parade for the Blues and Royals squadron at Wellington Barracks there was the Italian State visit (to Windsor), the State Opening of the General Assembly of the Church of Scotland, the State Visit of the President of Finland and the Investiture of the Prince of Wales at Caernarvon. On October 22, 1970, the Mounted Regiment rode out of their temporary accommodation at Wellington Barracks and into the new Hyde Park Barracks.

The Army's battle tank was now Chieftain, and Colonel Vickers, a leading exponent on tank tactics and battle drills and weaponry, welded The Blues and Royals with consummate success. Among the new

Regiment's 1969 sporting triumphs were the Rhine Army section of the Cavalry Cup and the inter-regimental polo. They led the way in that theatre, too, in skiing, canoeing, hockey and, of course, equitation. They also had much fun with, and scored renown with, too, the Weser Vale Bloodhounds. The Blues and Royals were at Lothian Barracks, Detmold, until 1971 when they were due for a first tour at Combermere.

A scene in the new barracks. (*Soldier* Magazine)

A Life Guards Scorpion crew in Norway. They were a part of the Force Reconnaissance Squadron Allied Command Europe (ACE), a role which helped to keep the Household Cavalry busy during the 1970s

Meanwhile, during the late 1960s, the Household Cavalry, who had hitherto always provided the basic training for their recruits, ceased to do so. For the following twenty-five years they were to be trained, along with the Foot Guards, at the Guards Depot, Pirbright Camp.

Next to Pirbright were the pavilions, horse lines and fields reserved for the Mounted Regiment's annual camps. Up to the early 1970s the two Squadrons spent their annual fortnight there by rotation. Subsequently, it was decided to camp the whole Regiment together, The King's Troop, Royal Horse Artillery, mounting the Queen's Life Guard for the period concerned. Since then the annual camp has been established at other sites, and the horses conveyed thither in boxes.

While The Blues and Royals were pulling together as a tank regiment, The Life Guards had been busy in Ulster and in providing the reconnaissance squadron for Allied Command Europe (ACE) Mobile Force – a role on the NATO flanks which took them anywhere between frozen Norway and blazing Turkey. There was also a squadron in Oman for nine months (at Sharjah again), whose principal duty was to patrol the Trucial States. In the autumn of 1971 it was The Life Guards' turn for Detmold. Nor were units in Rhine Army any longer exempt from tours of duty in Ulster. There was – in what was known as the 'Tin City', at Sennelager – a Northern Ireland Training and Advisory Team (NITAT) at which all BAOR units, or sub-units,

destined for duty in Ulster, were trained, with special emphasis on physical fitness, weapon handling and marksmanship. When required to act as infantry in the Province, the Household Cavalry formed 'rifle squadrons'. And they performed as infantry with the vigilance and expertise of the best of them.

This, too, was the era of the 'battle group' – two armoured regiments, one of gunners, a battalion of infantry and a field squadron of Sappers[5]. To train as a member of such a group the Household Cavalry Regiment stationed in Germany was flown for annual intensive combined exercises at the Suffield training area, in Alberta, Canada.

In 1988 the Household Cavalry's Rhine Army station was moved from Detmold to Sennelager. In 1990 there was a new battle tank, the Challenger, to be mastered. Meanwhile, for the armoured car role at Windsor, the wheeled Saladin and Ferret had been replaced with the cross-country tracked Scorpion and Scimitar.

The calendar for 1977, Jubilee Year, was, of course, prominently packed for the Mounted Regiment. Among other tasks they entrained their horses for the Queen's visit to Glasgow, where they billeted them in the freezing cold of a lairage (animal market); then advanced to Edinburgh where, among other duties, there was a Captain's Escort to be furnished for the Thistle Ceremony. As for the Blues and Royals, in Germany, they played a leading part in the Queen's review of the Rhine Army at Sennelager.

In 1979 both The Life Guards and The Blues and Royals lost their Colonels. Lord Mountbatten (Colonel Dickie),[6] who had succeeded Field Marshal Lord Harding (Colonel John) in 1965, was followed, as Colonel of The Life Guards, by Major General Lord Michael Fitzalan Howard, a former commander of the Household Division. The death, in October, of Field Marshal Sir Gerald Templer (Major General Sir Richard Howard Vyse's successor) demanded a new Colonel of the Blues and Royals. The Queen duly appointed Colonel Gerald's distinguished deputy, General Sir Desmond Fitzpatrick, a former commanding officer of the Royals.

The interchange between Windsor and Germany continued throughout the 1970s and '80s, with much the same hectic programmes. The ACE Mobile Force commitment ended in 1977, but there were a great variety of other roles for the squadrons. During the late 1970s the Windsor-based Regiment came to the rescue on the occasion of the bakers' strike and again for that of the firemen, and they provided escorts for the movement of American intercontinental Cruise missiles. In the 1980s a troop or two were flown to Belize (formerly British Honduras) as an added deterrent against threatening Guatemala. And, when the hijacking of aircraft was rife, the Household Cavalry were required to send armoured patrols to Heathrow.

BLUES AND ROYALS FOR THE FALKLANDS, MAY-JUNE, 1982

The Spring of 1982 found 'A' Squadron of The Blues and Royals in Cyprus, 'C' on block leave and 'B' at Combermere. On April 4, when the commanding officer (Lieutenant Colonel James Hamilton-Russell) received the order to provide two reconnaissance troops (each two Scorpions, two Scimitars) and a REME Light Aid Detachment for embarkation with the Task Force, for the reoccupation of the Falklands, on April 6, half 'B' Squadron were on Easter leave. Fortunately, however, there were two troops available at Combermere, those commanded by Lieutenant Mark Coreth (with Corporal-of-Horse Stretton) and Lieutenant Lord Robin Innes-Ker (with Corporal-of-Horse Thompson).

Having tested their guns on Ascension Island, crossed to the South Atlantic and been landed at San Carlos on May 21, the two

troops, the sole representatives of British armour in the campaign, proved their usefulness beyond all expectations. Their fighting vehicles rode the boggy ground well and they covered the distances much faster than the higher commanders had anticipated. They were strafed from the air, mined and sniped at. But, except for the loss of one Scorpion, they escaped injury. They did invaluable work setting up observaton posts and reporting Argentine movement, with casualty evacuation, and in re-supplying the forward troops with ammunition. Above all, their well-trained commanders and crewmen provided magnificent fire support with their 30mm Rarden cannons, 76mm guns and their respective coaxial machine guns. It was clear that, if they had been employed in support of the Parachute Regiment at Goose Green, many casualties might have been avoided. (In fact, Colonel H. Jones had asked for them but had been refused.) The Blues and Royals returned to their ship on June 24 and were back at Combermere by mid-July.

Brigadier Thompson, comanding 3 Royal Marines Commando, wrote to Colonel Hamilton-Russell: 'I was most impressed by both troops ... they did all that was asked of them in great style and were not deterred by anything ... I found everybody in both troops well mannered, well turned out in all circumstances, calm and collected – which is, if I may say so, what I would expect of Household Cavalrymen.' The Battle Honour 'Falkland Islands 1982' now adorns their Standards.[7]

A Squadron of Life Guards Chieftain tanks at Soltau, Germany in 1989. They are rehearsing a leaguer position prior to flying to the British Army training base at Suffield, Alberta, Canada

With the Airborne Forces asking for close light armoured support – following their Falklands experience – The Life Guards, their Scorpions and a number of their personnel were rendered parachutable in the late 1980s. (They manned the Pathfinder Platoon of the 5th Airborne Brigade.) That, coupled with the dismounted role in Northern Ireland, prompted the Regiments to set higher standards of physical fitness, a condition which is still very evident among all ranks.

ATTACK ON THE QUEEN'S LIFE GUARD, JULY 20, 1982

The Household Cavalry can never forgive the IRA for the iniquitous attack made on the Queen's Life Guard on July 20, 1982. That morning, at 10.40, as a Blues and Royals Guard rode along Hyde Park's South Carriageway, the IRA detonated, by radio control, a car bomb of gelignite-based explosive, containing 30lbs of nails. They thus murdered the Guard commander, Lieutenant Anthony Daly, his Corporal-Major, Roy Bright, Lance-Corporal Jeffery Young and Trooper Simon Tipper. Seven horses were killed, or had to be put down. Three other horses, though dreadfully injured, made remarkable recoveries. Of those Sefton, who lost over a gallon of blood, became a national legend and was nominated 'Horse of the Year' at Wembley.

Ever since that horrific incident of 1982

the Queen's Life Guard have brought their swords down from the 'slope' to the 'carry' to pay tribute, as they have passed the spot, with an 'eyes left' (or 'eyes right' returning to barracks).

LIFE GUARDS IN THE GULF WAR, 1990-1

The Iraqis, laying a false claim to the oilfields of Kuwait, invaded and annexed that State early in August, 1990 (and apparently threatened Saudi Arabia, too). The United States, Britain and France, along with the United Nations, demanded the unconditional withdrawal of the Iraqi forces, which was refused. Whereupon a resolution was made to drive them out and to restore the status quo ante. The Life Guards, then with Rhine Army, were required to provide a squadron to strengthen the 14th/20th Hussars in 4th Armoured brigade. 'B' and 'C' squadrons of The Life Guards being then at the Suffield Training Area, in Canada, the task fell to 'A' Squadron. Following a period of intensive training in Germany with the 14th/20th, 'A' Squadron flew to Saudi Arabia in December, while the remainder of the Regiment, 'B' and 'C' squadrons, were also dis-patched to the Gulf as back-ups and, in particular, to supply 'battle casualty replacements'.

By mid-January General Norman Schwarz-kopf, of the United States Army, the Allied commander-in-chief, had 350,000 men under his command. By that time, too, the worst of Saddam Hussein's Scud attacks on Israel and Saudi Arabia were over; and, by the third week of January, the Allied invasion of Iraq and Kuwait had begun.

Clad in protective suits, against the anticipated Iraqi 'chemical warfare' attacks, The Life Guards, with their Challenger tanks, entered Iraq alongside the Ist Battalion of the Royal Scots on February 25, their mission being to attack the enemy in three phases. Firing their 120mm main armament and coaxial machine guns they took the enemy in rear, and completely by surprise, inflicting many casualties, while Iraqi soldiers streamed past them, hands up, by the hundreds. And so the Household Cavalrymen drove on for phases two and three of their offensive, using their thermal observation gunnery sights to pick out targets during the hours of darkness.

Before dawn on February 27, they were ordered to a position on the north-west side

Life Guardsmen posing in front on one of their Challenger tanks during the Gulf War, 1991

The musical ride
practising in Hyde Park

of Kuwait City, and there they remained for a fortnight. They returned to Germany on July 1.[8]

(3) TWO REGIMENTS

In the meantime, the Cold War having ended and the Warsaw Pact having been dismantled, it was not long before the Treasury were demanding yet more severe Defence cuts. And the Army Board decided that the Household Cavalry must be reduced to one service Regiment. The compromise was that neither Regiment was to lose its identity but there should be a 'Union' of the two service Regiments.

In 1992, The Life Guards were withdrawn from Germany and a new armoured reconnaissance Regiment was formed at Windsor, composed of two squadrons of Life Guards and two from The Blues and Royals, with a mixed headquarters squadron. The establishment of the Mounted Regiment was, as it remains, unaffected by the 'Union'. Nor has there been any further reduction in the strengths of the two Regimental bands.

BANDS, TRUMPETERS AND THE MUSICAL RIDE

The bands of The Life Guards and The Blues and Royals have heavy programmes of engagements – State, charity and other events – throughout the year. Their three principal mounted commitments are for the Queen's Birthday Parade, Beating Retreat and the Lord Mayor's Show. They also furnish an integral part of the Household Cavalry musical ride, which, apart from the band, consists of 16 men (8 from each Regiment) of the display team (carrying lances), four trumpeters and a drummer (the drum horse being adorned with the famous kettle drums). The ride performs annually at the Royal Windsor Horse Show and the Royal Tournament, and tours throughout the summer, nationally and internationally, raising money for charities and helping to recruit for the Regiments – apart, of course, from providing magnificent entertainment.

All Household Cavalry musicians are trained as medical orderlies (and were employed as such during the Second World War). In 1989 they had an active role during the ambulance dispute. In 1991 they were included in the United Kingdom Casualty Evacuation (UKCE) plan; and, since then, some of them have been employed in a medical role in Bosnia.

The State trumpeters are to be seen – and heard blowing their fanfares – on nearly all State occasions, their two regular annual events being the State Opening of Parliament and the Garter ceremony.

The two bands interchange between Knightsbridge and Windsor every four years.

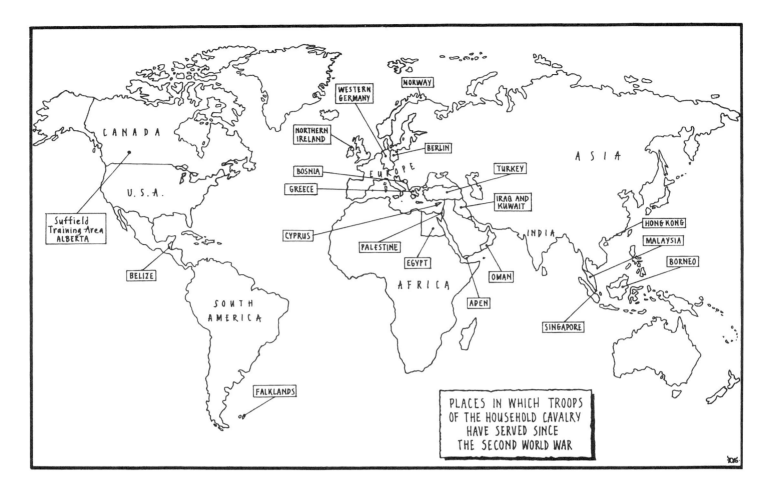

PLACES IN WHICH TROOPS
OF THE HOUSEHOLD CAVALRY
HAVE SERVED SINCE
THE SECOND WORLD WAR

Places in which troops of the
Household Cavalry have served
since the Second World War

THE HOUSEHOLD CAVALRY REGIMENT (ARMOURED)

The Regiment at Windsor is now (1996) based on the tracked armoured reconnaissance vehicle Scimitar, with its 30mm cannon and 7.62 mm coaxial machine gun. Of those there are three troops to each of the four sabre squadrons, each troop having four Scimitars, a total of 48 Scimitars. A fourth troop in each squadron contains four Striker anti-tank guided-weapon carriers. The establishment of a medium armoured car reconnaissance squadron also carries a fifth troop with four Spartans (turretless Scimitars), each designed to hold a crew of three, plus four troopers for dismounted work. But, at the time of writing, the Regiment lacks sufficient manpower to deploy those.

HCR is under command of the Third Division, for which it contributes a squadron for the Joint Rapid Deployment Force, a contingent of brigade strength prepared to go, at short notice, to any trouble spot. The 5th Airborne Brigade may also call upon the Regiment for both a squadron and an airborne troop, while the strength of 3

Commando Brigade also includes a potential squadron from Windsor. In addition the Regiment has a commitment in Cyprus. But, for the time being, HCR's principal task is in Bosnia.

BOSNIA

As most qualified observers in the world concede, the British contingent in the service of the United Nations in Bosnia-Hercegovina has been second to none in the execution of its duties.

At the time of writing, the Household Cavalry alternate with the Light Dragoons (who are stationed with I Division in Germany) in representing the British cavalry with two squadrons in Bosnia, operating as part of the International Peace Implementation Force. The tour of duty is for six months. Their first task is to assist the inhabitants of Bosnia-Hercegovina to live in the best possible conditions of peace and security, their second role being 'to enhance the provision of humanitarian assistance'. Apart from the routine convoy escorts the Household Cavalry squadrons have, often on

An armoured reconnaissance squadron of The Blues and Royals in full battle order, at Combermere Barracks, Windsor in the Summer of 1996

their own initiative, carried out a wide range of incidental missions – repairing schools, for example, laying on medical patrols to places normally inaccessible to doctors and providing aid for shell-damaged houses. Before proceeding to Bosnia the squadrons undergo several weeks of specialist refresher training. In an article in *The Guards Magazine* a former commanding officer of the Regiment concludes that

> ... The effort we have put into these tasks has been questioned by some. One can only say that unless we had done so we could have been perceived, in our own and the locals' eyes, as merely spectators in someone else's war. The work we have done has helped to give our presence legitimacy in the eyes of the local civil and military authorities and, by gradually returning life to a measure of normality, has given the local Croat and Muslim population a stake in avoiding a return to hostilities, certainly between themselves and, perhaps, in the longer term, between themselves and the Serbs. Last but not least ... the requirement to provide aid in an area where 50,000 of the estimated population of 150,000 are Displaced Persons,where the industry is in ruins and the principal towns are regularly shelled, has been indisputable.[9]

THE FUTURE

The army reforms of 1992 included the abolition of the Junior Leaders Regiment (Royal Armoured Corps) which had been an excellent, if small, fount of recruits.[10] The Guards Depot, which had served the Household Cavalry so admirably for a quarter of a century, was also done away with. But their recruits still go to Pirbright, to the Guards Company of the Army Training Regiment – where they fulfil the first 10 weeks of their service. The second-in-command and several instructors of that sub-unit being Household Cavalrymen, recruits are well briefed as to terms of service and what careers await them both at Windsor and Knightsbridge. The two Regiments have been receiving about half each of the volunteers from Pirbright. On principle, those going to Knightsbridge will complete a three-year tour there including their initial 20 weeks riding school, before being posted to Windsor. Those volunteering for the service Regiment must later fulfil their stint at Knightsbridge if they are to have a comprehensive future as NCOs.

In the days when the Household Cavalry rejoiced in two service Regiments the problem of reconciling the dual career – fighting role and mounted duty – presented few serious problems. The Life Guards and The Blues and Royals each looked after their respective mounted squadron, in terms of manpower, from relatively liberal resources. Since 1992 the situation has become much more brittle. And it is exacerbated by the fact that the 'teeth arms' – and particularly armoured and armoured car regiments –

have become increasingly technical and sophisticated. So that the contrast between being employed as an armoured vehicle commander or crewman and that of a mounted dutyman at Knightsbridge becomes more and more acute. This situation has a potentially adverse effect on careers, especially those of NCOs who, following, say a two-year tour at Knightsbridge, find themselves 'rusty' and probably behind, too, on the technical know-how when they return to Windsor.

However, the Regiments of Household Cavalry have found themselves in many fraught circumstances in their history of loyal service through fifteen reigns. From Sedgemoor to Bosnia they have trained and bivouacked and stabled and messed and crewed and fought together in happy comradeship. Being famous for their flexibility in the maintenance of the highest standards of performance, they have always contrived to meet new problems with a determined and cheerful approach. May that always be so.

1. The period 1952-69 on p.165 of this chapter is intended only to be a general survey of the Regiments' histories. For greater detail and chronological sequence see *Challengers and Chargers* and *The Story of the Blues and Royals*

2. Until the late 1960s the Regiments' staff personnel were incorporated in The Blues squadron, since when there has been a small, separate headquarters squadron.

3. The WVH had, in fact, been an inspiration of the Royal Horse Guards in 1968

4. Disbanded, October, 1975

5. The classic brigade group at this time was the 'square brigade' based on two armoured regiments and two battalions.

6. Lord Mountbatten was murdered by the IRA in Ireland a few days before the first Life Guards squadron was dispatched to Londonderry

7. For a fuller report on the Regiment's part in the Falklands Campaign see *The Story of The Blues and Royals*, pp271-85

8. For a fuller account of The Life Guards in the Gulf see *Challengers and Chargers* pp129-41

9. *The Household Cavalry Regiment in Bosnia – Winter 1994-5* by Lt Colonel W R Rollo, The Blues and Royals, in *The Guards* Magazine (Autumn, 1995)

10. It is hoped, at the time of writing, that the JLR (RAC) will be revived.

The Horse Guards, Whitehall

APPENDICES

A GOLD AND SILVER STICK

The following paragraphs from Regimental Standing Orders appertain to the Colonelcy-in-Chief and the Offices of Gold and Silver Stick.

The Colonel-in-Chief

Her Majesty Queen Elizabeth II is Colonel-in-Chief of both Regiments of the Household Cavalry.

The reigning Sovereign has been the Colonel-in-Chief since 1821 with the exception of Queen Victoria who never assumed the title of Colonel-in-Chief. Queen Victoria appointed the Prince of Wales to be Colonel-in-Chief of the Household Cavalry in 1880, an appointment which he retained on his succession to the throne.

The Colonels

The Colonels of each Regiment are appointed by Her Majesty The Queen.

The Colonels are to be consulted before any alteration of regimental privilege is agreed to and are to be kept informed by Headquarters Household Cavalry of all important matters affecting their Regiments.

The Gold Stick

The two Colonels of Household Cavalry hold the office of Gold Stick, an appointment in the Royal Household, and are in waiting on alternate months. The name of Gold Stick in Waiting is published each month in a Gold Stick Order. The duties of the Gold Stick are to protect the person of the Sovereign, and to receive and promulgate orders from The Sovereign concerning the Household Cavalry.

In the absence of both Gold Sticks the duties devolve on the Silver Stick in Waiting.

The Silver Stick in Waiting

The Lieutenant Colonel Commanding Household Cavalry holds the office of Silver Stick in Waiting, an appointment in the Royal Household. In the absence of the Gold Stick in Waiting he assumes his duties and precedence at any State Ceremony or Function.

The Silver Stick in Waiting is to be in general charge of all duties found by the Household Cavalry for The Queen in London and Windsor, and elsewhere when ordered. When he rides in carriage processions his place is close behind the Gold Stick. In the absence of the Gold Stick he rides by the right rear wheel of The Queen's carriage

The Silver Stick in Waiting is to be in attendance on the Sovereign on the following occasions:

a. The State Opening of Parliament
b. During a procession from Windsor Castle and in St George's Chapel following a Chapter of the Garter
c. When troops of the Household Cavalry are on duty for The Queen

He will also attend the Proclamation council after the demise of the Sovereign.

In the absence of the Lieutenant Colonel Commanding Household Cavalry, the Gold Stick in Waiting may appoint the Commanding Officer of one of the Regiments of Household Cavalry as Silver Stick in Waiting in his place.

The Adjutant to the Silver Stick in Waiting is called Silver Stick Adjutant. He is to accompany the Silver Stick in Waiting whenever a formed body of Household Cavalry troops are on duty. He is to be present on the Staircase of the House of Lords when The Queen drives in State to Open or Prorogue Parliament, and is to accompany the Silver Stick in the Garter Procession at Windsor. He is on no account to enter the Throne Room.

B COLONELS OF THE REGIMENTS

THE LIFE GUARDS

Captains-Commandant, and Colonels of the First (King's) Troop, 1660-1788.

May 1660	Sep 1668	Lord Gerard of Brandon
Sep 1968	Nov 1679	Duke of Monmouth (First Gold Stick)
Nov 1679	Aug 1685	Duke of Albermarle
Aug 1685	Apr 1689	Earl of Feversham
Apr 1689	Mar 1699	Earl of Scarborough
Mar 1699	Jul 1710	Earl of Albermarle
Jul 1710	Jul 1713	Earl of Portland
Jul 1713	May 1715	Earl of Ashburnham
May 1715	Sep 1721	Duke of Montagu
Sep 1721	Jul 1733	Earl of Pembroke & Montgomery
Jul 1733	Jun 1737	Lord Cutherlough
Jun 1737	Aug 1737	Duke of Montagu
Aug 1737	Mar 1766	Lord Delawarr
Mar 1766	Dec 1777	Earl Delawarr
Dec 1777	Jun 1788	Marquess of Lothian

Colonels of the two Regiments, 1788-1922

THE FIRST REGIMENT

Jun 1788	Mar 1789	Marquess of Lothian
Mar 1789	Dec 1792	Lord Dover
Dec 1792	Sep 1829	Earl of Harrington
Sep 1829	Feb 1865	Viscount Combermere
Feb 1865	Nov 1888	Earl of Lucan
Nov 1888	Nov 1902	Prince Edward of Sax Weimar
Nov 1802	Apr 1907	Lord de Ros
Apr 1907	Mar 1920	Lord Grenfell
Mar 1920	Jul 1922	Viscount Allenby

THE SECOND REGIMENT

Jun 1788	Aug 1797	Lord Amherst
Aug 1797	Jun 1843	Earl Cathcart
Jun 1843	Mar 1854	Marquess of Londonderry
Mar 1854	Apr 1863	Lord Seaton
Apr 1863	Sep 1863	Earl Beauchamp
Sep 1863	Oct 1876	Marquess of Tweeddale
Oct 1876	Jan 1890	Viscount Templeton
Jan 1890	Sep 1900	Earl Howe
Sep 1900	Apr 1905	Lord Chelmsford

THE SECOND REGIMENT *(Continued)*

Apr 1905	Apr 1907	Lord Grenfell
Apr 1907	Feb 1919	Earl of Dundonald
Feb 1919	Jul 1922	Hon Sir Cecil Bingham

THE PRESENT REGIMENT

Jul 1922	May 1936	Viscount Allenby
Jul 1922	May 1934	Hon Sir Cecil Bingham
May 1936	Jan 1957	Earl of Athlone
Apr 1957	Oct 1964	Lord Harding of Petherton
Jan 1965	Aug 1979	Earl Mountbatten of Burma
Aug 1979		Major General Lord Michael Fitzalan Howard

THE ROYAL HORSE GUARDS (THE BLUES)

Feb 1661	Feb 1688	Earl of Oxford
Feb 1668	Nov 1688	Duke of Berwick
Nov 1688	Dec 1688	Earl of Aran
Dec 1688	Mar 1703	Earl of Oxford
Mar 1703	Jan 1712	Duke of Northumberland
Jan 1712	Aug 1712	Earl Rivers
Aug 1712	Jun 1715	Earl of Peterborough
Jun 1715	Mar 1717	Duke of Argyle
Mar 1717	Aug 1733	Duke of Bolton
Aug 1733	May 1740	Duke of Argyle
May 1740	Feb 1742	Earl of Hertford
Feb 1742	Mar 1742	Duke of Argyle
Mar 1742	Feb 1750	Duke of Somerset
Feb 1750	Aug 1750	Duke of Richmond
Jan 1753	May 1758	Sir John Ligonier
May 1758	Oct 1770	Marquess of Granby
Oct 1770	Jul 1795	Field Marshal Conway
Jul 1795	Dec 1806	Duke of Richmond
Dec 1806	Jan 1813	Duke of Northumberland
Jan 1813	Jan 1827	Duke of Wellington (First RHG Gold Stick)
Jan 1827	Nov 1830	Duke of Cumberland
Nov 1830	Dec 1842	Viscount Hill
Dec 1842	May 1854	Marquess of Anglesey
May 1854	Jul 1855	Lord Raglan
Aug 1855	Mar 1869	Viscount Gough
Mar 1869	Oct 1885	Lord Strathnairn
Oct 1885	Mar 1895	Sir Patrick Grant
Mar 1895	Nov 1907	Viscount Wolseley
Nov 1907	Jul 1919	Sir Henry Evelyn Wood
Aug 1919	Jan 1928	Earl Haig
Jan 1928	Feb 1933	Sir William Robertson
Feb 1933	May 1951	Lord Birdwood
May 1951	Dec 1962	Sir Richard Howard Vyse
Dec 1962	Mar 1969	Sir Gerald Templer

1ST THE ROYAL DRAGOONS

King's Own Royal Regiment of Dragoons
(Formed 1683 from the Tangier Horse)

19 Nov 1683	Duke of Marlborough
1 Aug 1685	Viscount Cornbury
24 Nov 1688	Robert Clifford
31 Dec 1688	Viscount Cornbury
1 Jul 1689	Anthony Heyford

The Royal Regiment of Dragoons (from 1690)

21 Jun 1690	Edward Mathews
30 May 1697	Lord Raby (later Earl of Strafford)
13 Jun 1715	Viscount Cobham
10 Apr 1721	Sir Charles Hotham Bt.
12 Jan 1723	Humphrey Gore
1 Sep 1739	Duke of Marlborough (Charles, 3rd Duke)
12 May 1740	Henry Hawley

1st (Royal) Dragoons (from 1751)

5 Apr 1759	Hon Henry Seymour Conway
9 May 1764	Earl of Pembroke
28 Jan 1794	Philip Goldsworthy
7 Jan 1801	Thomas Garth
23 Nov 1829	Lord Edward Somerset
31 Mar 1836	Sir Frederick Ponsonby
20 Jan 1837	Sir Hussey Vivian Bt. (later Lord Vivian)
30 Aug 1842	Arthur Benjamin Clifton
8 Mar 1869	Charles De Ainslie
21 Mar 1889	John Yorke
29 Mar 1890	Sir Frederick Marshall
9 Jun 1900	Francis Russell
22 Mar 1912	Hon John Lindley

1st The Royal Dragoons (from 1920)

16 Apr 1919	Sir John Burn-Murdoch
22 Jan 1931	Sir Ernest Makins
Oct 1946	Francis Wilson-Fitzgerald
9 Dec 1954	Anthony Hilton Pepys
9 Dec 1964	Sir Desmond FitzPatrick

THE BLUES AND ROYALS
(ROYAL HORSE GUARDS AND 1ST DRAGOONS)

1969-79	Sir Gerald Templer
1979	Sir Desmond Fitzpatrick

APPENDIX C

LIEUTENANT COLONELS (SILVER STICK)

This appointment which carries the rank of Colonel was introduced into the Household Cavalry in March, 1943.

Mar 1943	Dec 1944	A H Ferguson	LG
Dec 1944	Sep 1946	Sir Robert Gooch Bt DSO	LG
Sep 1946	Jan 1950	H Abel Smith, DSO	RHG
Jan 1950	Jan 1953	F F B St George CVO	LG
Jan 1953	Mar 1956	E J S Ward MVO MC	LG
Mar 1956	Mar 1959	W H Gerard Leigh	LG
Mar 1959	Apr 1960	Marquess Douro MVO OBE MC	RHG
Apr 1960	Apr 1964	Hon J Berry OBE	RHG
Apr 1964	Oct 1966	D J St M Tabor MC	RHG
Nov 1966	Aug 1969	H S Hopkinson MBE	RHG
Sep 1969	Nov 1972	I B Baillie	LG
Nov 1972	Oct 1975	H D A Langley MBE	LG
Oct 1975	Sep 1978	J A C G Eyre	RHG
Sep 1978	Mar 1981	S C Cooper	LG
Mar 1981	Nov 1982	A J Hartigan	LG*
Dec 1982	Jan 1986	J G Hamilton-Russell MBE	RHG/D‡
Jan 1986	Apr 1987	J B Emson	LG
Apr 1987	Jul 1990	A H Parker Bowles OBE	RHG/D‡
Jul 1990		J D Smith-Bingham	RHG/D‡
		P B Rogers	RHG/D‡

*Colonel Hartigan died on 13 November 1982 from injuries received in a hunting accident. The duties of Lieutenant Colonel Commanding and Silver Stick in Waiting were carried out 'protem' by Lieutenant Colonel A H Parker Bowles, The Blues and Royals, Commanding Officer, Household Cavalry Mounted Regiment.
‡ Abbreviation symbol for The Blues and Royals.

APPENDIX **D** ORIGINS OF
THE LIFE GUARDS'
BRICKHANGING
CEREMONY

ORIGINS OF THE LIFE GUARDS BRICKHANGING CEREMONY
AS RELATED BY A VETERAN OF THE REGIMENT

In the year 1889, Mr Joe Holland a civilian forage master attached to the 2nd Life Guards, stationed at Hyde Park Barracks, was about to embark on his Christmas leave. He had arranged to join the senior Non Commissioned Officers for a couple of drinks. Just as he was about to climb the stairs to the mess, a runner arrived from the orderly room with an invitation for Joe to join the Commanding Officer for a pre-Christmas glass of sherry. Joe was none too pleased about this, and upon noticing a loose brick in the corner of the guardroom wall, he pulled it out and threw the brick up on to the sloping roof of the building, saying to some NCOs with him, 'whilst that brick stays up on the guardroom roof, I want the mess bar kept open. I will be back!' A few too many glasses of sherry later, Joe, forgetting his previous arrangement with the NCOs' Mess, went home to sleep off his over-indulgence. A while later he suddenly remembered his request that the bar should be kept open, and rushed back into barracks to find his friends had answered his request. The bar had remained open the whole time! From then on, the brick was hung every year at Christmas time – by Joe himself – for some 45 years until his death in 1934. A 'brickhanger's medal' can still be seen in the Household Cavalry Museum. Each subsequent brickhanger was, and still is, issued with a medal, including a number of commanding officers, who have hung the brick while the Regiment has been on active service, the last time being in Bosnia, in 1994. That year, a solid silver replica was hung by the Old Comrades back in Windsor. The brick is traditionally hung by the oldest living ex-Regimental Corporal Major who has not taken a commission.

There are various other stories relating to this unique regimental tradition, some involving Joe Holland and the navvies, who were digging the Regent's Park Canal at the time. Apparently, they used to throw bricks up into the trees, during the third week of December, until one remained lodged, and then disappear for their Christmas break. Perhaps Joe copied this custom and refined it for use in the 2nd Life Guards mess? No one knows the answer to that.

BIBLIOGRAPHY

The books and documents listed below dealing specifically with The Life Guards, Royal Horse Guards, 1st Royal Dragoons and Blues and Royals are available on private loan from the Household Cavalry Museum.

General

ANDREWS, Stuart, *Eighteenth Century Europe: The 1680s to 1815* (Longmans, 1965)

AINSLIE, General de. *Historical Record of the First or the Royal Regiment of Dragoons* (Chapman and Hall, 1887)

ARTHUR, Capt Sir George. *The Story of the Household Cavalry* (Constable, 1909 and Heinemann, 1926)

ATKINSON C T *History of the Royal Dragoons, 1661-1933* (University Press, Glasgow, 1934)

BARTHORP, Michael *British Cavalry Uniforms since 1660* (Blandford, 1984)

CANNON, Richard, *Historical Record of The Life Guards* (London, 1837)

CANNON, Richard, *Historical Record of the Royal Horseguards* (London, 1847)

CANNON, Richard. *The First or Royal Regiment of Dragoons* (Longman Orme, 1840)

CHILDS, John, *Armies and Warfare in Europe 1648-1789* (Manchester University Press, 1982)

COSENS, Lt-Col G P *Notebook on the Early History of the Royals 1661-1714* (Typescript held by the Household Cavalry Museum)

DAWNAY, N P *The Standards, Guidons and Colours of the Household Division, 1660-1973* (Midas Books, 1975)

FORTESCUE, Hon J W *A History of the British Army* (13 vols, Macmillan, 1899-1930)

HILLS R J T *The Life Guards* in Leo Cooper's *Famous Regiments* series (Leo Cooper, 1971)

Historical Records of the 1st and 2nd Life Guards, 1660-1922 (MS held in the Household Cavalry Museum)

PACKE, Capt Edmund, *An Historical Record of the Royal Regiment of Horse Guards, or Oxford Blues* (London, 1834)

The Royal Dragoons: Digest of Services of the Regiment. 1661-1929. A handwritten record kept by successive authors. (Held in the Household Cavalry Museum.)

WALTON, Clifford. *History of the British Standing Army* (Harrison and Sons, 1894)

Chapter Two

Angliae Notitiae, of The Present State of England, 1669-1700

CHILDS, John. Article: *Monmouth and the Army in Flanders* in the Journal of the Society for Army Historical Research Vol LII (1974) pp 2-12

CHILDS, John. Article: *The Army and the Oxford Parliment, 1681* in the English Historical Review, Vol XLIV (1978), pp 580-87

CHILDS, John. *The Army of Charles II* (Routledge and Kegan Paul, 1976)

LAFONTAINE, M de. *The Military Duties of the Officers of Cavalry containing the Way of Exercising the Horse according to the Practice of this Present time* (Robert Harford, London, 1678)

Chapter Three

CHANDLER, David G. *Sedgemoor 1685: An Account and an Anthology* (London 1985)

CHILDS, John. *The Army, James II and the Glorious Revolution* (Manchester University Press 1980)

EDE-BORETT, Stephen. *The Army of James II, Organisation and Uniforms* (Raider Games, Leeds, 1987)

THOMSON, G. M. *The First Churchill: The Life of John, 1st Duke of Marlborough* (Secker and Warburg 1979)

WATSON, J N P. *Captain-General and Rebel Chief: The Life of James, Duke of Monmouth* (George Allen and Unwin, 1979)

Chapter Four

CHILDS, John. *The British Army of William III, 1689-1702* (Manchester University Press, 1987)

VAN DER ZEE, Henri and Barbara. *William and Mary* (Macmillan, 1973)

Chapter Five

PETRIE, Sir Charles, Bt. *The Marshal Duke of Berwick* (Eyre and Spottiswoode, 1953)

SCOULLTER, R.E. *The Army of Queen Anne* (Clarendon Press, 1966)

TREVELYAN, G.M. *England under Queen Anne* (2 vols, Longmans Green, 1930)

WOODRUFF, Philip. *Colonel of Dragoons.* (Jonathan Cape, 1951). A novel very faithfully based on the Royals' service in the Peninsula, 1705-6

Chapter Six

MELVILLE, Lewis. *The First George* (2 vols, Pitman, 1908)

TAYLER, Alastair and Henrietta. *1715: The Story of the Rising* (Thomas Nelson, 1936)

Chapter Seven

CHARTERIS, Evan. *William Augustus, Duke of Cumberland* (Edward Arnold, 1913)

GRIFFITH DAVIES, J.D. *A King in Toils: George II* (Lindsay Drummond, 1938)

WHITWORTH, Rex. *Field Marshal Lord Ligonier: A Story of the British Army, 1702-1770* (Clarendon Press, 1958)

Chapter Eight

AYLING, Stanley, *George III* (Collins, 1972)

CALVERT, Sir Harry. *Journals and Correspondence* (contemporary)

GLOVER, Richard. *Peninsular Preparation: The Reform of the British Army, 1795-1809*

Chapter Nine

CHANDLER, David. *The Hundred Days* (Osprey, 1980)

CLARKE-KENNEDY, A.E. *Attack the Colour! An Account of the Royals in the Peninsula and at Waterloo* (The Research Publishing Co. 1975)

The Club Book. A record kept by a club composed of Royals officers below field rank from 1811 to 1816 and presented to the Regiment, in 1878, by Capt Green of the 49th Foot. Green's father was executor to Capt Sigismund Trafford, the last Royals custodian of this vivid document, which is held in the Household Cavalry Museum.

CROFTON, Sir Morgan, Bt. 2LG. *The Household Cavalry in the Waterloo Campaign* (Sifton Praed, 1912)

FULFORD, Roger. *George the Fourth* (Duckworth, 1935)

GUEDALLA, Philip. *The Duke* (Hodder and Stoughton, 1931)

McGUFFIE, T.H. *Peninsular Cavalry General (1811-13) The Correspondence of Lieutenant General Robert Ballard Long* (Harrap, 1951)

PAGET, Julian, *Wellington's Peninsular War* (Leo Cooper, 1990)

TOMKINSON, W. *Diary of a Cavalry Officer* (London 1894)

Chapter Ten

ANGLESEY, Marquess of. *A History of the British Cavalry, Vol 1* (Leo Cooper, 1973)

GORE ALLEN, W. *King William IV* (Cresset, 1960)

Chapter Eleven

ALEXANDER, Michael. *The True Blue: The Life and Adventures of Colonel Fred Burnaby, 1842-1885* (Rupert Hart Davis, 1957)

ANGLESEY, Marquess of. *A History of the British Cavalry, Vols 2 and 3* (Leo Cooper 1982)

HARRIES-JENKINS, Gwyn. *The Army in Victorian Society* (Routledge and Kegan Paul, 1977)

JAMES, Lawrence. *The Savage Wars: British Campaigns in Africa, 1870-1920* (Hale, 1985)

WRIGHT, Thomas. *The Life of Col. Fred Burnaby* (Everett, 1908)

Chapter Twelve

ANGLESEY, Marquess of. *A History of the British Cavalry, Vol 4* (Leo Cooper, 1986)

BELFIELD, Eversley. *The Boer War* (Leo Cooper, 1975)

HAMILTON, Ian. *The Happy Warrior: A Life of General Sir Ian Hamilton* (Cassell, 1966)

MAKINS, E (Ed). *The Royals in South Africa (1899-1902)* (Published by the Editor of *The Eagle*, 1914)

PAKENHAM, Thomas. *The Boer War* (Weidenfeld and Nicolson, 1979)

The Official War Diary of the Household Cavalry Composite Regiment for the South African War. (Held in the Household Cavalry Museum).

Chapter Thirteen

ANGLESEY, Marquess of. *A History of the British Cavalry, 1816 to 1919: Vol 7* (Leo Cooper, 1996)

ARTHUR Sir George. *The Story of the Household Cavalry (Vol III)* (Heinemann, 1926)

ASCOLI, David. *The Mons Star: The British Expeditionary Force 5 Aug-22 Nov 1914.* (Harrap 1981)

ATKINSON, G. *History of the Royal Dragoons, 1661-1934* pp 380-474

BICKERSTETH, J B. *History of the 6th Cavalry Brigade, 1914-1918* (Baynard Press, undated)

BICKERSTETH, John (Ed). *The Bickersteth Diaries, 1914-1918* (Leo Cooper, 1995)

War Diary of the 1st Life Guards, 1914-15 (Printed for Private Circulation. Copy in the Household Cavalry Museum)

Chapter Fourteen

BISHOP, Tim. *One Young Soldier: The Memoirs of a Cavalryman* (Ed by Bruce Shand. Michael Russell, 1993)

Chapter Fifteen

DE CHAIR, Somerset. *The Golden Carpet* (Faber, 1944)

DE GUINGAND, Sir Francis. *Operation Victory* (Hodder and Stoughton, 1947)

HEATHCOAT-AMORY, R. *Reminscences* (Privately Published, 1989)

ORDE, Roden. *The Household Cavalry at War: The Second Household Cavalry Regiment* (Gale and Polden, 1953)

PITT-RIVERS, J A. *The Story of the Royal Dragoons, 1938-1945* (William Clowes, 1957)

ROCKSAVAGE, Lord. *A Day's March Nearer Home* (Privately published)

ROSSE, Earl of, and Hill E.R. *The Story of the Guards Armoured Division* (Geoffrey Bles, 1956)

SMILEY, David. *Irregular Regular* (Michael Russell, 1994)

WILMOT, Chester. *The Struggle for Europe* (Collins, 1952)

WYNDHAM, Humphrey. *The Household Cavalry at War: The First Household Cavalry Regiment* (Gale and Polden, 1952)

Chapter Sixteen

LLOYD, William. *Challengers and Chargers: A History of The Life Guards, 1945-1992* (Leo Cooper, 1992)

ROLLO, Lt-Col W R. *The Household Cavalry Regiment in Bosnia – Winter 1994-95* (Guards Magazine, Summer 1995 issue, pp 76-77)

WATSON, J N P. *The Story of The Blues and Royals: Royal Horse Guards and 1st Dragoons* (Leo Cooper, 1993)

WATSON, J N P. *Sefton: The Story of a Cavalry Horse* (Souvenir Press, 1983)

WATSON, J N P. *Horse and Carriage: The Pageant of Hyde Park* (Sportsman's Press, 1990)

INDEX